Strategic Planning in Environmental Regulation

American and Comparative Environmental Policy
Sheldon Kamieniecki and Michael E. Kraft, series editors

Russell J. Dalton, Paula Garb, Nicholas P. Lovrich, John C. Pierce, and John M. Whiteley, *Critical Masses: Citizens, Nuclear Weapons Production, and Environmental Destruction in the United States and Russia*

Daniel A. Mazmanian and Michael E. Kraft, editors, *Toward Sustainable Communities: Transition and Transformations in Environmental Policy*

Elizabeth R. DeSombre, *Domestic Sources of International Environmental Policy: Industry, Environmentalists, and U.S. Power*

Kate O'Neill, *Waste Trading among Rich Nations: Building a New Theory of Environmental Regulation*

Joachim Blatter and Helen Ingram, editors, *Reflections on Water: New Approaches to Transboundary Conflicts and Cooperation*

Paul F. Steinberg, *Environmental Leadership in Developing Countries: Transnational Relations and Biodiversity Policy in Costa Rica and Bolivia*

Uday Desai, editor, *Environmental Politics and Policy in Industrialized Countries*

Kent Portney, *Taking Sustainable Cities Seriously: Economic Development, the Environment, and Quality of Life in American Cities*

Edward P. Weber, *Bringing Society Back In: Grassroots Ecosystem Management, Accountability, and Sustainable Communities*

Norman J. Vig and Michael G. Faure, editors, *Green Giants? Environmental Policies of the United States and the European Union*

Robert F. Durant, Daniel J. Fiorino, and Rosemary O'Leary, editors, *Environmental Governance Reconsidered: Challenges, Choices, and Opportunities*

Paul A. Sabatier, Will Focht, Mark Lubell, Zev Trachtenberg, Arnold Vedlitz, and Marty Matlock, editors, *Swimming Upstream: Collaborative Approaches to Watershed Management*

Sally K. Fairfax, Lauren Gwin, Mary Ann King, Leigh S. Raymond, and Laura Watt, *Buying Nature: The Limits of Land Acquisition as a Conservation Strategy, 1780–2004*

Steven Cohen, Sheldon Kamieniecki, and Matthew A. Cahn, *Strategic Planning in Environmental Regulation: A Policy Approach That Works*

Strategic Planning in Environmental Regulation

A Policy Approach That Works

Steven Cohen, Sheldon Kamieniecki, and Matthew A. Cahn

The MIT Press
Cambridge, Massachusetts
London, England

MIT Press books may be purchased at special quantity discounts for business or sales promotional use. For information, please e-mail special_sales@mitpress.mit.edu or write to Special Sales Department, The MIT Press, 55 Hayward Street, Cambridge, MA 02142.

This book was set in Sabon by SNP Best-set Typesetter Ltd., Hong Kong.
Printed and bound in the United States of America.
Printed on recycled paper.

Library of Congress Cataloging-in-Publication Data

Cohen, Steven, 1953–
Strategic planning in enviornmental regulation : a policy approach that works / Steven Cohen, Sheldon Kamieniecki, and Matthew A. Cahn.
p. cm.—(American and comparative environmental policy)
Includes bibliographical references and index.
ISBN 0-262-033410-0 (alk. paper)—ISBN 0-262-53275-1 (pbk. : alk. paper)
1. Industrial management—Environmental aspects—United States.
2. Pollution—Economic aspects—United States. 3. Environmental policy—United States—Case studies. 4. Butyl methyl ether—Environmental aspects—United States. 5. Underground storage tanks—Environmental aspects—United States. I. Kamieniecki, Sheldon. II. Cahn, Matthew Alan, 1961– III. Title. IV. Series.
HD30.255.C64 2005 363.7′0561—dc22 2005053445

10 9 8 7 6 5 4 3 2 1

To
Donna, Ariel, and Gabriella
Cindy, Millie, and Sofie
Diane, Arlo, Jonah, and Tobin

Contents

Series Foreword

Critics of U.S. environmental regulation often point to the liability of having ambitious policy goals joined with inadequate implementation and compliance. For that reason, policy analysts both within government agencies and in the scholarly community have sought to learn more about the variables that promote greater compliance and policy effectiveness, particularly those that increase the likelihood of achieving environmental quality goals. Such knowledge should have real value for policymakers and administrators seeking to improve environmental regulation, for example, by stimulating the desired behavior on the part of industry and other regulated parties. It should also be prized by scholars who are trying to develop explanatory models of regulatory policymaking and implementation.

Strategic Planning in Environmental Regulation updates and expands a study published by Steven Cohen and Sheldon Kamieniecki in 1991. The earlier book focused on leaking underground storage tanks (USTs) and the regulatory success achieved by the U.S. Environmental Protection Agency, in that case through its use of strategic planning. This book adds a comparative dimension by including the newer case of groundwater contamination caused by the gasoline additive methyl tertiary butyl ether (MTBE). It also thoroughly updates the previous description of the UST program. The two cases are linked because many USTs store gasoline.

The central question guiding this research is how policymakers and regulators can do a better job of crafting responses to the pollution control challenges they face. At a time when regulators struggle with implementing command-and-control environmental policies and many analysts pin their hopes on alternatives to conventional regulation such as use of market incentives, self-regulation, and information disclosure, the authors look to strategic planning as one way to improve agency performance. Strategic planning is another way of thinking about the application of policy design principles—the selection of policy tools that are most likely to achieve certain objectives. In particular, strategic planning requires careful consideration of the regulatory objectives, the target audiences for regulation, their beliefs and motivation, their resources and interdependence, the political and economic circumstances that affect their behavior, and the characteristics of the regulatory agency. Ideally, those who write the laws would work closely with those who must implement them, and they would also take into account how these factors affect policy success. Sad to say, reality often falls short of this ideal for policy formulation and implementation.

In an effort to document both success and failure in these efforts, Cohen, Kamieniecki, and Cahn present a theoretically grounded model of strategic regulatory planning, with an emphasis on stakeholder processes and facilitated negotiation. They then show how its use helped to produce favorable outcomes in the case of the USTs and how the absence of its use may be an important explanation for the considerably less successful effort to deal with MTBE contamination. Analysis of these two cases forms the heart of the book, and the authors provide enough scientific and historical detail for readers to draw their own conclusions about the hypotheses being tested.

The result of this comparison is a richly detailed analysis of why regulation works better in some cases than in others. For those who recognize that regulation is, as the authors say, a "practical necessity" in modern society and not merely an "ideological preference," the book offers intriguing insights into alternative approaches to environmental regulation and a practical guide to the application of strategic planning principles. As such, the research reflected in the book draws from and significantly contributes to the scholarly literature on policy design, policy implementation, administrative behavior, regulatory policy, and environmental policy and politics.

The analyses presented in this book illustrate well our purpose in the MIT Press series in American and Comparative Environmental Policy.

We encourage work that examines a broad range of environmental policy issues. We are particularly interested in books that incorporate interdisciplinary research and focus on the linkages between public policy and environmental problems and issues both within the United States and in cross-national settings. We welcome contributions that analyze the policy dimensions of relationships between humans and the environment from a theoretical or empirical perspective. At a time when environmental policies are increasingly seen as controversial and new approaches are being implemented widely, we especially encourage studies that assess policy successes and failures, evaluate new institutional arrangements and policy tools, and clarify new directions for environmental politics and policy. The books in this series are written for a wide audience that includes academics, policymakers, environmental scientists and professionals, business and labor leaders, environmental activists, and students concerned with environmental issues. We hope they contribute to public understanding of environmental problems, issues, and policies of concern today and also suggest promising actions for the future.

Michael Kraft, University of Wisconsin–Green Bay
Coeditor, American and Comparative Environmental Policy Series

Preface

In late 1984, Paul Light, then director of studies at the National Academy of Public Administration (NAPA), hired Steve Cohen to assemble and manage a staff to conduct a study for the Environmental Protection Agency (EPA) of the implementation of the new amendments to the nation's hazardous waste laws. NAPA's Hazardous Waste Management Project was guided by a distinguished panel of academic and professional experts and chaired by Alan Altshuler, one of the nation's eminent scholars in public administration. To provide expert advice to the project, Cohen recruited Sheldon Kamieniecki to join the project as its senior consultant. After one year, NAPA produced a strategic plan for EPA's new underground storage tank (UST) program.

When the project ended, Cohen and Kamieniecki decided to write about the concepts that informed the planning process, the process itself, and the early implementation record of the federal underground tank program. This resulted in a book: *Environmental Regulation Through Strategic Planning* (1991). The authors concluded that at least until the publication of the book, EPA's UST program had been a success.

Throughout the 1990s, Cohen and Kamieniecki continued discussing the issues addressed by that book—principally, How can environmental regulation be made more effective? One issue that dominated these discussions was first raised by Columbia University Professor Richard Nelson during a seminar session that covered the development of EPA's tank strategy: Was the tank program unique? Could strategic planning be of value in other areas?

In continuing this conversation, Cohen and Kamieniecki thought that the next step in this process of exploration would be to take an environmental program that was failing and examine it for evidence of strategic thinking. This new study would also analyze the potential usefulness of strategic planning for improving the failed program. After considering a number of emerging environmental issues, the issue of methyl tertiary butyl ether (MTBE) contamination seemed a good fit. MTBE was a substance that was added to gasoline to prevent air pollution, and yet it turned out to be a danger to the nation's supply of groundwater. It was a new problem created by an attempt to solve an old problem. Kamieniecki enlisted Matthew Cahn, his former student and now professor of political science at California State University, Northridge, to join the team and help develop a case study on the development and implementation of MTBE policy. Cahn had used Cohen and Kamieniecki's book extensively in his courses and was quite familiar with its theoretical framework and underlying thesis.

Another part of the study was to revisit the original theoretical framework on strategic regulation based on lessons learned in the 1980s and 1990s. We also reexamined the underground tank program to see if the promise it demonstrated in the late 1980s had resulted in performance in the early twenty-first century. Finally, we sought to compare the two processes and see if we still thought that strategic planning could contribute to effective environmental regulation.

Twenty years after NAPA's Hazardous Waste Management Project, we find the process of strategic planning a useful reform to standard environmental policymaking. We also find that it continues to be rare and underused and that the old misguided trade-off between environmental protection and economic growth persists in the halls of government. This misinformed debate is one reason that the stakeholder analysis and engagement that characterized tank regulation would be so useful in other areas. Regulated parties need to understand why they are targeted for change. However, as the MTBE case demonstrates, stakeholder engagement alone is not sufficient for effective policymaking. The other steps of strategic planning are needed to increase the probability of effective regulation.

As policy analysts, we must confess our bias that additional facts and analysis can improve decision making and public policy. We know that there are those who do not agree with us and believe that one result of analysis is a type of policy paralysis. Still, the alternative to facts and analysis is guessing and magic, and we would just as soon take our chances with policy based on good data and knowledge. We think it is important to document success and failure and learn from both where we can. We offer this new book in the hope that the lessons within it can be applied. Our purpose in writing it is to contribute to making our planet a little more sustainable.

Acknowledgments

We acknowledge Mark Kaswan for his research assistance on methyl tertiary butyl ether. His contributions to chapters 5, 6, and 7 are substantial. We are grateful to Alison Gilmore for her work on the index. We appreciate Michael Kraft's support and encouragement throughout the development of the book project and the assistance and guidance provided by Clay Morgan at MIT Press. We are also indebted to the four anonymous reviewers of an earlier draft of the book manuscript, and we are thankful for their excellent comments and suggestions for revision. Steve Cohen acknowledges the support of Dean Lisa Anderson and Professor Jeffrey Sachs as well as the support and patience of Louise Rosen, Kelly Quirk, and Yana Chervona. As is always the case, we take full responsibility for all errors and omissions.

Introduction

When this work began, we conducted a fairly exhaustive review of the literature on regulation. Specifically, we sought research on how to improve compliance with regulation. Although we discovered a rich literature on macroissues such as market alternatives to regulation and the regulation-deregulation debate, there was surprisingly little on the microissue of how to make regulation effective.[1]

Direct command-and-control regulation has been criticized on many fronts in recent studies. Salamon, for example, notes the political difficulties inherent in the use of coercive policy tools and how government, as a consequence, has steadily moved toward the adoption of less coercive measures.[2] Kagan presents a picture of an increasingly fragmented and dysfunctional system.[3] Neither Salamon nor Kagan suggests how regulatory power can be made politically acceptable in instances where direct command-and-control regulation is required. Sparrow, in contrast, advises practitioners on specific ways to make their policy programs more successful.[4] He believes that regulators can be more effective by adopting promising enforcement approaches for improving regulatory performance.

It is reasonable to focus on the issue of regulatory effectiveness because regardless of the normative values and preferences of researchers, it is clear that regulation is here to stay.[5] Policymakers in the United States continue to rely on regulation as a means of influencing individual and corporate behavior. Yet regulation has been too narrowly construed as command-and-control standard setting and enforcement. More accurately, the concept of regulation includes the full range of activities intended to influence private behavior to conform to public goals. Given the tendency of Congress to regulate, it makes little sense to focus academic study solely on the wisdom of regulation and ignore the issues of regulatory effectiveness and compliance.

In a real sense, the issue of overregulation is a phony one. Given the high level of corporate influence in the policymaking process,[6] truly ruinous regulation is either safely ignored or lightly enforced. The issue is less dramatic than it appears to be. It is in the public interest for American industry to produce as many goods and services as efficiently as possible. It also is in the public interest for government to prevent industry from harming people in the process of accumulating wealth. In most cases, the public will have to pay for increased levels of safety. From double-sealed drug containers to hazardous waste cleanup, the public pays. In other cases, regulation can actually improve productivity by forcing modernization and the adoption of new technologies. For example, recycling regulations have helped promote energy efficiency, and new equipment for engine emissions control has improved air quality.

A problem with the debate over whether to regulate is that it diverts attention from the real trade-offs policymakers must make. Instead of learning how to develop a viable, creative, interactive relationship between business and government, policymakers focus their analytical guns on a war that will never be fought. Regulation is not an ideological preference; it is a practical necessity. Given the complexity of modern economies, government must play a role in mitigating the harsh side effects of economic development.

Even in the antiregulatory environment of the Reagan administration of the 1980s, regulation never ceased.[7] In many areas, it was only slightly curtailed, and in other areas it even expanded.[8] The reason that President Reagan was unable to "end" regulation was that ending regulation was never his goal. It could not have been. There is, in fact, a fairly broad consensus that certain industries must be regulated in order to avert negative consequences. This is a matter of practical necessity and a result of the complexity and interconnectedness of modern economies.

Despite the political appeal of decentralization and despite our society's attraction to the concepts of "small is beautiful" and "back to nature," the future is likely to see the country's (and world's) economy become even more complex and interdependent. Few are about to return to the land and farm. If anything, the need for regulation is likely to grow. Therefore, the ability to regulate effectively must improve, or the efficiency of the economic system will suffer. Regulation should be seen as a method of social and economic management in need of improvement.

If our regulatory process is unable to grow out of its relatively primitive state of symbolic politics and posturing, the country will face one or more of the following unwelcome outcomes:

- Economic inefficiency due to unnecessary compliance costs
- Negative externalities caused by unregulated economic behavior (unsafe technology, tainted food and drugs, and environmental pollution, for example)
- The development of nonsustainable societies

Despite its economic problems at the turn of the century, the Japanese, among others, have demonstrated the importance of close government-corporate relations in competitive modern economies. Unless an effective partnership is created, American business will be overwhelmed by foreign businesses that have learned to combine state and corporate power. Effective regulation is a critical component of a sophisticated government-industry relationship.[9]

This book introduces the concept of strategic regulatory planning and presents an overall approach for achieving compliance with hazardous materials laws. Although this book primarily focuses on the decision to include and later exclude methyl tertiary butyl ether (MTBE) in gasoline and the implementation of a critical provision of the Hazardous and Solid Waste Amendments of 1984, specifically the regulation of underground storage tanks (USTs), many of its conclusions are applicable to other pollution control programs and probably to other policy areas (e.g., education, health care, and transportation). Little research has been conducted on how to design effective regulatory programs, and the design of such programs is the principal concern of this study.

This introduction provides a general introduction to issues pertaining to the management and regulation of hazardous waste and materials and reviews the problems and policies in this area. Specific attention is paid to the use of MTBE in gasoline as a way to lower air pollution emissions and efforts to abate leaking USTs. Although both the MTBE issue and the UST issue represent separate policy dimensions, they are interrelated in that MTBE is a gasoline additive and a large percentage of USTs store gasoline. This provides a good balance between shared policy similarities and differences across the two issue areas and makes comparisons meaningful and potentially insightful. The chapter concludes with an overview of the book. The discussion begins with an analysis of the issues concerning the delegation of authority by Congress.

Congressional Delegation of Authority

Lowi offers an insightful and compelling indictment of contemporary American government in general, and of congressional delegation of power to regulatory agencies in particular.[10] Although he does not object to delegation in principle, he does criticize delegation without guidelines and standards, a practice he attributes to widespread acceptance of interest-group liberalism. He later writes that the congressional delegation of authority "is an inevitable and necessary practice in any government," and "no theory of representative government is complete without it."[11] Nonetheless, "the delegation of broad and undefined discretionary power from the legislature to the executive branch deranges virtually all constitutional relationships and prevents attainment of constitutional goals of limitation on power, substantive calculability, and procedural calculability."[12] He reasons that "every delegation of discretion away from electorally responsible levels of government to professional career administrative agencies is a calculated risk because politics will always flow to the point of discretion; the demand for representation would take place at the point of discretion; and the constitutional forms designed to balance one set of interests against another would not be present at the point of discretion for that purpose."[13] As a consequence, liberalism is undoing itself because public policies are resulting in privilege, and private goods are going not to the deserving but to the best organized.

Fiorina questions the correctness of Lowi's explanation, pointing out that there are a number of good reasons for legislators to delegate regulatory authority (e.g., lack of technical information and time).[14] He demonstrates how these reasons are empirically supported by previous research. He then turns his attention to the role that uncertainty plays in the literature on regulatory origin, and he offers various formal models of the role of uncertainty in the regulatory process.[15]

The Rule-Making Process

Despite Lowi's concerns, rule making has become an important component of public policymaking.[16] Numerous government agencies, such as the U.S. Environmental Protection Agency (EPA), are required by legislative mandates to draft and implement specific guidelines and regulations that are broadly referred to in enacted legislation. The Administrative Procedure Act (APA) of 1946, written by Congress to bring consistency and predictability to the decision-making processes of government agencies, states that a "rule means the whole or part of an agency statement of general or particular applicability and future effect designed to implement, interpret, or prescribe law or policy."[17] Rules provide the specific information often missing in laws, and rule making brings a capacity for adaptation to changing conditions that a statute alone would lack.[18] Rules originate in agencies, stipulate law and policy as directed by authorizing legislation, have either a broad or narrow focus, and attempt to influence future conditions. According to Kerwin, "Increasingly, rulemaking defines the substance of public programs. It determines, to a very large extent, the specific legal obligations we bear as a society. Rulemaking gives precise form to the benefits we enjoy under a wide range of statutes. In the process, it fixes the actual costs we incur in meeting the ambitious objectives of our many public programs."[19] The process of rule making, as Kerwin explains, is central to the formulation and implementation of public policy in the United States. It differs and is separate from the legislative and judicial process, but it also is a critical part of the overall policymaking effort.

The New Deal and the 1960s and 1970s were eras of sharp growth in governmental programs that required extensive rule making to meet ambitious goals.[20] Rule making also expanded during the 1980s and 1990s. Today, despite criticisms and attempts at reform, it is an indispensable governmental process, and this is unlikely to change in the future. The manner in which rule making is carried out has significant implications for the functioning of democracy and the nation's well-being.

Although rule making was intended to be efficient, factually oriented, nonpolitical, and objective, it has become something quite different.[21] Rule making appeared to grant bureaucrats an immense amount of freedom of action. Instead, they must adhere to a long list of procedural guidelines and are subjected to political pressure from different quarters—the White House, Congress, interest groups, and the public.[22] The rule-making process has become increasingly open and information driven, thereby providing stakeholders an opportunity to influence the final outcome of the process.[23] Opportunities for participation have grown and diversified since the passage of the APA, and agencies are under pressure to take public comments seriously.[24] The Office of Management and Budget plays a crucial role in the rule adoption process by reviewing new regulations and assessing their economic impact.[25]

Kerwin identifies and discusses eleven stages of rule making.[26] Briefly, they include origin of rule-making activity, origin of individual rule making, authorization to proceed with rule making, planning the rule making, developing the draft rule, internal review of the draft rule, external review of the draft rule, revision and publication of a draft rule, public participation, action on the draft rule, and post-rule-making activities. It is a mistake to assume that the rule-making process has a clear start and finish; components of rules can be challenged and altered at any time.

Due to congressional impatience with the length of time certain government agencies took to promulgate rules, Congress has inserted "hammer" provisions in particular types of legislation. These regulations are required to go into effect by a specified date unless the agency adopts its own regulations. These "regulations by statute" normally include regulatory requirements that no one, including Congress, truly prefers. They are used to place pressure on agency officials to accelerate the rule-making process. Hammer provisions, along with deadlines, have become a widely used popular accountability tool of Congress.

The APA suggests that there are three categories of rules: legislative or substantive, interpretive, and procedural.[27] Legislative or substantive rules are promulgated when, by legislative mandate or authorization, agencies draft what in essence is new law. Interpretive rules explain to the public how agencies interpret existing law and policy and do not create new legal requirements. Procedural rules outline the organization and processes of agencies and often concern matters of importance to the public.[28] Rules can also be classified by the segment of society they influence and direct (e.g., rules for private behavior).

Negotiated Rule Making

Regulatory negotiation, or "reg-neg" as it is frequently referred to, offers competing interests a direct and meaningful role in rule making. A fairly recent concept, this idea began to take shape in the early 1980s with the changing political climate and as academics and practitioners began to write about the approach. Writings at the time discussed the rationale for regulatory negotiation, its likely benefits, the necessary conditions for success, and the obstacles to its execution.[29] Harter, for example, severely criticized contemporary rule making for its adversarial process, distortion of information, foundation for litigation, and the lack of progress that had resulted.[30] As a consequence, announcements of rules were often delayed, and their quality was frequently poor. Affected parties were frustrated and disillusioned by the process, and compliance suffered as a consequence. Instead, Harter recommended the adoption of an alternative process, one in which conflict was resolved through face-to-face negotiations, bargaining, and compromise.[31] Agency officials would organize and participate in the negotiations rather than remain aloof from the process. In this way, information would flow more freely, thereby producing higher-quality regulations in less time than in traditional rule making. Stakeholders would also be much less likely to litigate after the rule was issued because they were part of the process and therefore would perceive the regulation to be legitimate.[32] Compliance was predicted to increase, saving taxpayers money on enforcement costs.[33] In 1990 the federal government responded to these and other criticisms and calls for reform by passing the Administrative Dispute Resolution Act and the Negotiated Rulemaking Act.[34] In 1993 the National Performance Review, chaired by Vice President Al Gore, made a number of recommendations, including widening the use of reg-neg to improve rule making.[35]

Since the adoption of regulatory negotiation by certain agencies, including the EPA, there has been considerable research of the process. Coglianese, for example, has analyzed the timeliness and litigation experience of rules developed using negotiation.[36] He finds that negotiated rules are not produced more quickly than are rules developed using standard procedures.[37] He also reports that rules developed using negotiation are, on average, challenged in court more frequently than those that resulted from traditional processes.[38] In another study, Langbein and Kerwin examine the quality of the experience of participants in both reg-neg and conventional rule making.[39] Based on their interviews with random sets of participants, they find that those involved in negotiated rule making give that process higher ratings on the quality of information it generated, the amount learned, economic efficiency, cost-effectiveness, compliance, legality, overall quality, net benefits for the organization, and the personal experience of the respondents than participants in the conventional rule-making process. In contrast, Siegler, who represents the American Petroleum Institute in regulatory negotiations, believes that reg-neg is a cumbersome process "for everyone involved."[40] Coglianese reports that "negotiated rulemaking has not lived up to its promising potential to save regulatory time or prevent litigation."[41] He concludes that regulatory negotiation is not worth the additional time, money, and resources required for its operation. Overall, Coglianese and Coglianese and Allen argue that reg-neg does not necessarily lead to improved policy design and more effective regulation.[42]

The Time It Takes to Make Rules

The time it takes to make rules in government agencies, especially in the EPA, has been a topic of research. Kerwin and Furlong, for instance, analyze the average time it takes to formulate rules in four major programs at EPA: air, water, toxic substances, and waste.[43] They report that rule making takes anywhere from just over two years to a little under five years.[44] Although it is difficult to say how much time EPA should take in issuing rules since conditions vary from one policy context to another, Congress has clearly grown frustrated with the pace of rule making in the EPA. By 2003, Congress had passed approximately one thousand statutory deadlines for the issuance of regulations under a variety of environmental laws.

The EPA, for example, experienced serious delays in the rule-making process for the Resource Conservation and Recovery Act (RCRA) of 1976. The law is designed to regulate generators, transporters, and disposers of solid waste (garbage). Initially, the EPA's Office of Solid Waste and Emergency Response (OSWER) concentrated its efforts on trash collection and disposal services provided by local governments because these activities generated the greatest amount of trash. By the early 1980s, however, it became clear that a much greater threat to the environment and public health was posed by the inclusion of toxic wastes in garbage. Reports of serious groundwater contamination led Congress to amend RCRA and pass the Hazardous and Solid Waste Amendments (HSWA) in 1984. This new law, among other things, substantially altered OSWER's mission and approach to rule making, greatly expanded its jurisdiction, and imposed tight deadlines for the issuance of the numerous regulations needed to implement the new statutory provisions.[45] As a consequence, OSWER became the most efficient rule-making unit in EPA, issuing regulations quicker than any other program office in the agency. However, in an EPA report titled "The Nation's Hazardous Waste Management Program at a Crossroads," it was observed that the great volume of rule making within a short period of time resulted in low morale, high staff burnout, and turnover in the RCRA program.[46] Thus, although many rules were issued in record time, the result was an inconsistent, incoherent regulatory program that may not have been fully understood by the target population.[47] Clearly, then, speed in rule making can have costs.

EPA and Rule Making

Despite these earlier problems, the EPA has become quite efficient and effective at rule making.[48] McGarity, for instance, observes, "With the very notable exception of the turbulent early 1980s, EPA has acquired a well-deserved reputation as one of the most intelligently run agencies in the federal government. While its output has never been high, it has . . . been of increasingly high quality."[49] Over the years EPA has moved away from, for example, its practice of appointing a work group for all rules and has fashioned a new, more sophisticated tier system. Rules are now assigned one of three tiers depending on the rule's importance, its cross-environmental media implications, and the potential for controversy inside or outside the agency. Kerwin believes other agencies in the federal government are likely to adopt this model.[50]

Coglianese, in his examination of negotiated rule making in the EPA, however, cites the failure of the Clean Fuel Negotiated Rulemaking Committee to head off conflict concerning the requirements for reformulated gasoline under the Clean Air Act of 1990.[51] In its effort to secure consensus, the reformulated gasoline rule led to the adoption of MTBE. Immediately following its adoption, however, citizens complained about headaches and dizziness associated with the additive. Others complained about the increase in fuel prices. These complaints were widely covered in the media. Coglianese concludes, "To this day, press reports about the rule continue, though now they focus on cases of groundwater contamination with MTBE, a substance which is reported to be a possible carcinogen."[52]

As Harter points out, the EPA has valued negotiations and partnering highly, and it has strongly promoted negotiated rule making.[53] The aim has been to reach a consensus in rule making. Although there have been some complaints, most applaud the EPA's effort to pursue and improve negotiated rule making. More generally, and in opposition to Coglianese, Harter believes that negotiated rule making has worked well throughout the bureaucracy.[54]

The Hazardous Waste Problem

There is widespread agreement among scientists and policymakers that the production and disposal of hazardous materials has become an enormous and complex problem in this country. The data certainly bear this out. At the end of World War II, the United States produced about 1 billion pounds of hazardous waste per year.[55] Since then, the generation of hazardous waste has increased at an alarming rate, approximately 10 percent per year.[56] About a ton of waste is now generated annually for every citizen in the United States. According to Rosenbaum, "Today, about thirty-five thousand chemicals are used daily in U.S. industry. Between five hundred and one thousand new chemicals are created annually. Currently the EPA has more than ten thousand new chemicals pending review, as required by the Toxic Substances Control Act (TSCA) of 1976."[57]

Hazardous materials and hazardous wastes differ from one another. Hazardous materials are potentially toxic substances used in manufacturing processes. Hazardous wastes are potentially toxic substances that are the unwanted by-products of manufacturing processes. Unfortunately, a significant amount of these wastes are not disposed of in an environmentally safe manner.[58] Though no estimates are available on the amount of hazardous materials used in manufacturing, that number should be considerably higher than the figure for waste.

A wide variety of industries, led by the organic chemical and metals industries, generate hazardous wastes and dispose of them in different ways.[59] Although exact figures on waste generation, transporters, and disposal sites are unavailable, Plehn, a former director of the EPA's Office of Solid Waste, estimates, "Over 750,000 businesses generate hazardous waste, and over 10,000 transporters move it to treatment or disposal at over 30,000 sites. Up to 50,000 sites have been used at some time for hazardous waste disposal."[60] About 2,000 of these sites pose a serious and imminent threat to the environment and, in many cases, to public health. Among the dangerous substances transported and stored at hazardous waste dumps are flammables, heavy metals, asbestos, acids and bases, and synthetic organic chemicals. Even radioactive material has been discovered at some sites. A large number of these substances are carcinogenic, cause birth defects, or affect the central nervous system. Clearly, hazardous waste management is one of the most important and pressing issues policymakers at all levels of government face today.[61]

Although agreement exists on the pervasiveness of the problem, there is much disagreement over how best to regulate the handling of toxic materials and the disposal of hazardous waste. Environmentalists, for example, demand direct government intervention to ensure compliance with standards in the handling of dangerous materials. Industry leaders, however, argue that such actions will require huge expenditures on their part, possibly forcing them out of business. As a result, they will have no choice but to ignore strict regulations and procedures. Policymakers, who are in the middle of this controversy, must therefore choose regulatory approaches that will satisfy the most intense concerns of involved parties and also protect the environment and public health. How to select and implement the most acceptable and effective regulatory plans is a major concern of both legislators and environmental officials.[62]

Background of Hazardous Materials Policy

In an attempt to ameliorate the hazardous materials problem, the federal government has enacted several laws directly concerning dangerous materials. The passage of the Toxic Substances Control Act in 1976 signaled a new awareness among policymakers of the need to regulate the introduction each year of thousands of new chemicals into the environment. The well-publicized tragedy at Love Canal, New York, led to the enactment of the Comprehensive Environmental Response, Compensation, and Liability Act (CERCLA) in 1980. Better known as Superfund, the bill established a five-year, $1.6 billion program to clean up the nation's worst abandoned, hazardous, and toxic waste dumps.[63] Superfund was reauthorized in succeeding years and funding was increased; however, its implementation proceeded slowly. By the late 1990s, it became clear that the magnitude of the abandoned waste problem and the money required to clean up the worst sites far exceeded initial expectations. By 2004, 883 sites on the National Priority List had been cleaned up substantially. Although the progress of Superfund site abatement improved considerably in the 1990s, the program still faces a backlog of seriously contaminated sites (about 475), cost overruns, technical complexities, and political controversy.[64] President George W. Bush decided not to reauthorize and continue funding the program during his first term in office, and as of late 2004 the restoration of funding for this program was still in the hands of Congress. RCRA requires the federal government to formulate specific rules for handling and disposing of hazardous waste.[65] States are expected to ensure that private parties obey these rules within their borders. The major incentive that a corporation has for spending money to comply with RCRA is avoidance of punishment.

Underground Storage Tanks

HSWA regulates, for the first time, the owners and operators of over 1 million underground storage tanks. In contrast to previous hazardous waste laws (e.g., Superfund in 1980), the regulation of USTs was passed without any widespread outcry from the public. Following the allegations of mismanagement in the EPA's hazardous waste program, Congress was searching for a vehicle to demonstrate that it was aggressively controlling toxic pollution. The revisions of RCRA became a forum for demonstrating Congress's "get tough" policy.

HSWA is one of the most detailed pieces of environmental legislation ever written.[66] After battling over interpretations of environmental legislation during the reign of EPA administrator Anne Gorsuch-Burford in the early 1980s, Congress decided to leave nothing to chance. EPA was placed on tight schedules, and regulations were required to conform to detailed congressional specifications. If EPA did not meet the deadlines for promulgating guidelines, Congress included statutory "hammer clauses" in HSWA. Thus, industry understood that the result of contesting and delaying standards would be stricter standards.

In addition to tightening hazardous materials regulation, HSWA significantly expanded the number of individuals and firms subject to regulation. Prior to 1984, toxic-bearing municipal garbage dumps, small-quantity generators of hazardous waste, and UST operators were not regulated by federal law. HSWA placed all those parties under federal control.

The single most dramatic expansion of regulatory power is the provision of the law regulating USTs. Every gasoline station in America is now regulated under HSWA. (Therefore, the consumer product gasoline, not a hazardous waste, is the primary target of the legislation.) To comply with the law's edicts many tank owners have replaced their tanks (at a cost ranging from $10,000 to $100,000) and cleaned up tank leaks (at costs ranging into the millions). This authority was expanded when Superfund was reauthorized in October 1986. The Superfund Amendments and Reauthorization Act (SARA) required owners of USTs to carry insurance and provided EPA with a $100 million per year trust fund to pay the cost of abating tank leaks.

The complexity and challenge of this regulatory task was staggering, primarily because of the large and diverse size of the target group. Tens of thousands of firms were included in the UST program, most of them small businesses with unique problems and characteristics. Management of the UST program presented EPA with a formidable and nearly unprecedented challenge since it rarely has had to oversee a target population of this nature or magnitude. The only truly analogous program is the regulation banning leaded gasoline in new automobiles, a program that required the installation of smaller gasoline pump spouts. In 1985, when the UST program began, EPA senior management believed that to achieve adequate rates of compliance in the UST program, it would have to develop a new approach to regulation.

In December 1984 the EPA's OSWER contracted with the National Academy of Public Administration (NAPA) to analyze the long-range implementation issues associated with the UST provisions of the newly enacted HSWA. In the mid- to late 1980s, EPA adopted a unique, strategic, and results-oriented approach to implementing one part of that new act: the regulation of USTs. Working with senior staff and management in the EPA, NAPA developed a strategic regulatory plan for USTs. Enough time has now passed to evaluate accurately this regulatory effort. Accordingly, this book presents a case study of this unique regulatory program. The EPA and NAPA analysts who developed the plan are referred to as the program's planners in the text.

Methyl Tertiary Butyl Ether

The administration of George H. W. Bush worked with environmentalists and key members of Congress to revise substantially the 1970 legislation by passing the Clean Air Act Amendments of 1990. Rosenbaum believes the legislation represented "the most important, and imaginative, regulatory reform in more than a decade."[67] The new law added to the original legislation two sections concerning acid precipitation and ozone protection and significantly revised a majority of the remaining provisions. Title II addressed mobile sources and outlined numerous new emission standards for automobiles and trucks. Among the requirements was that oil and gasoline companies must produce and sell cleaner-burning fuel in the most polluted areas by 1992 and in all areas with ozone problems by 1996.[68] Among other things, this required the use of oxygenated gasoline (gasoline that has been blended with alcohol or ethers that contain oxygen) in areas that did not meet the federal ambient air standards for carbon monoxide. California was one of these designated areas and is a focus of this study. Ambient carbon monoxide levels are highest during the cold-weather months, and oxygenated gasoline, which reduces carbon monoxide emissions, was to be used during these months in various states. The 1990 Clean Air Act (CAA) required at least 2.7 percent oxygen content in gasoline, which is typically achieved by the addition of about 15 percent of MTBE, an effective oxygenate.

California requested a waiver by the EPA of the 2.7 percent oxygenate requirement to one that is 2 percent oxygenate, which is the amount California's winter gasoline has contained since November 1992. In addition, California adopted the federal reformulated gasoline program in 1995, which required the use of reformulated gasoline in the smoggiest regions of the state. It was at this point that MTBE's importance and dependence began to increase substantially.

Under the CAA of 1990, the California Air Resources Board (CARB) determined the need to reduce vehicle emission beyond federal standards to deal with the state's excessive air pollution problem. CARB sought to reduce volatile organic compounds by 55 percent as well as achieve the maximum feasible reductions in vehicle emissions of particulate matter, carbon monoxide, and toxic air contaminants by December 31, 2000. The agency thus introduced Phase II Reformulated Gasoline, which is capable of providing significant reductions beyond those of federally mandated reformulated gasoline. Therefore, by federal law, gasoline must contain an oxygenate to be in compliance with the California Phase II Reformulated Gasoline measure in order to reduce air pollution. Oxygenates are used for this purpose, and many states, including California, have largely turned to MTBE in their effort to stay within these clean air standards. MTBE as a fuel oxygenate was therefore added to gasoline.

California quickly implemented the use of reformulated gasoline in its most polluted areas. Initially, the benefits of this cleaner-burning gasoline were apparent and seemingly legitimate. Gasoline containing MTBE was to reduce immediately emissions from all existing on-road, gasoline-burning automobiles, trucks, and other motorized equipment. The reduction in ozone-forming emissions from the use of cleaner-burning gasoline was to account for approximately 25 percent of the total ozone reductions expected from all new pollution control measures to be adopted in

California. This emissions reduction from using reformulated gasoline was equivalent to removing approximately 3.5 million motor vehicles from the state's roads and highways and producing the largest emission reductions of any control measure since the adoption of unleaded gasoline.[69] As a consequence, significant amounts of carbon monoxide as well as cancer-causing pollutants, such as benzene, were prevented from entering the atmosphere. Although gas mileage suffered somewhat, leaders and the public believed the air was cleaner. Refiners favored MTBE over other oxygenates because of its ability to boost octane levels and blend with gasoline.

Not much time passed before problems began to arise with the use of MTBE. Almost immediately after its introduction, people reported headaches and nausea after coming into contact with gasoline containing MTBE. This prompted the federal government and the oil industry to finance jointly a study on the possible health hazards associated with the additive. Initial studies were conducted by the Lawrence Livermore National Laboratory, and the research showed MTBE to cause cancerous tumors in rats. Reproductive and developmental studies on MTBE also revealed that inhalation exposure could result in maternal toxicity and adverse effects on a developing fetus. At the end of 1998, a team of researchers from four University of California campuses submitted a report to California governor Gray Davis and the state legislature titled, "Health and Environmental Assessment of MTBE."[70] The ten-month study provided detailed information and data on human health effects, air quality and ecological effects, groundwater and surface water, risk and exposure assessment, water treatment, and cost-benefit analysis. Based on the findings of the research, the principal recommendation of the study was that a phase-out over several years should take place (rather than an immediate ban) so that refiners could be given the flexibility to achieve air quality objectives in their modifications. Overall, the researchers demonstrated that the gasoline additive MTBE posed a serious risk of contaminating water supplies, particularly underground aquifers.

The first discovery of MTBE in groundwater came in 1995 in Anaheim, California. The Orange County Water District, the first agency in the state to test for MTBE, found high levels in wells used to monitor groundwater. In February 1996, Santa Monica first detected its groundwater to be contaminated by the chemical, and the wells were promptly closed. Officials began a search for the source of the pollution and found that it came from a leaking underground gasoline tank. Shortly after, three other municipal drinking water wells in Santa Monica were found to be contaminated by MTBE. In the months that followed, Santa Monica city officials were forced to shut down seven wells, losing more than half their water supply. The cost of the cleanup was estimated to be about $100 million over the next decade. Since the discovery of MTBE in Santa Monica's drinking water, reports of MTBE contamination in groundwater have become widespread in California. This includes South Lake Tahoe, where at least twelve of its thirty-four wells had to shut down; the San Francisco Bay Area, where MTBE has been found in at least three of ten Santa Clara Valley Water District drinking reservoirs; and in more than three hundred shallow groundwater monitoring wells within Santa Clara County.

The majority of MTBE in groundwater was discovered to come from leaking underground gasoline tanks and their associated piping. Well over 32,000 leaking underground storage tank sites have been found in California alone. The average cost of an industrial cleanup is approximately $150,000. Since the widespread introduction of oxygenated gasoline, the treatment of water contaminated with MTBE has become problematic. MTBE, due to its small molecular size and solubility in water, does not readily attach to soil particles and moves rapidly and far into groundwater. This makes widespread MTBE contamination a real and serious problem.

Overview of the Book

This book examines the concept of strategic regulatory planning and presents an overall regulatory program for achieving compliance with policies designed to improve air quality through the use of a gasoline additive, MTBE, and with the UST provisions of HSWA. The book contains three parts with ten chapters and a Conclusion. Part I offers a model for regulatory strategy formulation. Parts II and III apply the model to the cases of MTBE and UST regulation, respectively.

Part I comprises four chapters. Chapter 1 discusses the concept of strategic regulatory planning. The design of strategic regulatory plans is the principal focus of this study. Chapter 2, the theoretical core of the work, presents a model of a tactical approach to regulatory planning. Chapter 3 develops a framework for selecting specific regulatory devices. The framework directs agencies to evaluate regulatory activities according to cost of implementation and degree of coerciveness. Chapter 4 reviews a number of specific regulatory devices available to program planners.

Part II contains three chapters. Chapter 5 explains how MTBE was selected as a gasoline additive and the negative impact it was later found to have on water quality. Chapter 6 discusses the lack of strategic regulatory planning in the selection of MTBE as a gasoline oxygenate. Chapter 7 analyzes the effort to adopt a strategic approach for resolving the MTBE issue.

Part III has three chapters. The model for developing strategic regulatory plans introduced in chapter 2 (and elaborated on in chapters 3 and 4) is applied to the case of USTs in chapters 8, 9, and 10. The Conclusion then assesses the applicability of strategic regulatory planning to other environmental programs and to other policy areas. It also summarizes the major findings of the book and offers possible future avenues for policy research.

I

Strategic Planning and Effective Regulation

1

The Problem of Regulatory Strategy Formulation

The previous chapter presented an overview of government efforts to regulate hazardous materials, with particular attention paid to the issues involving the management of leaking USTs and the introduction and subsequent phase-out of MTBE as a gasoline additive.[1] When both programs began, policymakers believed that a new approach to regulation would have to be developed in order to achieve adequate rates of compliance. Perhaps most notably, attempts to manage USTs and include an oxygenate in gasoline would require environmental policymakers to deal with a huge target population with modest profit margins, something the EPA had rarely been asked to do before.

This was clearly a unique situation; policymakers are infrequently put in a position where a considerable amount of experimentation is required in order to meet specific goals. Most government agencies avoid experimenting with alternative policy approaches, building their new programs directly on the model of existing programs. As experience has shown, this tendency seriously underestimates the complexity of the problems government is often called on to solve and probably explains a certain amount of policy failure.[2] In the case of underground tanks, Congress had given EPA a major new regulatory task, and, in recognizing this, agency officials devised a fresh approach to controlling leaking USTs. In an effort to lower automobile emissions as required by the 1990 Clean Air Act Amendments, EPA and many states, including California, were required for the first time to select a new gasoline additive.[3] EPA had to experiment to some extent as a result.

This chapter discusses the major problems and issues involved in the formulation and implementation of a regulatory plan. While the book itself mainly addresses the formulation of regulatory programs, a number of critical and related implementation issues must first be considered. The chapter begins with a discussion of public policymaking theories relevant to regulation. After indicating exactly what is meant by regulation and identifying the factors that affect compliance, the question of why regulation planning is rarely strategic is addressed. The chapter then examines the difficulties in developing and implementing regulatory approaches.

How Policies Are Normally Developed

Public policies, including regulation, are typically incremental and partial rather than rational and comprehensive. Braybrooke and Lindblom observe that "the synoptic [rational] ideal is not adapted to man's limited problem solving capabilities."[4] Rational policymaking is problematic because it does not account for the inadequacy of information, cost of information, difficulty of truly separating ends from means, and openness of the system of variables with which it contends. Most policies are incremental because of limits on human capabilities to employ rational methods of policymaking. Steinbrunner indicates that something akin to incremental policymaking is quite common in nature.[5] He gives the example of the tennis player's returning an opponent's serve. Due to the speed of the ball, the player does not collect all the data relevant to the decision-making process and rationally calculate a response to the situation. The player does not formulate a response based on air currents, the exact velocity of the ball, measurement of the angle of the approach, and so on. Rather, the player scans the situation for the one or two most critical variables needed to return the ball. Steinbrunner explains: "We have already seen the secret of the ability [of simple decision-making mechanisms] to handle variety. The simplest cybernetic mechanisms do not confront the issue of variety at all, for they make no calculations of the environment. The mechanisms merely trace a few feedback variables and beyond that are perfectly blind to the environment. Hence degrees of complexity in the environment are of no concern within the decision making mechanism itself, and the burden of calculation which the analytic (rational) paradigm seems to impose is not a problem for cybernetic assumptions."[6]

Policymakers, using cybernetic mechanisms, deal only with what they must, reacting only when the environment changes the variables the mechanism deems critical (as a thermostat would react to the cooling of a room by turning on the heat while ignoring all other stimuli). In this sense, incremental policymaking is simply the survival of those procedures and institutions best suited to handle complexity, and the rational ideal is never attained.

Usually, government applies standard operating procedures (roughly analogous to cybernetic mechanisms) that deal with complexity by addressing only a few variables. Similar to the tennis player returning a serve, a policymaker usually has a limited amount of information and must react quickly. Decisions are made when the policymaker has correctly identified the few significant variables and has accurately interpreted the available information on these variables.

In a crisis situation, the policy environment is unstable, and confusion abounds. This was dramatically evident during and immediately following the attack on the World Trade Center twin towers and the Pentagon on September 11, 2001. Policymakers at all levels of government were forced to make decisions with little time to gather all the information necessary. Most quickly collected whatever data they could and took calculated risks in deciding what should be done. Perceived threats and time pressure did not allow officials the luxury of comprehensive data collection and extensive policy deliberation.

In noncrisis situations, the policy environment is stable and "decomposable" (it can be divided into segments that can be separately acted on). Although some confusion nearly always exists, the amount is obviously less than in crisis conditions. When the degree of change required is small and existing knowledge of the situation is slight, a strategy of disjointed incrementalism is pursued. This strategy is remedial, serial, and exploratory; policymakers move away from problems rather than toward solutions.[7] Braybrooke and Lindblom note that "analysis and evaluation are socially fragmented, that is, they take place at a very large number of points in a society. Analysis of any given problem area and of possible policies for solving the problem is often conducted in a large number of centers."[8]

The concept of overlap, or where one policymaker leaves off, another will pick up, is central to cybernetic theory and is central to the incremental model's response to the need for comprehensiveness suggested by rational theory. Although incrementalism is an accurate description of traditional policymaking, it is less useful in explaining policymaking during revolution, crisis, and what Braybrooke and Lindblom term "grand opportunities." In these situations Dror's "extra rational processes," Steinbrunner's "cognitive based inference machines," and Jones's nonincremental (and one might argue "cognitively based") "speculative augmentation" are core elements of the policymaking process.[9] In these situations, traditional policymaking procedures cannot produce required outputs. Basing decisions on a few obvious information sources that can trigger appropriate cybernetic mechanisms does not permit solution of the problem at hand. In crisis situations, humans infer from available theory and data and make a decision. Essentially, public officials estimate; they project in order to augment their normal ability to produce policies. It is in these situations that incrementalism cannot explain policy processes. Neither the need to control leaking USTs nor the need to include an oxygenate in gasoline to reduce air pollution was considered a crisis. Nevertheless, policymakers believed these two issues were important and wanted both of them effectively addressed as quickly as possible.

Hazardous Waste Policy

Typically, environmental regulatory programs, if not most other regulatory programs, are often products of disjointed policymaking. Components of complex policy issues are identified, separated, categorized, and subjected to detailed analysis. A difficulty with this approach is that it sometimes focuses agencies on means and encourages them to lose sight of ends. Due to complexity, the "whole" is so fragmented that policymakers and staff have little incentive to consider the big picture. Rather than worrying about whether a regulatory program will allow an agency to reach a legislative goal, many policymakers strive to improve the efficiency of the regulation development process.

EPA's hazardous waste regulatory program is a case in point. As reflected in the Resource Conservation and Recovery Act (RCRA) program, federal hazardous waste regulation was purely a paper exercise until 1982.[10] For seven years, EPA made numerous attempts to promulgate hazardous waste rules under RCRA before finally succeeding. While these rules were being developed, hazardous waste remained unregulated by the federal government. Difficulties in promulgating regulations stemmed from legal challenges to requirements and shifts in EPA policy. EPA's Office of Solid Waste became more concerned with process and policy issues than with implementation and improving environmental quality.[11]

This was apparent in EPA's interim permit program for hazardous waste treatment facilities. In order to receive interim permit status, a facility simply had to send in a postcard (a part B application) notifying EPA of its existence. Although this interim permit enabled facilities to operate with legal sanction, firms receiving permits were not required to make any changes in pollution control practices. Considerable organizational resources went into identifying facility operators and processing their interim permits. These steps were the necessary beginnings of a new regulatory process, though they did nothing to improve environmental quality.

As a result of the lessons learned from the RCRA program, one objective of this book is to investigate the possibility of introducing strategic planning into the regulatory process and to inject a genuine concern for implementation—resulting in compliance—into that process. Regulatory planning, however, is a disjointed and segmented process. Adding a concern for implementation cuts against the grain that establishes such policymaking practices in the first place. Nonetheless, it is advantageous for policymakers to address issues of feasibility prior to program execution. Although implementation is difficult to incorporate into the regulatory process, it is critical to do so. Formulating a strategy for implementing rules is an analytical or rational process difficult to graft onto an incremental process. It asks policymakers to project the behavioral impact of the policies they formulate. Strategic regulatory planning is therefore potentially useful since it requires a concern for both the formulation and implementation of specific regulatory policies.

The amount of analytical information that can be absorbed by a detailed, highly incremental regulatory process is questionable. Nevertheless, the issue is well worth exploring: Can regulation programs become more strategic? The following discussion defines strategic regulatory planning, discusses the difficulty of developing such a process, and points out why such a process might be valuable.

Defining Strategic Regulatory Planning

Meier defines regulation as "any attempt by the government to control the behavior of citizens, corporations, or subgovernments."[12] Strategic regulatory planning is an effort by government to develop a comprehensive strategy or tactic for controlling behavior. Hoffer and Schendel define strategy as the basic pattern of current and planned resource deployments and environmental interactions that indicate how the organization will achieve its objectives.[13] In strategic regulatory planning, the formal regulation itself is only one component among several available to control behavior. Funding, technical assistance, exhortation, and publicity are examples of other techniques that can be used to influence the behavior of regulated parties. Strategic planning seeks to place the promulgation of formal regulations within the context of other tools available to affect behavior. In the broadest sense, a regulatory strategy projects the impact of government action on the organizational environment of regulated parties.

Implementing a regulatory plan is different from implementing other types of governmental plans. It differs from a general implementation plan because its main objective is not to alter the behavior of implementing agencies, but rather to influence the actions of private regulated parties. In this sense, the goal of a regulatory plan is to achieve the highest rate of compliance possible. The chain of actors involved is far more complex and far more weakly connected than the chain of actors presented by Pressman and Wildavsky in their classic "decision point" analysis.[14] Implementing nonregulatory programs is difficult and requires tactical thinking. Implementing regulatory programs is typically even more difficult, and therefore tactical thinking may be even more important.

Strategic Thinking and Regulation

The search for market-based regulation, while a worthy endeavor, partially results from a misinterpretation of the relative success of regulation. First, as Meier indicates, most regulation has in fact been quite successful.[15] Certainly, an analysis of methods for influencing the behavior of regulated parties is a critical and frequently neglected element of the regulatory process. In some cases, market mechanisms may be reasonable, in others grant programs may be appropriate, and in some instances typical regulatory standard setting and enforcement (direct command-and-control regulation) may be necessary. Neither should be automatically favored without careful investigation or analysis. The point of strategic regulatory planning is to focus attention on the behavior of regulated parties in order to identify the positive and negative incentives government can offer or stimulate others to offer to increase compliance among target groups. Attention is shifted from bureaucratic and legalistic processes to the behavior of the regulated community. It is hoped that the emphasis on "wordsmanship" is replaced by an emphasis on behavior that is feasible in the real world.

The counterargument to this line of reasoning is that strict regulatory standards set clear and defensible rules of law and that a concern for feasibility should not be allowed to water down standards.[16] It is understood that the implementation process will inevitably cause rules to be compromised. Additionally, compromises from strict standards are preferred to compromises from debased standards. The difficulty with this argument is that unrealistic, infeasible regulations undermine respect for standards and may result in unanticipated and unwanted side effects. Realistic standards coupled with a concern for feasibility undermines internal opposition to regulation within the regulated community, or at the very least does not reinforce a common source of resistance to regulation. A concern for implementation directs attention to problems of that portion of the regulated community willing to comply. Particularly in new areas of regulation, a focus on those most willing and able to comply can result in dramatic progress toward reaching regulatory objectives. When moving from a condition of no regulation to a condition of regulation, compliance initially is often near zero. An emphasis at the outset on capacity building and co-opting regulated parties may result in greater change in behavior than a rigid policy of enforcing preestablished rules. The key is to maintain a credible enforcement threat to motivate compliance.[17]

Table 1.1
Factors affecting regulatory compliance

1. Capability + motivation + feasibility = Highest probability of compliance
2. Capability + motivation – feasibility = Low/no probability of compliance
3. Capability – motivation + feasibility = Low/no probability of compliance
4. Motivation + feasibility – capability = No probability of compliance
5. Feasibility – capability – motivation = No probability of compliance
6. No feasibility – motivation – capability = No probability of compliance
7. Motivation – feasibility – capability = No probability of compliance

Three critical factors logically affect whether regulated parties can and will comply with regulation. First, do they have the capability to improve their performance and come closer to behaving as expected by regulators? Second, are the regulations themselves feasible—that is, can competent firms or individuals comply? Third, if a firm is capable of complying and the regulations are feasible, is it at all motivated to modify its practices? This third factor hinges in part on the credibility of the enforcement threat. Table 1.1 lists some of the possible combination of factors and the effect of these factors on the probability of compliance. A variety of combinations is imaginable where the probability of compliance is either low or nonexistent. Where capability and feasibility are not issues, the emphasis on implementation leads to a focus on motivation and enforcement. Where feasibility is an issue, a concern for implementation leads to the development of more reasonable regulatory rules. Where capability is an issue, the emphasis is on working with the regulated community to develop the capacity for behavioral change. Regulatory strategy formulation involves an analysis of these factors and proposals for specific enforcement and assistance programs, and suggestions for feasible methods of achieving regulatory objectives.

The Promulgation of Regulation

Legislative bodies, in conjunction with executive leaders of government, enact laws designed to ameliorate certain problems in society. Whereas such legislation spells out the goals and intent of the law, legislative bodies often leave it up to agencies to write specific rules and guidelines and enforce them.[18] As the previous chapter explained, this is the primary aim of the rule-making process. Regulation writing by agencies, however, should be seen as a unique and important component of the larger policy formation and implementation process. As such, rule making should be viewed as a means for achieving policy goals, determined by the legislature, in conjunction with other mechanisms.

The promulgation of regulation is meaningless and can be misdirected when separated from a concern for implementation. The common perception that the concept of regulation is ineffective may be based on nonrepresentative experiences with particularly ineffective rules. This ineffectiveness may stem from the separation of policy formulation and implementation, not from any flaw in the concept of regulation. The success of the regulatory approach probably can be increased if it is adopted along with other policy tools in the overall implementation process.

Why Regulation Formulation Is Rarely Strategic

Regulations are typically promulgated with public and interest group input, and feasibility is often an important factor. There are many examples of guidelines, however, that are issued without assessing ability to implement. There also is a tendency for the regulatory process to focus on procedural and ideological issues rather than on practical concerns. Often, symbolic or emotional stands are taken on issues, or issues are raised that have little practical relevance in the real world. These tendencies have not developed because participants are ignorant, but rather because of the dictates or mandates of legislation, the notion that the rule of law will prevail and must be maintained, separation of policy formulators from policy implementers, or length of time and complexity of promulgation.

The Dictates of Legislation

Lowi complains that legislative mandates are often so vague that bureaucrats have little legislative guidance in writing rules.[19] Since the publication of his work, Congress has become much more diligent about specifying regulatory goals and standards.[20] Meier indicates that though fairly vague, "goals were normally used before 1970; since 1970 regulatory goals have been more specific."[21] The increased specificity of goals has tended to circumscribe administrative options and has encouraged regulators to adhere as closely as possible to the dictates of the legislature. Although Lowi's concern about interest group co-optation of bureaucracies is still warranted, a decline in interest group access and influence could remove a constraint previously imposed on regulators.[22]

The Notion That the Rule of Law Will Prevail

Drafters of symbolic regulations can take comfort in the fact that they are "right": their regulatory rules are an interpretation of a legal statute that represents the "will of the people." Regulators can assume that they have the law on their side and that regulated parties must obey that law. Certainly, a nation of laws must adhere to such a principle. Unfortunately, the world does not operate according to black and white principles. Unbending insistence on the sanctity of the law on the part of policymakers can make outlaws of firms that would like to live within the law but lack the means to do so. In a judicial system where plea bargaining is the rule rather than the exception, legal principles become relative rather than absolute concepts. Given the pervasive atmosphere of negotiation and compromise surrounding the judicial process, it is naive to believe that regulation can avoid such bargaining. Nevertheless, a clear obstacle to strategic regulation is the assumption that the rule of law is absolute and must prevail.

The Separation of Policy Formulators and Implementers

Another hindrance to strategic regulatory planning is that the people who write regulations (in agencies) are often not involved in program implementation.[23] This creates an artificial atmosphere somewhat divorced from reality. Often policy debate revolves around abstract or symbolic issues. Communication between policy formulators and implementers is frequently inadequate. Communication channels between writers of rules and regulated parties are even more attenuated.[24]

Promulgating rules and standards is complex and requires a set of highly specific skills. Substantive concerns must be balanced against the need for clear and legally defensible provisions and language. Unfortunately, process and legal concerns sometimes dominate because operational concerns are under represented. General counsel offices lose face if their regulations are poorly crafted. Regulatory or program offices are often judged on their ability to meet schedules rather than regulate wisely. Difficulties stemming from the separation of policy development and administration are exacerbated by these internal dynamics of regulation development.

The Length of Time and Complexity of Promulgation

The process of drafting regulations is dominated by a concern that the regulation be successfully promulgated. Those who write rules worry about the ability of their regulations to withstand court challenges and about internal and Office of Management and Budget (OMB) reviews. As discussed in the Introduction to the book, they also are increasingly concerned about the length of time it takes to promulgate regulations and the number of pages the regulation fills in the *Federal Register*.[25] The requirements for regulatory impact analysis, Paperwork Reduction Act compliance, internal agency review, OMB review, and public comment have produced a lengthy and complicated process. Work plans for promulgating even simple rules can have hundreds of decision points over many months.

Difficulties in Developing and Implementing Regulatory Strategies

There are a number of potential obstacles to developing and implementing regulatory strategies. Among them are the difficulty of projecting behavior, estimating resources, setting priorities, explicit strategies, obtaining the resources and authority to develop a regulatory plan, and implementing a strategic regulatory plan. This section briefly reviews each of these problems.

The Difficulty of Projecting Behavior

The critique of rational decision making levied by Braybrooke and Lindblom also applies to regulatory strategy formulation.[26] It is likely to be difficult and costly to obtain all the information needed to project the impact of government action on regulated parties. Even cooperative firms may not be capable of projecting their own response to specific government actions, and noncooperative firms may provide misleading information. Thus, the cost of making such projections can be quite high.

Still, it is critical for government to obtain an accurate picture of the regulated community's capacity for change. Rather than conducting major studies to project corporate behavior, it may be far more fruitful to use Peters and Waterman's strategy and conduct small-scale, short-turnaround pilot projects.[27] For example, perhaps policymakers could allow different states or regions to experiment with a variety of regulatory approaches to see which approach provides the most desirable results. The best regulatory plan may simply set up a number of distinct cybernetic mechanisms. Policymakers could then determine which devices are most able to produce the outputs desired. In this vein, Mintzberg has written of the need to craft strategies through incremental organizational learning: "Our craftsman tries to make a freestanding sculptural form. It doesn't work, she rounds it a bit here, flattens it a bit there. The result looks better, but still isn't quite right. She makes another, and another and another. Eventually, after days or months or years, she finally has what she wants. She is off on a new strategy."[28]

The Problem of Estimating Resources

With a variety of governmental and even nongovernmental organizations involved in regulation, it may be difficult to estimate the full range of resources available. It also is difficult to project the level of state, local, and private resources that will be allocated in response to federal regulatory initiatives. Even currently deployed resources are difficult to track. New regulatory tasks can sometimes be piggybacked on existing functions. Established educational institutions and mechanisms, analytical laboratories, inspection facilities and personnel, reporting and control systems, and other resources may be accessed for regulatory objectives at bargain rates.

Setting Priorities

Identifying mechanisms for implementing rules may be difficult and costly, but setting strategic priorities can be even more problematic. In some cases, the statute being implemented may be so vague that it is difficult to justify priorities. In other cases, such as the Hazardous and Solid

Waste Amendments (HSWA), the statute is so specific that priority setting is often problematic. In the case of HSWA, however, the paucity of administrative resources made such priority setting a practical necessity.

Although it is easier to develop a regulatory strategy by articulating and prioritizing goals, agencies are frequently not eager to set such priorities. Programs often require explicit value trade-offs. Congress, like the rest of the government, prefers to avoid such choices. Sometimes it avoids responsibility by using vague standards and simply telling the agency to "somehow solve the problem." At other times, it is overly specific in detailing the work it wants an agency to perform. Under this approach, trade-offs are avoided by telling the agency to promulgate rules immediately. In the absence of substantial additions to the agency's resource base, such specificity is symbolic and often meaningless. Priorities must still be set. However, priority setting takes place in an atmosphere of extreme time and resource pressure rather than in a programmed planning exercise.

The Danger of Explicit Strategies

Trade-offs made in the heat of the moment may not be noticed and may be an easily ignored case of "non decisionmaking."[29] Strategic choices committed to paper and analyzed can easily be used against the regulatory agency. The danger of an explicit strategy is that the agency must specify what it will *not do* in addition to what it *will do*. This is particularly problematic when legislation has "overspecified" a great number of activities that are not prioritized and that are trivial. On the one hand, administrative necessity forces an agency to make choices, and explicit approaches can improve the quality of those choices. Unfortunately, a reasonable regulatory plan might also be a political liability. On the other hand, a caveat-laden strategy might succeed in obscuring hard choices, but it also might be an inadequate guide to action.

The Difficulty of Obtaining the Resources and Authority to Develop a Regulatory Plan

Perhaps the greatest difficulty in developing a regulatory plan is obtaining the turf and resources that are required. Program or line offices that control the turf may not control all the turf and will almost never have the unencumbered resources needed to develop a thorough plan. Staff or policy offices may have the resources and expertise needed to develop a meaningful plan, but may not have the legitimacy or access to data needed to succeed. Clearly, a joint effort of some kind stands the greatest chance of success. Unfortunately, without firm and clear direction from a legislative or executive body, it is difficult to see how such cooperation is in the immediate short-term interest of either the program or staff office.

This is the previously discussed problem of grafting a rational planning process onto an incremental decision-making structure. Organizational units are divided and subdivided to narrow the scope of complexity that must be addressed by a given unit. This enables complex issues to be acted on, but it does not ensure that the separate components of the issue are ever analyzed as a whole. In the typical regulatory process, feedback from the regulated community and the public is articulated by and through regional field offices, state and local governments, and interest groups. The most unreasonable aspects of a regulatory policy are gradually adjusted to conform to the dictates of reality. In this sense, the regulatory process is actually an evolutionary process nearly always requiring modifications and midcourse corrections over time. Success is achieved when such adjustments lead to continued improvements in the given problem, which happened in the case of water pollution control.[30]

This typical process creates generally satisfactory results. Where results have not been satisfactory, it has been assumed that the problem is with regulation as a concept rather than the specific characteristics of a given regulation. Economists have advocated using prices, taxes, and the market to regulate business behavior.[31] Conservatives have advocated deregulation and a reliance on free enterprise and market choice to ensure attainment of social good.[32] When Vice President George Bush headed a panel on regulatory reform early in the Reagan presidency, he judged the panel's success by the number of regulations eliminated rather than the number of regulations improved. Those who maintain that business is always more successful than government in getting things done seem to ignore the record number of bankruptcies and the savings and loan crisis that occurred in the late 1980s and early 1990s, as well as the sudden collapse of several of the nation's largest companies (along with the indictments of their top executives for using illegal accounting practices) at the turn of the century.

Given these economic, political, and analytical biases, it is not surprising that there have been few meaningful attempts at improving the effectiveness of regulation. In addition, it is difficult for such an activity to find a place in government. The most likely possibility would be in the policy offices of agency chief executives or their principal deputies. Agency policy and management shops, the other likely formulators of regulatory programs, have become something of an endangered species. While the 1960s and 1970s saw dramatic growth in these organizations, they suffered a sustained attack at the federal level under the Reagan administration. They did not significantly grow in succeeding presidential administrations.

The Difficulty of Implementing a Strategic Regulatory Plan

Even if an organization manages to develop a strategic regulatory plan, it may be quite difficult to update and implement such a plan. First, the rules that are promulgated must conform to the plan's parameters. Determining conformity is a fairly straightforward analysis; however, imposing conformity may be a different matter. If the program is not developed and overseen by the office promulgating the rules, it may very well be ignored. Even if all the organizations responsible for drafting standards are involved in strategic planning, it is possible that conflicts and contradictions may arise between the dictates of the program and the mandates of the legislation. Assuming that rules are made to conform to strategic requirements, the next step is to ensure that the regulatory program is executed as written. If a plan requires contributions from a variety of organizational units—private, federal, state, and local—then simply tracking activities may be a challenge. It often is difficult to develop realistic operational measures and quantify certain variables. Moreover, it may be impossible to collect data from a multitude of actors. Beyond tracking, there is the problem of motivating these institutions to perform as desired. Such motivation will require a careful blending of incentives and well-trafficked, two-way communication patterns.[33]

Even if a strategic regulatory plan is developed and rules adhere to regulatory techniques, other activities aimed at influencing target groups adhere to strategic requirements, and the institutions involved in implementing the plan perform as expected, a plan may still not be successfully executed. In the final analysis, a program is successfully implemented if the behavior of regulated parties changes in the manner desired. A proposed plan must be flexible and capable of evolution. In the real world, approaches must be modified, institutional arrangements must be solidified, and incentives must be fine-tuned. In many cases, regulated parties will not alter their behavior without a credible threat of punishment for noncompliance. An effective regulatory process will test the tolerance of the regulated party and adjust accordingly. Changing target group behavior is a slow process at best. It should be expected that inducing behavioral change will be a difficult and often painstaking undertaking.

Regulatory Reform and Innovation

In recent years, efforts have been made to promote regulatory reform and innovation, primarily as an attempt to overcome the shortcomings of traditional command-and-control regulation. Many of the reforms and innovations are quite creative and include, for example, cap-and-trade programs to reduce airborne emissions, markets for water pollution permits, voluntary strategies, coregulation, greater stakeholder involvement, and community-based environmental protection and natural resource conservation. Some approaches emphasize entrepreneurship and reinvention, attempt to reduce red tape, and promote market or network strategies. Thus far, the new reforms and techniques have had mixed success.

One of the most important innovative approaches has been the rise of grassroots governance efforts in western communities and elsewhere across the country. Those promoting these efforts have tried to reconcile competing values through collaborative and participatory decision making that brings together citizens, key stakeholders, and government agencies in search of acceptable and effective solutions. These ad hoc and voluntary arrangements have sought to develop consensus on habitat conservation plans for protecting endangered species, restoration efforts for degraded ecosystems, planned communities and smart-growth strategies for suburban areas, and redevelopment of brownfields. Weber's study, for example, explores the use of grassroots governance processes (grassroots ecosystem management, or GREM) in rural communities in the West, where local economies have been heavily dependent on natural resource use, such as timber harvesting.[34] He concludes that GREM can produce win-win outcomes and help to integrate environmental and economic values.

Cooperation and collaboration between business groups and the federal government increased during the 1990s, with certain companies publicly announcing that they now wish to go "beyond compliance" and join the "greening of industry" movement. Taking advantage of this change in perspective on the part of corporate America, the EPA launched a number of voluntary government programs to encourage even more companies to follow this path. The 33/50 program was begun in 1991, just prior to President Clinton's taking office, with the goal of reducing releases of seventeen high-priority chemicals by 33 percent by 1992 and 50 percent by 1995. According to the U.S. General Accounting Office, the program has achieved moderate success.[35] The Energy Star program, which began in June 1992, certifies energy-efficient appliances, electronic equipment, personal computers and computer equipment, and many other products. By 2001 there were more than 11,000 Energy Star–compliant products widely used in the United State and in other nations, resulting in considerable energy and cost savings.[36] Project XL (e*X*cellence and *L*eadership), launched in November 1995, was an attempt to reward superior corporate environmental performers with greater statutory and regulatory flexibility. The program permits industry a certain latitude in seeking cleaner, cost-effective environmental management strategies. According to Beardsley et al., the program has had few environmental benefits and requires new authorizing legislation to enhance its limited incentives for participation.[37] The Common Sense Initiative (CSI) was designed to move environmental protection beyond the traditional command-and-control, pollutant-by-pollutant approach to a novel industrial sector-by-sector approach aimed at developing integrated, comprehensive strategies for protecting air and water quality and land.[38] Coglianese and Allen reveal that despite claims by federal government officials, only a handful of the projects developed under CSI have produced technological innovations or pollution prevention, or have resulted in any other significant policy change.[39] Instead, most of the projects resulted only in the development of educational material or the collection of information. In 2002 and 2003 EPA established the Design for the Environment (DfE) program and the Sector Strategies program, respectively. The DfE assesses the potential environmental impacts of a product, as well as the materials and processes used to make that product. EPA's Sector Strategies Program works directly with industry sectors, along with their stakeholders and trade groups, to make production processes less damaging to the environment.[40]

Industry, too, has taken the initiative and developed voluntary programs that attempt to improve its environmental management practices. The Responsible Care program, for example, was instituted by the Chemical Manufacturing Association (CMA) in the wake of the explosion at a chemical plant in Bhopal, India, in 1984.[41] Responsible Care is a comprehensive program containing a variety of elements from community education and emergency response to pollution prevention, process safety, and employee health. The CMA openly admits that the purpose of this program is to quiet criticism of their industry by improving the environmental, health, and safety performance record of their members.[42] Garcia-Johnson argues that multinational companies in the U.S.-based chemical industry are successfully exporting corporate voluntarism in the form of environmentalism through Responsible Care.[43] This program, however, has had mixed success in the United State until now. Regardless of its motives, in recent years industry has indeed shown some willingness to address difficult pollution and natural resource problems on its own.[44]

The chemical industry and others have severely criticized Superfund for being unfair, misdirected, and wasteful, and EPA has adopted a number of new implementation measures as a result. Nakamura and Church assess these new measures in their study of regulatory reform in the Superfund program.[45] They discuss why coercive policy approaches meet frequent challenges to their legitimacy and why attempts to reform such programs present unique administrative and implementation challenges. They convincingly argue that regulation and other coercive approaches remain effective and necessary strategies for meeting public policy goals. The two researchers show how changes in the Superfund program were formulated and implemented, and they explain why the reforms generally succeeded.

A number of studies by Resources for the Future address the movement from direct command-and-control regulation to new, innovative regulatory strategies. Fischbeck et al., for example, note that despite criticisms of regulation, the progress that has been made in protecting the environment is due to regulation.[46] They believe the United States has succeeded in controlling significant environmental, health, and safety problems and that pollutants and other harmful emissions have declined. In their view, the challenge is now to improve the regulatory system by dealing with problems that are more subtle, especially when our evolving knowledge of science and engineering paves the way for more nuanced forms of measuring and understanding environmental degradation. They argue that existing regulatory approaches must be made more flexible so that they can be tailored to each regulatory context and objective.[47]

The National Academy of Public Administration (NAPA) examined regulatory reform at EPA and issued a report to Congress in 1997.[48] The report focuses on two aspects of improving environmental regulation: an increased emphasis on performance and a search for alternatives to traditional command-and-control regulation. NAPA's report discusses the goal of strategic regulation: the drive for cost-effective environmental performance and results. According to the report, "The hallmark of performance-based management is a focus on measuring and achieving specific environmental outcomes rather than agency activities or 'inputs.' "[49] Although the data collected on performance-based management will help EPA and state officials make better decisions for the environment, the data will not make the decisions easier for the agency. This study adopts the NAPA definition of strategic regulation and planning in its analysis of MTBE and USTs.

Summary

This chapter has analyzed the issues and problems concerning regulatory strategy formulation. It began with a theoretical discussion of how public policies are usually developed. The point was made that public policies, including regulation, are normally incremental and partial rather than rational and comprehensive. After reviewing how process and policy issues took precedent over implementation in hazardous waste management, the analysis defined the concept of strategic regulatory planning and examined why regulation formulation is rarely strategic. The difficulties associated with developing and implementing regulatory strategies were addressed. Recent research on regulatory reform and innovation was summarized at the conclusion of the discussion.

This investigation provides an example of EPA's developing one program with strategic elements and developing a second program without a systematic effort to develop a strategic regulatory plan. There are a number of reasons why underground tank regulation was strategic and most EPA policy development is not. The political context of the policy is perhaps the central element of the difference. While private firms tend to resist regulation reflexively, the regulation of leaking underground storage tanks was not a particularly contentious political issue. As already noted, the tanks were not leaking valueless wastes but a valuable product. The owners of these tanks had no economic interest in allowing the tanks to leak. In fact, the larger and more powerful oil companies may have had a reason to support regulation as a method of increasing the capital requirements to sell gasoline and driving smaller companies out of business. This relative lack of political heat gave EPA the opportunity to develop a program focused on the behavior of regulated parties. While the regulatory process included conflict and active participation of interest groups, compared to other EPA policy areas, it was relatively noncontentious.

In contrast, the regulation of the content of gasoline as a method of reducing air pollution is among the most contentious policy areas in which EPA works. Due to differing environmental conditions, the content of gasoline varies by region. The cost and complexity of refining gasoline mean that regulations affecting gasoline content can have a direct impact on the price of fuel that the mass consuming public pays at the pump. EPA is under extraordinary cross-pressure from the environmental community, the oil industry, consumer groups, and elected officials. After a while, just getting a regulation promulgated is seen by the agency as a priority. Policymakers often consider strategic thinking under these conditions to be a luxury. When attempted, it is often overwhelmed by changes made to respond to interest group demands.

This study recognizes the needs and requirements of the political process and does not call for eliminating politics in environmental policymaking. Still, even when dealing with contentious political issues, it is possible for administrative agencies to develop strategic plans that may influence the political dialogue and eventually be implemented when nonstrategic efforts fail or the level of political heat dies down.

2

A Strategic Approach to the Regulatory Planning Process

Linder and Peters provide an extensive analysis and critique of the policy implementation literature.[1] They divide previous implementation studies into two broad groups that they label "The Horrors of War" and "The Search for Theory." Scholarship belonging to the first group dwells on the various obstacles to effective implementation.[2] Studies in the second category reflect four major theoretical views of implementation: the top-down perspective, the bottom-up perspective, evolution and background mapping, and the bottom-down approach.[3] Linder and Peters's main critique of the existing implementation literature is its tendency, especially evident in the bottom-up approach, to combine empirical and normative statements. They argue that "the selection of *goals* and the mechanisms for attaining those goals should be made foremost on the basis of what we want to do, not what we can do easily."[4] Consequently, policy research has moved away from "developing better mechanisms for designing policies and designing implementation systems."[5] At the conclusion of their work, they call for greater consideration for the application of carefully thought out design criteria in policy formulation and implementation.[6]

The previous chapter discussed regulation as policy formulation, and it pointed out how formulation and implementation are frequently uncoordinated. In addition to the unique features of the regulatory process that distinguish it from other policy areas, it has a distinct goal: achieving compliance. As a result, the regulatory process requires analysts to conceptualize outputs and outcomes somewhat differently than it does in other policy domains (e.g., redistributive programs).[7] Obvious as it may seem, analysts must take this into account in the design and implementation of regulatory plans and in the assessment of their performance. Whether a public housing program has been successfully implemented, for example, might depend on such diverse factors as the number of housing units built over a given period of time, the overall quality of the housing, the percentage of units occupied to date, complaints about crime and services, and other similar variables. Whether a regulatory program has been successfully designed and implemented, in contrast, is primarily dependent on the level of compliance achieved among predefined target groups and, for the purpose of this study, improvement in environmental quality.

This chapter identifies a series of steps that the EPA could have taken in UST regulation and the gasoline additive program. Although these steps were developed with the Hazardous and Solid Waste Amendments (HSWA) in mind, they are applied to the selection of MTBE as an oxygenate as well. The approach adopted here should be applicable to the regulatory planning process in most other environmental and public policy areas and should be especially helpful in instances where some experimentation in regulation is required in order to achieve legislative aims. At the outset of the chapter, a schematic model is offered as a guide for policymakers. The suggested steps are then followed in Parts II and III of this book. Thus, this chapter provides a broad overview of the issues, trends, and interdependencies involving the various actors in the regulatory arena.

In contrast to other studies, this investigation views the regulatory planning process in a strategic manner. Regulators are encouraged to examine the actors in the process tactically, addressing such questions as: What are the motivations of the actors? What internal and external resources are available to them to conform, ignore, or fight? How motivated are they to use these identified resources? What supports or conflicts exist between the desired change in behavior in question and other regulatory programs already in operation?

Most important, strategic regulatory planning involves a close examination of the legislative goals concerning the given policy. Among the questions that must be addressed are: Do policymakers understand the goals of the legislative body? Are these goals attainable? The ultimate end of strategic regulatory planning is to control behavior through methods that agree with legislative aims and societal values regarding the issues at hand. Thus, a strategic approach demands careful consideration first of whether enforcement is appropriate; second, if enforcement is appropriate, to what degree the parties involved should be pressured to comply; and third, how coercive the regulatory device should be. Prior to introducing the strategic regulatory planning model, the next section discusses the meaning of compliance.

Defining Compliance

How compliance is defined can vary markedly depending on the actors involved and the policymaking context. In this study, compliance means the degree to which members of a target group conform to the directives of an agency, court, legislative body, or some other governmental unit. Since compliance implies behavior of some sort, we use the term *compliant behavior* in the study. One way to determine whether members of a target group are in compliance with an environmental law is to monitor levels of pollution on a regular basis. The EPA and other state and local agencies often use sophisticated equipment to track, for example, possible changes in air and water pollution levels in designated areas. In theory, the greater the number of firms that are in compliance with rules, the more likely pollution will decrease and environmental conditions will improve in a given locality.

One way to determine the proportion of individuals or institutions (public or private) in compliance is to survey the target population. However, sometimes it is difficult to discern whether a particular mode of behavior on the part of certain individuals or organizations satisfies the objectives of policymakers. This is often true when statutes and regulations are ambiguous or when the level of compliance cannot be scientifically and accurately determined. In such cases, analysts might rely on the perception of regulators to help judge the overall effectiveness of an enforcement program. Although such perceptions also are subject to error, they are sometimes the only information available for evaluative purposes.

A Model for Strategic Regulatory Planning

This section presents a model for strategic regulatory planning to encourage policymakers to approach regulation through a tactical, step-by-step process and to link policy formulation with implementation. The steps are derived from a schematic outline of political strategy formulation developed by MacMillan and Jones.[8] Research conducted by Hoffer and Schendel was also helpful in identifying specific elements of the model.[9] As readers will note, the model incorporates elements of both incremental decision making (e.g., the need to take previous actions into account) and rational decision making (e.g., the recommended use of cost-benefit analysis). Figure 2.1 lists the seven major steps that should be followed in designing an effective regulatory program.

Step 1	Problem Recognition	What is at issue?
Step 2	Identification of Parties	Who is involved?
Step 3	Historical analysis	How have different levels of government and the parties involved responded to this issue in the past? Why?
Step 4	Situational Analysis	
	A. Mission/objectives	What outcomes are desired?
	B. Party analysis	What are the motivations, goals, positions, and resources of each party to comply with, ignore, or fight the desired behavioral changes?
Step 5	Strategic Regulation Formulation	Determination of the conditions in the regulated community, regulating agency, and the outside arena that affect the cost and level of coerciveness of alternative regulatory devices. The most appropriate devices are then chosen to influence target group behavior and achieve compliance.
Step 6	Ex Ante Review	Addresses the fit and feasibility of the regulatory plan before implementation.
Step 7	Ex Post Review/Revision	Following implementation, how successful has the regulatory plan been at modifying behavior? Is further modification needed?

Figure 2.1
A seven-step model for strategic regulatory planning

The approach outlined in figure 2.1 differs markedly from traditional approaches to the regulatory planning process. All too often, policymakers skip directly to the strategic regulation formulation step, bypassing entirely the preliminary stages that are necessary to create a dynamic rather than static formulation process. Perhaps this proclivity is due to impatience on the part of officials to solve the problem at hand immediately. Operating within a very short time frame or believing the issue to be extremely serious can nurture this feeling. In many cases, however, a lack of thoroughness is the culprit. The result generally is the adoption of regulatory devices that are neither cost-effective nor in agreement with legislative intentions. Policymakers overseeing the most successful regulatory programs are likely to have followed the preliminary steps in the model. While some may believe that following the seven steps lengthens the regulatory process, each stage is vital to a tactical approach to regulatory planning. The following sections discuss each of the seven steps in detail.

Step 1: Problem Recognition

The first step of the strategic regulatory planning process is problem recognition. Before taking any action, the following questions must be considered:

- What issue is being addressed?
- What is the source of the undesirable behavior?
- Why does this behavior persist?
- What parties are responsible for perpetuating the undesirable behavior?
- How serious is this problem now? Potentially?
- How long has this problem persisted?

The problem recognition stage serves to focus efforts on a clearly definable problem or issue. Policymakers are encouraged to examine the issue in a dynamic rather than static process; that is, the problem should be recognized as a logical result of dynamic forces. Admittedly, there is often a lack of information or some degree of uncertainty at the outset. The problem recognition stage serves to identify the issue and players and provide an introduction to the question at hand.

All too often, the problem recognition statement is either forced into one sentence or hopelessly lost in pages of prose. And although a one-sentence statement clearly forces the policymaker to think succinctly and serves to focus further efforts, the questions posed above cannot be properly addressed in only a few words. Nevertheless, care should be taken to make the product of this stage concise.

Step 2: Identification of Parties

This step serves to identify all individuals and groups that are directly or indirectly involved in or affected by the problem. Most, if not all, of these actors are frequently referred to as stakeholders in the public policy literature. Five primary categories of parties should be examined:

- Legislative parties (e.g., Congress and state legislatures)
- Regulatory parties (federal agencies, state agencies, and local officials)
- Target groups
- Victim groups
- Interested third parties

The legislative parties usually serve as the impetus to the regulatory planning process. Moreover, they provide the legal authority for successful implementation and enforcement. The regulatory parties are usually considered the implementation and enforcement agents. In addition to serving this role, they are also knowledgeable and interested about the issue being regulated. They should be considered facilitators as well as enforcement agents.

Target groups are private or public groups or individuals whose behavior is considered counter to societal goals as determined by a legislative body. They can vary by such characteristics as size, wealth, business, political and economic self-interest, and geographic location. Members can be organized into professional associations, or they may exist independent of one another. In the public sector, agencies (e.g., the Tennessee Valley Authority) and individuals (e.g., county health officials) are potential target groups. As explained before, regulation attempts to control the behavior of target populations so that other individuals, groups, or society as a whole are protected.

Victim groups are those who are adversely affected by the persistent behavior (past, present, or future) of the target population. Victims can be individuals or groups, or even society as a whole. In many cases, the outcry of these groups forces legislative bodies to enact regulatory statutes.

Finally, interested third parties are groups or individuals who have some direct or indirect stake in the issue, generally through the market system. Automobile insurance companies, for example, would constitute interested third parties in deliberations over proposed regulations concerning the installation of a new safety feature (e.g., the air bag) in automobiles. Whether and to what degree they become involved in a controversy often depends on their economic position in the controversy.

The identification of stakeholders is an essential step in the strategic regulatory planning process. Often, traditional approaches focus only on regulatory parties and target groups. Failure to consider the role or position of other groups, such as interested third parties, can result in the development of misguided and unnecessarily expensive programs. Without question, regulatory parties and target groups are the primary actors in the regulatory process. However, it also is important to recognize and consider the roles of others that are affected by the issue.

Step 3: Historical Analysis

This stage requires policymakers to gain an understanding of the history and seriousness of the problem, as well as the effectiveness of previous regulatory attempts at different levels of government. The following questions should be addressed:

- How long has this suboptimal behavior persisted?
- What previous attempts have been made at prevention?
- regulatory attempts
- legislative attempts
- market pressure
- How successful or unsuccessful were these attempts? Why?
- How have the regulated parties responded to these efforts?
- How have the other involved or affected parties responded? Why?

This step encourages policymakers to learn from the past. In the regulatory planning process, historical analysis is crucial. For various reasons, many prior regulatory efforts may have been unsuccessful at changing behavior, while other efforts may have changed the behavior in question but produced unwanted side effects. The historical analysis stage not only ensures that prior mistakes are avoided but, more important, identifies the underlying party motivations and external causes that precipitated prior regulatory failure.

Step 4: Situational Analysis

The situational analysis phase serves two purposes. First, it identifies, conceptually and operationally, the specific goals and desired outcomes. Second, it assesses the strengths, weaknesses, resources, and motivations of each party involved. From a tactical standpoint, policymakers attempt to predict the responses of each party to the regulatory stimulus and explain the motivations or reasons for responding in such a manner. Public choice theory might be helpful in this regard.[10] Meetings, documents, and surveys can provide important data during this phase of the model. A thorough situational analysis will help identify and eliminate unwise regulatory approaches at the outset, thereby increasing the potential for developing a successful plan. The situational analysis is divided into two segments: mission/objectives and party analysis.

Mission/Objective The mission/objective segment identifies the goals of the pertinent legislative and regulatory bodies. Why are they interested? What do they want to accomplish? How do they want to change behavior? How much change do they believe is needed or desired? The importance of this exercise is self-evident: a regulatory policy must follow from an attempt to achieve a set of clearly stated goals. Where the strategic approach to this step differs, however, is that the mission/objective must be addressed on two levels, policy and operational.

At the policy level, what does the legislative body or regulatory agency want to have happen, and why? This question should be answered in broad, nondescriptive terms. The value of the policy mission/objective is to provide an overall direction to the rule-making process. The policy level also helps to identify legislative and regulatory priorities. Such questions as the urgency of the issue and the seriousness of the existing or future problem should be addressed at this level.

In addition to the policy mission/objective, operational guidelines and goals also must be identified. Operational objectives should be concrete, quantifiable, and attainable and identify measurable results. These objectives provide a basis for assessing the success or failure of the regulatory strategy in modifying target group behavior.

Party Analysis Policymakers at this level are required to examine each of the affected parties identified in step 2 of the model and ask a series of questions aimed at further anticipating party reactions to varying regulatory approaches. In general, the following question should be addressed: What are the motivations, goals, positions, and resources of the party to comply with, ignore, or oppose the proposed behavioral changes? Broken down by specific party group, additional questions and activities might prove insightful.

Legislative Parties

- How much of a priority is this issue?
- How does this issue fit with other priorities?
- What political pressure is associated with this issue?
- What type of resources has the legislative party devoted to this issue?

Regulatory Parties

- Examine the existence and viability of roles by federal, state, and local governments, as well as the public, trade associations, and other actors (e.g., oil and gasoline companies).
- Examine the possibility of a combination of regulatory actors.
- Assess the resources (political, financial, reputation, personnel, and others) of each actor and the relationship between the resources of actors and the task at hand. If the relationship is inadequate, perhaps another player needs to be substituted or another combination of regulatory players is needed.
- What motivation does each party have to deploy its available resources to comply with regulation? If the motivation or incentive for resource deployment is not substantial, how can the situation be manipulated to provide adequate incentive?

- What is the reputation of each actor? Does the reputation of an actor prevent effective implementation by that party?

Target Groups

- How large is the target group? (There may be more than one.)
- How diverse is the target group (size diversity, geographic diversity, industry diversity, and degree of violation diversity)?
- What resources (e.g., political, economic, reputation, and personnel) are available to comply with, ignore, or oppose the regulation?
- What motivation does the group have to apply these resources toward compliance? Toward ignoring the regulation? Toward fighting the regulation?
- What type of market pressures can be exerted on the target group to force compliance? How susceptible is the target group to this pressure?
- How organized is the target group? What is the probability of the target group's attempting to block the regulation?
- How does the regulatory goal fit with the personal goals of the target group?

Victim Groups

- How directly is the victim group affected?
- How apparent is it that the target group is the guilty party?
- How motivated is the victim group?
- What resources does the victim group have available?
- How susceptible is the target group to victim group pressures?

Interested Third Parties

- How close are the parties to this issue? How close are the regulatory objectives to the personal objectives of the parties?
- How motivated are the parties to participate in the resolution of this problem?
- What resources do the parties have available?
- How susceptible are these parties to outside (market or political) pressure?

In general, these questions and activities are intended to promote a broad and in-depth analysis of the resources and motivations of each party to act in a desirable or undesirable manner. Interplay between the groups is very important, and for this reason each of the five groups must be carefully examined. One might hypothesize, for instance, that the greater the potential influence of a market mechanism and the greater the motivation and resources of the victim parties, the less effort is required by the regulatory parties to ensure the successful implementation of a regulatory program. Less regulatory party involvement translates directly into lower costs—and a larger bang for the buck.

Dunn outlines a procedure that provides possible insights into the future behavior of policy stakeholders.[11] The procedure, which he refers to as the feasibility assessment technique (FAT), allows analysts to produce forecasts about the likely impact of stakeholders in supporting or opposing the adoption or implementation of various policy alternatives. Dunn believes that FAT is "particularly well suited for problems requiring estimates of the probable consequences of attempting to legitimize policy alternatives under conditions of political conflict and the unequal distribution of power and other resources."[12]

More specifically, FAT measures different aspects of political and organizational behavior, including the issue positions, available resources, and relative resource rank of third parties. An index of total feasibility is created using a mathematical formula. From Dunn's standpoint, FAT "forces the analyst to make explicit subject judgments, rather than treat political and organizational questions in a loose or arbitrary fashion. Feasibility assessment also enables analysts to systematically consider the sensitivity of issue positions and available resources to changes in policy alternatives."[13] This approach is not used in the examination of the MTBE and UST cases in this study due to the enormous number of stakeholders involved. Nonetheless, future researchers may wish to consider employing FAT in their work.

Step 5: Strategic Regulation Formulation

This stage is what is most often considered the regulation planning process. Here, specific regulatory devices are selected and the actual regulatory program takes shape. Many policymakers consider this step to be the most critical part of the process. Due to the importance of this phase, the next chapter expands on the current discussion and develops a conceptual framework for the selection of specific regulatory devices.

The goal of strategic regulatory planning is to develop a program that follows from and is consistent with the tactical analysis. The general premise is that the more consistent the regulatory program is with the tactical analysis, the more successful the program is likely to be in terms of compliance and improved conditions. There are three main activities in the strategic regulation formulation stage: determination of desired degree of compliance, determination of the viability of self-regulation as a regulatory mechanism, and determination of degree, type, and method of direct regulatory involvement.

Determination of Desired Degree of Compliance When legislators pass laws, they generally expect them to be vigorously enforced and fully obeyed. Only idealists, however, actually believe that this is possible or even necessary in all cases. Political and economic factors usually force policymakers to take a realistic approach to enforcement by setting a desired and attainable level of compliance prior to program implementation. At this stage, policymakers must consider whether 100 percent compliance is necessary. If it is not, they must determine what degree of compliance is needed in order to meet environmental quality goals. Although the desired degree of compliance is often only a rough estimate, several factors must be kept in mind. Policymakers must take into account, for example, the resources of the target and enforcement groups. The susceptibility of the target group to the influence of the market system, victim groups, and interested third parties should also be considered.

If it is either unrealistic or undesirable to aim for total compliance on the part of the target population, a clear decision rule must be formulated concerning enforcement priorities. In a policy area where polluters vary a great deal in size and how much they pollute, for example, it probably would be prudent to concentrate enforcement efforts on the largest polluters. If firms are roughly the same size and pollute about the same amount, however, alternative guidelines for identification and discrimination must be set. For instance, will businesses be selected randomly for compliance checks? Is systematic enforcement, perhaps based on location, possible? Or is self-regulation the most preferable approach?

The decision rule should relate to the strategic goals, resources, and motivations thus far discussed. Further considerations include the legal authority for enforcement, the resources of the enforcement agency, and the fragmentation of the enforcement agency (or agencies).

Determining the Viability of Self-Regulation Self-regulation, if viable, has several advantages over direct regulation, including greater efficiency through the market system, less government involvement, fewer regulatory resources expended, fewer transaction costs, and the promotion of a positive relationship between government and industry. For these reasons, whenever viable, self-regulation is preferred over direct regulatory intervention. The problem lies in identifying the conditions necessary for self-regulation to be a feasible and potentially effective regulatory alternative.

The flowchart in Figure 2.2 provides a brief outline of the conditions necessary for self-regulation to be practical as well as a rudimentary decision rule. If the resources of the target group are sufficient to permit self-regulation and there is motivation to commit these resources, self-regulation is a viable alternative. Also, if the threat of enforcement

Might self-regulation be enough? ---------no-------► Active government involvement is needed.

yes

Are target group's resources enough to allow self-regulation? ---------no-------► Active government involvement is needed.

yes

Is there a motivation to commit these resources? ---------yes------► SELF-REGULATION

no

Is threat of enforcement enough to insure compliance? ---------no-------► Active government involvement is needed.

yes

Can noncompliance be hidden? ---------yes------► Active government involvement is needed.

no

SELF-REGULATION

Figure 2.2
Self-regulation flowchart

is sufficient to ensure compliance, and noncompliance cannot be hidden by members of the target group, self-regulation is feasible.

The decision rule provides a basic framework for determining when self-regulation will work. When conditions favorable to self-regulation are not present, policymakers must consider whether it is more efficient and cost-effective to attempt to create conditions that increase the viability of self-regulation than to expend energy and resources developing a direct regulatory approach. Admittedly, conditions favorable to self-regulation may be rare. The obvious advantages of this approach, however, justify serious consideration of its adoption.

Direct Regulatory Intervention After determining that self-regulation alone insufficiently motivates the target group to modify its behavior, more direct government involvement must be considered. The key questions to ask here are:

- How much government involvement is necessary?
- What means (or methods) of involvement best fit with the analyses performed above?
- What relationship or atmosphere is best maintained between the regulatory party and the target group?

The specific regulatory tactics and devices available are discussed in detail in chapter 4. The methods available include:

- Market solutions and economic incentives
- Insurance programs
- Taxes, fees, and other negative incentives
- Education, information disclosure, and media involvement
- Reporting and formal compliance tracking
- Licensing
- Permits
- Standard setting
- Penalty setting
- Inspection
- Adjudication

Each of these regulatory devices has advantages and disadvantages. The strategic regulatory planning process requires that these devices be adopted (either individually or in combination) so that an optimal fit is obtained between fulfillment of regulatory goals, advantages and disadvantages of selected regulatory tactics, and party goals, motivation, and resources.

Step 6: Ex Ante Analysis

The ex ante analysis addresses the fit and feasibility of the selected regulatory program before implementation. This acts to avoid wasted effort, resources, and time spent in implementing a poor regulatory program by identifying potential trouble spots before it is too late. The following questions should be asked:

- Can the regulated party understand what is expected? Does it understand how its behavior is to be changed?
- Are the goals and methods specific enough to serve as operational incentives?
- Will the implementation of this strategy have the desired effect on behavior?
- Are the enforcement mechanisms too lenient? Should the cost of noncompliance be raised?
- Does the program produce subsequent undesirable behavior in other areas (either by the target group or any other population)?

Although definitive answers to many of these questions cannot be determined prior to implementation, it may be possible to make some rough estimates. At the very least, addressing these issues will serve to identify serious flaws in the proposed regulatory plan that previously may have been overlooked. As flaws are singled out, policymakers should trace back through the strategic plan to the problem point and reformulate the regulatory plan using the modified knowledge base.

Step 7: Ex Post Review and Revision

At this stage policymakers determine the effectiveness of the regulatory program after it has been implemented by using feedback and

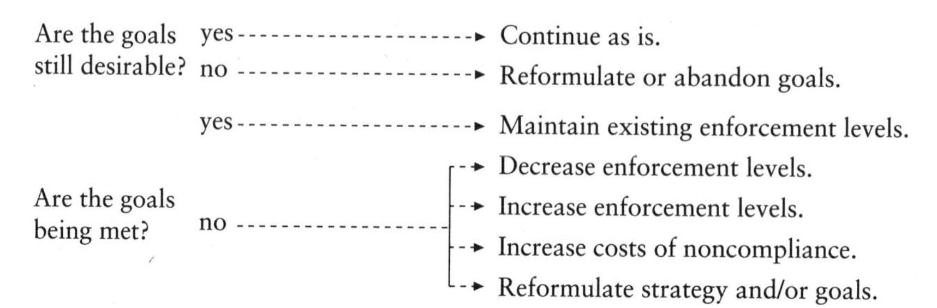

Figure 2.3
Ex post review/revision flowchart

evaluation. The operational objectives identified in step 4 serve as the basis for comparison.

The decision analysis shown in Figure 2.3 serves as a simple framework for ex post review and, if necessary, revision. If policymakers determine that the program goals are still desirable, they ought to continue the same course. If they determine that the goals are being met, they should either maintain the enforcement levels or perhaps decrease enforcement efforts. The latter decision should be made only if policymakers believe they can save time and money and feel reasonably certain that compliance rates and environmental quality will not suffer. Appropriate and immediate action is required, of course, if the objectives are no longer desirable or are not being achieved. In nearly every case, the aim of revision will be improved compliance and environmental quality.

Conducting an ex post review and revision of a government program is a difficult task. Ingram's framework for analyzing policy implementation is a useful starting point for framing the questions that must be addressed in a rigorous review. According to Ingram, success in policy implementation is extremely difficult to evaluate in any general sense.[14] While meeting the goals prescribed by statute, or compliance, may be the simplest criterion of successful implementation, this may not be appropriate in all policy analysis. Some goals may be symbolic and will not be useful measures of success. The critical factors affecting implementation will vary according to the type of constraints of the policy, leading to different problems and different criteria for measuring success.[15]

In presenting a framework for analyzing implementation, Ingram, as in this study, sees policy formulation, implementation, and outcome as interrelated and describes the process as "a seamless web."[16] Beginning with policy formulation, in table 2.1, she draws from Salisbury and Heinz in pointing to the costs imposed on policymakers as important determinants of the type of legislation that is likely to result.[17] Distinguishing between negotiation costs, or the costs of coming to agreement, and information costs, which involve the costs of identifying the possible impacts and linkages among the related parties, she predicts the type of legislation that is likely to emerge. Negotiation costs will be low when there is little congressional argument about the goal to be accomplished, while information costs will be low when the results of government actions are clearly predictable with few unintended consequences. The type of structure of the enacted policy will depend on the level of the costs.

The legislation's structure determines the tasks in which implementers will have to engage, hence the approach that implementation is likely to follow. The clarity of the goals or lack thereof, as well as the level of procedural flexibility or specificity, will govern the approach that is taken. Each approach has different criteria for evaluation, running from achievement of statutory goals, to simply forging agreement that did not exist prior to implementation of the legislation.

The types of problems that may emerge are different according to the characteristics of the implemented policy, and policymakers are encouraged to anticipate the particular variables that might affect their specific policy, ranging from changes in the environment to clientele relationships. Implementation strategies should seek to avoid, or at least minimize, these critical variables.

Overall, Ingram believes that the implementation phase of a statutory program "should contribute toward policy improvement or the evolution toward more tractable problems for which there are more doable and agreeable responses."[18] Clearly, realization of the statutory goal, or compliance in the context of this study, is not the only way to gauge the success of program implementation. Her framework, when discussed in reference to the application of the strategic regulatory planning model introduced in this study, serves well as a realistic assessment of the practical limitations and expectations of regulatory policy.

Table 2.1
Flexible framework for analyzing implementation

Nature of decision costs	Structure of statute	Appropriate approach	Criteria for evaluation	Critical variables affecting implementation
Low negotiation costs/ low information costs	Clear goals; procedural flexibility	Command-and-control; programmed	Achievement of goals	Changes in external circumstances or policy environment
High negotiation costs/ low information costs	Open-ended goals; procedural flexibility	Adaptive; backward mapping	Grassroots creativity; modifying proximate policy behavior	Bureaucratic entrepreneurship; "fixers" and "double agents"
Low negotiation costs/ high information costs	Clear goals; procedural specificity	Oversight; policy reformulation	Policy learning	Administrative capability
High negotiation costs/ high information costs	Open-ended goals; procedural specificity	Bargaining	Broad agreement and support; avoidance of agency capture	Clientele relationships

Source: Helen Ingram, "Implementation: A Review and Suggested Framework," in Naomi B. Lynn and Aaron Wildavsky, eds., *Public Administration: The State of the Discipline* (Chatham, N.J.: Chatham House, 1990), p. 477. Copyright © 1990 by Chatham House Publishers, Inc. Reprinted by permission.

Summary

This chapter presented a model containing a series of recommended steps to follow in the formulation and implementation of regulations. The main objective of the model is to permit policymakers to achieve the highest rate of compliance possible under existing conditions and constraints. Each step was discussed separately. In particular, the importance of step 5, strategic regulation formulation, was noted. The next chapter adds to our understanding of this step by presenting a conceptual framework for the selection of specific regulatory techniques.

The strategic approach to regulatory policy formulation leads directly to a set of identifiable steps to assist policymakers in structuring successful regulatory plans. The approach places a heavy emphasis on the motivations, resources, and interdependencies of affected parties. Moreover, it directs policymakers to examine closely the legislative and regulatory goals and objectives. The overall aim is to fit the devised regulatory program with both the environment from which it is authorized or enforced as well as the environment in which it is implemented. Only by creating the best possible fit between strategy and environment will the behavior of the target population be controlled efficiently and effectively.

The planning steps outlined in this chapter serve as a guideline for tactical formulation of any regulatory issue; the model is both generic and universal. What is important is that the strategic planning steps be considered a dynamic process. In other words, in designing regulatory plans, policymakers should examine all steps of the planning process rather than considering only one or two steps within a static environment.

The evolutionary nature of the regulatory process, where improvement over previous actions is often desired, will require policymakers to return to the model on numerous occasions. The structure of the model is flexible enough to permit and even facilitate this activity until compliance goals are eventually met.

3

A Conceptual Framework for Selecting Regulatory Devices

A difficult question often confronting environmental policymakers is how to achieve compliance in regulatory programs.[1] Answers to this question are elusive because of tight budgets, interest group pressures, vague statutes and directives, and other factors. Obviously, the failure to obtain compliance with environmental regulations threatens the nation's environmental quality and, in many cases, the public health.[2] If policymakers possessed a well-defined conceptual framework for the selection of regulatory devices, they would be more likely to increase compliance rates and, in turn, environmental quality and public safety.

In order to analyze the effectiveness of MTBE and UST programs later in this book, this chapter develops such a framework. It first examines the possible conditions that can affect the cost and coerciveness of regulatory devices required to attain compliance and then presents a conceptual framework for choosing regulatory mechanisms.

Conditions Affecting the Cost and Coerciveness of Regulatory Techniques

Much of the literature on regulation in the United States is primarily devoted to concerns such as deregulation,[3] the capture of regulatory agencies by regulated parties,[4] the applications of cost-benefit analysis to regulatory strategies,[5] and the extent to which regulatory performance is influenced by presidential administrations.[6] Although research on these topics has provided students with a firm theoretical foundation for understanding regulatory performance at the macro level, little is known about specific conditions that can affect compliance at the micro level.

Major works on regulation allocate little space to this subject, and only a few studies have addressed the topic directly.[7] This is somewhat surprising given the practical value of knowing the effect of various factors on compliance.

In most cases, policymakers want to steer the outcomes of regulatory efforts as close to compliance as possible with the least amount of coercion and at the lowest financial cost to government. Usually the most coercive techniques (e.g., on-site inspections) necessitate the greatest government involvement and therefore are more expensive to oversee than the least coercive techniques (e.g., voluntary self-regulation). The presence of certain conditions, however, will tend to influence how much coercion is required and at what cost. In theory, the adoption of the most expensive and restrictive regulatory devices should guarantee a high rate of compliance. Yet as Rosenbaum shows, certain conditions (e.g., a poor business climate) can force outcomes toward noncompliance for even very costly and coercive regulatory techniques.[8] In other instances, additional considerations might permit the adoption of the least costly and coercive regulatory devices to achieve compliance. If environmental policymakers are to devise mechanisms to produce desired results, they must carefully read existing conditions and be alert to changes.

Accordingly, this investigation analyzes the possible economic, political, and administrative factors that can color the outcomes of regulatory activities in programs such as the use of an oxygenate in gasoline to reduce emissions and the management of USTs. Due to space limitations, only the most important conditions are identified and discussed. Admittedly, the conditions examined in this study are not mutually exclusive. Also, the relative prominence of the different factors vary from one case to the next, and they nearly always act in combination with one another. The study examines conditions in the regulated community, regulating agency, and outside arena.

Conditions in the Regulated Community

Several conditions in the regulated community can influence level of compliance within a policy field. Among them are the presence of constituency organizations, size and diversity of target population, resources of target groups, amount of behavioral change required, the ability to hide noncompliance, and risk preference.

Presence of Constituency Organizations Previous research has shown how the presence of constituency organizations (i.e., professional or trade organizations) can influence the overall cost of regulation. Welford Wilms's study of the California Energy Commission's program to enforce mandatory building standards to save energy partially drew on personal interviews with architects, builders, and building officials, who were asked their views on this largely unsuccessful program.[9] His research indicated that architects, builders, and building officials usually looked to their professional or trade associations rather than a government agency for guidance, advice, and training.[10] The associations, according to two-thirds of the respondents, played an important role in this respect by notifying members about forthcoming standards, interpreting complex regulations, and providing well-focused training. The Sheet Metal and Air Conditioning Contractors' Association of North America, for instance, offered seminars on solar heating and other energy-conserving new equipment on the market. Wilms's analysis suggests that constituency organizations, when included in the policymaking process, can help defray the cost of regulation by offering services normally provided by a government agency.[11]

Of course, the presence of constituency organizations can also hinder compliance. If leaders of such groups strongly oppose a particular regulatory program, they can persuade their members to demonstrate dissatisfaction with the program by ignoring government requests for changes in behavior. This can increase the cost of compliance and make the adoption of the most coercive regulatory devices necessary.

Size and Diversity of Target Population The size and diversity of a target population can have an impact on the required cost and coerciveness of a regulatory plan. When many diverse businesses fall under one law, it might be necessary for policymakers to adopt a set of varied regulatory techniques in order to address the different circumstances surrounding each industry. Such an approach has the potential for making regulation complex and expensive. Furthermore, when firms are part of a large target population, it is easier for them to ignore regulations and escape detection than when they are part of a small target group.[12] In such cases, coercive strategies may be required to achieve a desired level of compliance. Breyer and Tobin suggest that the huge size and diverse nature of the automobile industry and reliance on self-regulation by the National Highway Traffic Administration, respectively, has led to low rates of compliance in the agency's automobile safety program.[13] Therefore, the greater the size and diversity of a target group, the more costly and coercive regulatory mechanisms will have to be to achieve compliance.

Resources of Target Groups The resources of target groups, especially expertise and funds, can be an important variable.[14] Assuming target groups wish to comply, those with abundant expertise and funds will be better able to follow regulatory guidelines than those deficient in expertise and funds. Prakash's study of Baxter and Lilly's attempt to go beyond compliance with environmental regulations supports this observation.[15] Thus, for example, large, financially sound companies are in a better position than small, struggling companies to develop mechanisms to dispose hazardous waste themselves or to contract with outside treatment facilities. Businesses with limited staffs and operating budgets usually do not have a choice and must hire outside disposal companies. The additional costs they must incur to satisfy regulations force them to oppose orders to manage their wastes in a certain way. Government technical or financial assistance could reduce financial pressures, temper opposition, and lead to desirable compliance rates.

Wealthy firms are in a better position than struggling firms to avoid regulation.[16] If wealthy firms oppose a law, for example, they have the legal expertise and resources to take the government to court. Appeals can take years, often at considerable cost to taxpayers and the environment. Moreover, if fines are small relative to the cost of compliance, profitable companies can choose to ignore regulations and pay the fines. This was a common practice in environmental policy for some time until higher fines and stricter penalties were adopted.[17] Therefore, the amount of resources a target group possesses and its willingness to comply can influence how coercive and expensive regulatory techniques must be to achieve compliance and protect the environment.

Amount of Behavioral Change Required The greater the expected degree of behavioral change required by a regulation with regard to bureaucratic routines, organizational expenditures, or company autonomy, the greater is the likelihood of long-term delay.[18] The amount of behavioral change will vary according to whether a target firm's mission is inconsistent with, alien to, or hostile toward a policy. The greater the amount of behavioral change required, the more likely there will be difficulties achieving compliance.[19] Thus, the more that target groups oppose a particular regulation and the more that group practices must be modified, the greater the need is for expensive and coercive regulatory devices.

Ability to Hide Noncompliance Extensive previous experience with government regulation may influence the ability of an industry to hide noncompliance. Firms that have secretly and successfully avoided compliance with environmental laws in the past will probably be more informed about techniques that can be used to circumvent proposed regulations than companies with a strong compliance record. In addition, some types of regulatory activities, such as self-regulation, tend to increase the ability of certain firms to avoid compliance because they require less direct outside supervision.[20] In contrast, continuous monitoring through regular on-site inspections will tend to diminish the ability of firms to ignore the law.

Risk Preference The risk that firms are willing to take to avoid compliance with environmental regulations can be influenced by any number of variables.[21] The pressure to turn a profit and keep afloat in competitive markets, for example, can affect risk preference. The pressure to make money is probably greatest when economic conditions are poor and losses have occurred over a long time. But even when economic conditions are good, persistent foreign competition can cause industry leaders to take a greater risk and avoid compliance. These leaders may feel that the federal government has done little to curtail the flow of cheap imported goods manufactured by companies that are exempt from similar environmental regulation in their own countries. The general orientation of particular industrial leaders toward taking risks also can affect risk preference. Regardless of what exactly determines risk preference, policymakers must estimate the chances firms are willing to take to avoid compliance. Such estimates will influence the cost and restrictiveness of regulatory techniques necessary to induce compliance.

Conditions in the Regulating Agency

A number of conditions in the regulating agency can also affect compliance rates. Among these are the commitment of actors, the regulatory timetable, the resources of the regulating agency, and the precision of the rule.

Commitment of Actors Establishing open communication between government, industry, and the public when developing regulatory requirements for handling hazardous materials tends to foster commitment among the different actors in the policy process.[22] Leaders of competing interests will be most willing to bargain and compromise when information exchange is free and unobstructed. Commitment among enforcers and target groups to upholding regulations is a necessary element for achieving compliance.[23] A lack of support, particularly on the part of those in the field, can destroy a program and lead to noncompliance.

Rourke demonstrates how esprit de corps can be a critical factor in an agency's attempt to meet its policy goals.[24] In his opinion, organizational esprit relies to a large extent on the development of an appropriate ideology or sense of mission on the part of an agency as a means of binding outside supporters to the agency and a strategy for intensifying the loyalty of the organization's employees to its purposes.[25] During the 1960s, the Peace Corps was an excellent example of a charismatic government agency that evoked faith and enthusiasm that transcended rational calculation. While such esprit is difficult to induce and sustain, it could be the driving force behind national, state, and local efforts to achieve high rates of compliance with agency rules at low cost and with limited coercion. A lack of commitment among government officials, of course, can have the reverse effect.

Regulatory Timetable As Coglianese and Kerwin point out, the time it takes to draft, adopt, and implement regulations can be significant.[26] Often the regulatory process proceeds too slowly, and compliance is postponed. Barke demonstrates how lengthy delays in the promulgation of rules have hurt the regulatory activities of the Interstate Commerce Commission and the Federal Communications Commission.[27] West reports the same malady at the Federal Trade Commission.[28] Durant reports a similar finding in his research on EPA's efforts to bring the Tennessee Valley Authority into compliance with air and water quality standards.[29] Sometimes agencies act too quickly due to outside pressures. Thompson argues that Occupational Safety and Health Administration officials in the early 1970s were impatient in promulgating and enforcing new rules.[30] Alternatively, firms can forestall compliance through the use of delay tactics unless such tactics are viewed as detrimental to the operation of the firms over the long haul (e.g., by generating negative media attention or risking substantial long-term costs).

In California the automobile industry has used delay tactics in order to avoid having to produce, market, and sell zero emission vehicles (ZEVs), specifically electric-powered vehicles. The industry has accomplished this by intensely lobbying the public and the California Air Resources Board (CARB), arguing that the battery technology is not well developed and that the vehicles are too costly to produce and sell. Deadlines for the major automobile manufacturers to make available a certain percentage of ZEVs have been postponed more than once. The threat of setting deadlines, however, has spawned the development of new technologies to lower automobile emissions. Given the pressure on California to meet air quality standards set under the Clean Air Act of 1990 by 2010, the automobile companies have been forced to provide a viable substitute for ZEVs. CARB will probably require the automobile industry to produce a large number of low-pollution vehicles, such as hybrid gasoline- and electric-powered automobiles, and a relatively small number of ZEVs powered by fuel cells and battery-powered electric engines.[31]

Resources of the Regulating Agency The number of staff and amount of funds available for enforcement are undoubtedly among the most crucial factors influencing cost, coercion, and rate of compliance.[32] Heffron and McFeeley attribute many of the problems associated with the implementation of the Occupational Safety and Health Act to a lack of inspectors and funds, particularly given the size of the target group (over several million business establishments).[33] Inadequate enforcement resources are, in fact, a general problem in federal and state environmental programs.[34]

The amount of collective expertise possessed by a regulatory agency also is critical. Although EPA and some large states have a sufficient number of highly trained personnel with considerable experience in managing complex environmental problems, other state and local agencies do not always have sufficient expertise. This is an important issue, since much of the burden of achieving compliance is placed on the shoulders of state and local officials. Agencies that have little or no history of dealing with complicated environmental problems may not perform as well as those that have experience in this area. Some accommodations should be made where trained and qualified staffs are lacking. Sensitivity to this issue during the selection of regulatory devices can lead to increased compliance.

Precision of the Rule A wide range exists in the degree of precision with which environmental policymakers can articulate their rules, and their choice usually affects compliance. Officials should not always attempt to achieve the maximum possible precision. Rather, they should decide how precisely to convey their rules based on the nature of the regulatory program and the implications of their choices for the rate of compliance by the target group, the cost of rule making, the cost of applying the rule and of resolving disputes about its application, and the extent and impact of divergence between the actual results and those intended.

Usually a precise rule is likely to cost more in agency resources and may be under- or overinclusive of possible behaviors. An extensive investigation in initial rule making to sharpen the clarity of a regulation is often justified when:

- Potential compliance problems are serious.
- The costs of applying a regulation are likely to be high.
- The expense of initial rule making is offset by the reduced cost of subsequent policy clarifications.

- The risk of misinterpretation of an ambiguous regulation is large compared to the risk that a clear regulation will be under- or overinclusive.

In general, precise rules promote voluntary compliance because they are easy to comprehend and enforce. Environmental policymakers should therefore consider enhancing the clarity of guidelines if efforts to control costs and increase voluntary compliance are most important.

Conditions in the Outside Arena

Conditions in the outside arena also may have a bearing on rates of compliance. Among the most important conditions in the outside arena are the political sphere, the openness of the process, the economic climate, and decision structures and demand patterns.

Political Sphere The political sphere can affect the cost and coerciveness of regulatory devices.[35] Certainly, a harmonious political atmosphere can allow the adoption of the least restrictive regulatory mechanisms. West finds that such a setting for the operations of the Securities and Exchange Commission tends to facilitate the regulation of both buyers and sellers.[36] Yet the literature implies that the general antiregulatory mood in the American business community, particularly among small firms, may pose a serious obstacle to compliance with environmental regulations.[37] If this is the case, then the most costly and coercive regulatory devices could actually have a negative impact on compliance in policy areas involving small businesses, such as in the MTBE and UST programs.

A second political obstacle may arise from the relative clout of a regulating agency and a target group. When an agency has more clout than a target group, it will be comparatively easy for government officials to take whatever actions they deem necessary. When a target group has more political power than the regulating agency, however, it will be difficult for government officials to impose restrictions on the group.[38] Sufficiently influential businesses or business associations can call on elected leaders to block attempts to regulate their activities. Or, according to O'Leary, firms can delay compliance with statutes in the courts, possibly until a new administration with different views on the issue enters office.[39]

The level of cooperation between regulators, members of the target group, and other factions also can influence the selection of regulatory techniques and rate of compliance.[40] Cooperation is most critical when the size of the target group is unusually large and the enforcement staff is small. Such collaboration allows the adoption of the least costly and restrictive regulatory devices. Hence, as the level of cooperation between agencies and target groups increases, so does the likelihood that compliance goals will be met.

Openness of the Process According to democratic theory, citizens must be given an opportunity to participate fully in the affairs of government, and leaders must be held accountable for their actions. When citizen participation is broad and regular, policymakers can discern the public's views on the controversial issues and act accordingly. Congress has included requirements for public involvement in environmental legislation. Yet many government officials still consider citizen participation requirements a nuisance and sometimes try to circumvent them.

Previous research underscores the importance of the level of openness of public policymaking. Weber's study, for instance, shows that the more open the decision-making process is, the less costly and restrictive regulatory devices have to be to persuade target groups to obey the law.[41] In addition, Hermanson investigates the Offeror System administered by the Consumer Product Safety Commission (CPSC).[42] As part of this program, industry personnel, consumer groups, and the public are invited by the CPSC to participate in the development of safety standards for a particular category of products that the agency had already determined presented an unreasonable risk of injury to users. (This is similar to the negotiated rule-making process described earlier in the book.) All interested parties are asked to propose standards and to meet with the agency to review specific criticisms and objections. Once the CPSC evaluates the suggested regulations, it selects a proposal and publishes it in the *Federal Register*, thereby providing an additional opportunity for public comment. The CPSC employed this system successfully in the development of standards for such products as architectural glass, book matches, power lawn mowers, television sets, and public playground equipment. In Hermanson's view, consensus achieved in the Offeror

System through bargaining and negotiations leads to a high level of compliance.[43] Additional research by Dunlap, Kraft, and Rosa, O'Brien, Clarke, and Kamieniecki, and Weber also points out the political advantages of broadening a policymaking process to include all concerned parties.[44]

Economic Climate Economic conditions in the nation as a whole and in specific regions of the country can have a significant impact on the ability of regulatory agencies to impel compliant behavior. Business is less likely to resist agency directives when the national economy is strong than when it is weak. But even when the nation's economy is healthy, disparities in economic conditions between states and localities always exist and can interfere with efforts to achieve compliance in environmental programs.[45] In areas where economic conditions are poor, businesses will be likely to oppose attempts to modify their behavior than in areas where conditions are good. Moreover, most state and local officials will be subject to severe cross-pressures from industry, workers, environmental groups, and the federal government in regions where economic conditions are poor. While federal law and the EPA will often require state and local officials to enforce pollution control regulations, industry might ask them to relax requirements in order to save money.

Decision Structures and Demand Patterns The structure of decision systems and demand patterns can be crucial factors in the selection of regulatory devices. Salisbury describes how the interaction between integrated or fragmented decision structures and demand patterns may affect policy outcomes.[46] An integrated decision system has numerous, interconnected levels with a direct line of authority. An integrated system, by definition, is hierarchical in structure (like the military). A fragmented decision system is one that has many levels with no lines of direct authority (similar to legislative bodies). A fragmented demand pattern is characterized by many competing factions, each pressing for its own interest independent of the others. More often than not, this second type of demand pattern leads to self-regulation. An integrated demand pattern results from collective pressure from groups with shared attitudes, values, and interests. Potentially, this can facilitate direct command-and-control regulation. Whereas an integrated decision structure is an important requirement for imposing increasingly coercive regulatory mechanisms successfully, a fragmented structure is likely to encourage the opposite. Wilms shows this to be the case in his analysis of an attempt by the California Energy Commission to regulate building standards in order to conserve energy.[47]

Sabatier and Mazmanian also emphasize the need for substantial hierarchical integration within and among government agencies.[48] The goal here is to minimize the number of veto or clearance points by providing supporters of statutory objectives with inducements and sanctions sufficient to guarantee acquiescence among those with a potential veto. The problem is particularly acute in federal statutes that rely on state and local administrators to carry out the details of program delivery and for which some field level officials or target groups (or both) display substantial resistance toward statutory directives. To the extent the system is fragmented, there will be significant variation in the degree of compliant behavior among officials and target groups—as each responds to the incentives for modification within its local setting—and thus a lower attainment of statutory objectives.[49]

A Conceptual Framework for the Selection of Regulatory Devices

The conceptual perspective developed in this investigation relies on Lowi's policy classification scheme, with further elaboration by Salisbury.[50] Lowi classifies policies as distributive (non-zero-sum policies in which nearly everyone benefits), redistributive (policies that approach zero sum, in which some benefit and some lose), and regulatory (policies that also tend toward zero sum, and in which government prescribes rules of behavior for particular groups). Salisbury added a critical dimension to Lowi's typology by identifying self-regulation policies as a fourth policy type. Self-regulation policies are frequently offered as a noncoercive alternative by sectors of society targeted for external regulation, and they are invariably not zero sum. These policies also impose constraints on a group, but are perceived only to increase, not decrease, the beneficial options to a particular segment of the population.[51]

Under this classification scheme, policies are either self-regulatory or regulatory. Thus, the Lowi and Salisbury typologies suggest that regulatory policies are either noncoercive (through self-regulation) or coercive (through direct command-and-control regulation). In the real world, however, regulatory devices tend to fall at different points along a continuum of coerciveness. In other words, devices intended to control behavior tend to vary according to their restrictiveness. Noncoercive approaches (through self-regulation) occupy one end of the continuum and coercive approaches (through direct command-and-control regulation) the other end. Conceptualizing regulation in these terms provides a flexible framework in which to study alternative regulatory mechanisms.

Cost is a second dimension that characterizes regulatory mechanisms. Cost refers to the amount of money government must spend to administer a particular regulatory approach. In general, the most coercive activities (e.g., imprisoning polluters) require the greatest government involvement and therefore are more expensive to administer than the least coercive activities (e.g., economic incentives). Limited government revenues make this an important variable.

The total cost and coerciveness of the selected regulatory program represents the overall government effort necessary to attain compliance and control pollution. Compliance can be achieved in varying degrees and is best conceptualized along a continuum ranging from avoidance to adherence.

Figure 3.1 shows the theoretical relationships between different types of conditions, the noncoercion versus coercion and low-cost versus high-cost dimensions, overall government effort, and level of compliance. The conceptual framework presented in the figure is nested in step 5 of the strategic regulatory planning model and, in conjunction with the previous stages, fosters a concern for implementation. In more general terms, it provides policymakers with a guide for formulating a regulatory plan to meet specific legislative goals—in this study, the requirement under the Clean Air Act of 1990 to add an oxygenate to gasoline and the UST provisions of the Hazardous and Solid Waste Amendments.

Under optimal conditions (e.g., a harmonious political environment), policymakers can use the least coercive enforcement techniques (e.g.,

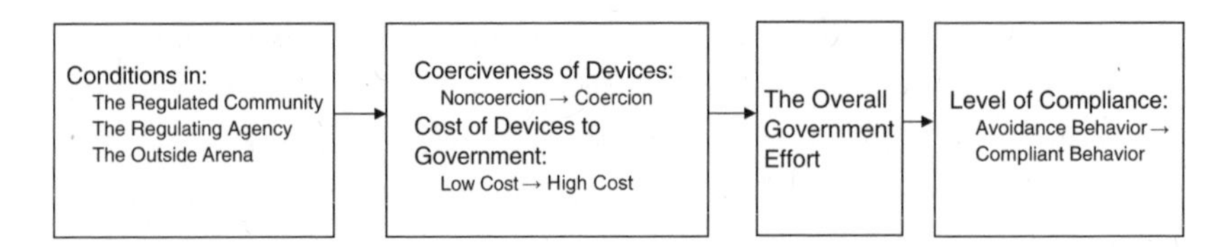

Figure 3.1
A conceptual framework for the selection of regulatory devices

reporting by firms and formal compliance tracking) at the least cost to achieve full compliance. The assumption is that the least coercive mechanisms are always preferable to more coercive mechanisms if only because the former devices are more cost-effective than the latter. In contrast, extremely restrictive enforcement arrangements (e.g., court injunctions) necessitate direct government involvement and thus incur substantial costs. Under ideal conditions, therefore, policymakers will select regulatory devices that are the least coercive and least costly and that lead to compliant behavior.

Unfortunately for policymakers, optimal conditions are rare. Many times the conditions that do exist (e.g., a lack of agency funds or a small staff) tend to diminish the effectiveness of the least coercive approaches, often to the point that the outcomes are in danger of moving toward avoidance behavior. In order to prevent outcomes from moving in this direction, policymakers must select techniques, either singularly or in combination, that are affordable and coercive enough to produce compliant behavior.

Policymaking is a dynamic process, and circumstances tend to change over time. Decision makers are continuously gauging the potential impact of given conditions on regulatory mechanisms and making adjustments as they see fit.[52] Eventually, they may be forced to adopt expensive and restrictive approaches that will result in compliant behavior in an attempt to prevent outcomes from moving toward avoidance behavior. When accurate information is available and incorporated into deliberations, policymakers usually will achieve the greatest level of compliance possible with the least effort and expense regardless of the conditions existing at the time. This underscores the importance of obtaining the most accurate data available as changes occur.[53]

In a pluralist, multilevel system like that in the United States, some communities may favor avoidance behavior in the face of unpopular regulations. Relaxing enforcement of gun control laws is one example. Though such situations may arise from time to time, in most cases policymakers want their regulatory devices to achieve the highest level of compliance possible under given conditions.

Summary

This chapter developed a conceptual framework for policymakers to employ in the selection of regulatory devices for enforcing environmental rules. It began by presenting an in-depth examination of the conditions in the regulated community, regulating agency, and outside arena that might affect the cost and coerciveness of regulatory devices. The discussion of these conditions led to the construction of a conceptual framework for choosing regulatory techniques and achieving compliance. The application of this framework should improve levels of compliance in environmental policy as well as in other public policy areas.

Given the complicated nature of environmental problems, policymakers will want to employ several regulatory devices in combination with one another. It is difficult to say exactly which combination of devices will yield the greatest level of compliance at the least cost. Moreover, past experiences in environmental management, or in other policy areas for that matter, do not always provide clues about which regulatory techniques will be the most appropriate in a given instance. Consequently, policymakers need to be flexible, open-minded, innovative, and willing to experiment. They also must be willing to collect accurate and detailed information on the variables that affect the cost and coerciveness of regulatory mechanisms. Once this is done, they can choose the devices that will best minimize costs and maximize compliance.

Regardless of which combination of techniques is selected, a policy feedback and evaluation system can greatly improve the chances for success in achieving compliance. Whatever the source of proposed changes, it is important that policymakers encourage independent evaluation studies to analyze accurately the actual impacts of the policy. Such systematic assessment serves both to correct imperfections in program design and performance and counteract the tendency for complaints to dominate the informal feedback process.[54] (A policy feedback and evaluation system belongs in step 7, the ex post review/revision stage, of the strategic regulatory planning model.) The adoption of this strategy can help diminish the political problems that often accompany regulatory efforts on a large scale.

4

A Menu of Regulatory Devices

The previous chapter presented a conceptual framework for the selection of specific regulatory devices. This framework represented step 5, strategic regulation formulation, in the strategic regulatory planning model discussed in chapter 2. An examination of this stage of the strategic regulatory planning process would not be complete without an in-depth study of the individual regulatory tools available to environmental policymakers. This chapter therefore identifies a number of regulatory devices and analyzes the strengths and weaknesses of each. The discussion focuses on the potential ability of a technique to control behavior.

As Freeman notes, economists have criticized direct command-and-control regulation in two respects.[1] First, such regulation necessitates a pattern of pollution control devices that tends to be excessively costly and therefore not cost-effective. Second, the direct command-and-control approach creates an inappropriate incentive structure for businesses and individuals. Since compliance is very costly, no positive incentive exists to control pollution and there is negative incentive to avoid penalties. Thus, in Freeman's view, "Not only is there no incentive to do better than the regulations require, but also the incentives to comply with the regulations themselves may be too weak to overcome the disincentive of bearing the costs of compliance, resulting in a high rate of noncompliance with the rules."[2] Regulatory tools exist that offer alternatives to traditional direct regulation.

Some of the regulatory devices examined in this chapter are interrelated. This is evident, for example, in the discussion concerning standard setting, the permit system, and inspections. Prior to implementing a permit system and an inspection program, a regulatory agency must develop a set of rules for the type of regulated activity (e.g., waste disposal) in question. Once this is done, permits can be granted to specific facilities. Whether firms are in compliance with the requirements in their permits is determined through inspections. This combination of regulatory devices has been used in the administration of the Clean Water Act. Although permit and inspection techniques will be described separately, in practice these techniques are used in combination with one another.

The following discussion is roughly organized according to the level of coerciveness of the regulatory devices. Self-regulation and innovative market solutions and economic incentives are considered to be the least coercive mechanisms and are examined first. Increasingly coercive regulatory techniques that traditionally government has used to achieve compliance are analyzed next.

Self-Regulation

Self-regulation has been both praised and criticized by policy analysts. On the plus side, there are several advantages to self-regulation. This approach allows policymakers to project a positive, action-oriented public image while entailing none of the risks associated with aggressive enforcement. Government officials can assume that some progress toward compliance is probably being made. Moreover, in the current antiregulatory climate, the voluntary compliance implied by self-regulation and efforts to educate members of a regulated industry is more appealing to target groups and the public than is mandatory compliance. Making compliance voluntary also is consistent with the prevailing political ethic of state and local control. Vigorous enforcement, however, can unify opposition to a regulatory program. Finally, of course, self-regulation costs less, at least in the short term.

A major disadvantage of this strategy can be gleaned from Tobin's analysis of self-regulation in the automobile industry.[3] Examining the National Highway Traffic Administration self-regulating program on the recall of motor vehicles, the definition of defects, the frequency of defect reports, and the notification of vehicle owners, Tobin concludes that self-regulation—while minimizing governmental cost and involvement in the private sector—has serious faults. Specifically, it gives motor vehicle manufacturers too much latitude in determining the existence of a defect and makes government overly dependent on company officials for information. As a result, consumers and the government must rely almost exclusively on industry to provide accurate information. An incentive therefore exists for the manufacturers to cut corners and avoid the letter of the law.

Nevertheless, as Miller, Rosenbaum, and Marcus, Geffen, and Sexton observe, cooperation and collaboration between business groups and government increased during the 1990s, with certain companies publicly announcing that they now wish to go "beyond compliance."[4] Taking advantage of this change in perspective on the part of corporate America, the EPA launched a number of voluntary, self-regulation government programs to encourage even more companies to follow this path. These programs were discussed and evaluated in chapter 2. As noted, EPA's efforts to stimulate cooperation between business and government has had mixed results.

Market Solutions and Economic Incentives

Market solutions and economic incentives have received considerable attention and strong endorsement in the environmental policy and economics literature. According to Walter Rosenbaum, "The most commonly proposed reform for the command-and-control approach is to substitute or add market-based approaches that rely fundamentally on economic incentives and markets to accomplish the environmental improvements intended."[5] Bryner writes that "market incentives are believed by many to be the key to ensuring that environmental goals are achieved at lower costs than are possible using bureaucratic, centralized approaches."[6] A number of innovative regulatory tools incorporating the pull of the market and economic incentives have been suggested. One technique is the establishment of so-called property rights for pollution, in effect creating a "market for pollution" to limit overuse of scarce natural resources like air and water. Under this approach, the government determines the allowable level of each pollutant and then auctions off to firms the rights to use the environment to pollute. These rights are exchangeable with discharge rights for certain limited areas. In theory, the law of supply and demand works to determine the costs of these rights to pollute and ultimately lower emission levels.[7]

Along these lines, EPA has been developing "offsets" and "banking" policies for controlling pollution and has implemented the "bubble" policy as an alternative to traditional command-and-control directive regulation.[8] Offsets allow new sources of pollution in locations that have not met air quality standards. Under this program, new pollution sources must be balanced by reductions in existing pollution in the location. Firms are permitted to trade pollution rights in order to encourage the most efficient means of control at a given pollution level while still allowing economic growth. Offsets are most useful when it is cheaper to reduce an old source's emissions than to implement control of the same quantity of pollution at the new site. In banking, offsets are created by companies with comparatively lower control costs, banked, and then either sold to other companies at a later date or used in their own expansion. Banking therefore permits offset trades to occur over time, allowing for growth in individual firms and in the region as a whole. Finally, the bubble policy allows owners to choose which sources of pollution to control as long as the facility's overall emissions of a specific pollutant do not exceed a given level. In effect, an imaginary bubble is placed over the plant. This approach permits companies to reduce emissions for the entire facility in the most cost-effective fashion.

These regulatory devices have received support from economists and many policy analysts because of their unobtrusive nature, potential cost-effectiveness, and emphasis on planning rather than direct regulation.[9] Stone thinks these techniques can lead to additional flexibility in the response of companies to changing economic circumstances, increased production efficiency, and an enhanced ability to direct innovation into socially desirable directions.[10] Eads and Fix, however, identify several serious difficulties with the adoption of market approaches and economic incentives.[11] First, these devices appear to give industry the "right to pollute" and therefore many environmentalists strongly oppose them. Second, pollution markets are not simple to create and sustain. Third, although perhaps fewer than those of direct regulation, information requirements are by no means trivial. Fourth, businesses are already acclimated to the regulatory game, and they may be dubious about launching into a new type of control, possibly threatening their current position in the marketplace. Finally, Meier points out that transaction costs, which are often downplayed by proponents of these devices, can actually be quite high.[12] Perhaps most important is the question of how to maintain an open and competitive marketplace. Research by Wilms and Hahn and McRae describes how these problems can affect compliance.[13]

Kamieniecki, Shafie, and Silvers analyze whether the move from direct government regulatory control of air pollution to the 1993 adoption of the Los Angeles Regional Clean Air Incentives Market (RECLAIM) emissions trading system, a market-based form of air quality management, has led to greater effectiveness and efficiency in an equitable and democratic manner as promised.[14] Evidence from the sulfur dioxide emissions trading program, established under the Clean Air Act of 1990, is also reviewed in their study. Overall, the three researchers find that emissions trading programs are fairly effective and efficient at meeting their goal of improved air quality, especially when compared to traditional direct command-and-control regulatory efforts. Questions remain, however, as to whether market-based approaches can satisfy environmental justice concerns and involve the public in an open, ongoing, and meaningful way.

Two years following the publication of Kamieniecki, Shafie, and Silvers's research, the South Coast Air Quality Management District (SCAQMD), a regional state agency that oversees pollution control efforts in southern California, reported that after eight years into the RECLAIM program, "smog cuts have been minimal, companies are failing to meet pollution reduction targets, and proposals to rescue the operation are mired in controversy."[15] Over the course of the program, the SCAQMD has received very few applications from companies to upgrade pollution control capacity. Instead, industry has done everything it can to buy credits or use other means to avoid purchasing costly pollution control equipment. The sulfur dioxide program, in contrast, has been considered a major success.[16] RECLAIM is still a relatively new program, and certain corrections, if adopted, could improve the performance of the program and the region's air quality. Future analysts will want to take into account variations in weather and economic conditions, as well as improvements in technology, in their evaluations of the long-term effectiveness and efficiency of the program.

Insurance Programs

Insurance programs, in effect a type of market approach, have been proposed as a means by which risk can be spread and damages compensated for at relatively low costs.[17] A major advantage of such programs is that they transfer most of the costs and oversight responsibilities typically required in a regulatory effort from government to private insurance companies. Ferreira has examined the circumstances under which insurance might replace direct command-and-control regulation in reducing risk.[18] His study focuses on the transportation and storage of liquid natural gas and the crashworthiness of automobiles. He finds that the effect of insurance on behavior depends on how the insurance is priced and how accident costs would be distributed without it. Accurate risk assessment is important but difficult to achieve. The two programs Ferreira analyzes indicate that insurance is a viable alternative, given good risk assessment, financially responsible parties, and enough information.[19] Insurance is required under the Resource Conservation and Recovery Act (RCRA) for corrective action at hazardous waste treatment, storage, and disposal facilities.

Certain conditions must prevail if insurance is to work. First and foremost, a competitive market for insuring members of a target population must exist on a continuous basis. Yet the environmental impairment liability (EIL) market has experienced considerable fluctuation. When RCRA became law in 1976, several insurers in London, England, had been developing liability policies for pollution accidents that do not happen suddenly.[20] On the passage of the Superfund legislation in 1980, a handful of American firms entered the market and began offering similar policies. By 1983, over a dozen primary insurers were selling pollution liability policies, and at least forty insurers and reinsurers had established a pool, somewhat resembling the nuclear liability pools.[21] By the end of 1984, however, several English and American insurers withdrew from the market. Today there are only a small number of pollution insurers, several of which insure "light" risks (e.g., gasoline stations and dry cleaning stores).[22]

Probst et al. have conducted an extensive investigation of the role of insurance in Superfund.[23] Among other things, they examine what could happen to insurance markets if insurers were required to cover substantial Superfund-related costs. Based on low-cost and high-cost scenarios for current and future Superfund sites, they estimate that the financial impact on the insurance industry would be considerable and possibly devastating. They believe reforms are needed to moderate the insurance industry's liability for Superfund-related costs.

Katzman argues that several court rulings best explain the collapse of the market.[24] In his view, "An unwritten criterion for insurability is the predictability of the tort process and the sanctity of insurance contracts. While an insurer can expect the tort law to evolve and contracts to be reinterpreted in unanticipated ways, judicial decisions have virtually undermined the predictability of insurance policies when pollution is at issue."[25] Insurance companies contend that court rulings "rewrite insurance contracts in an arbitrary way, and that the 'deep pocket' of the insurance industry is being used to finance a social program rather than to spread risks."[26] As a result, insurers no longer believe it is profitable for them to offer EIL coverage for light or heavy risks.

Katzman suggests several possible solutions to this dilemma.[27] One is to establish forward-looking occurrence policies that indemnify businesses for accidents that originated in the policy year, regardless when the consequences (e.g., an increase in cancer rates) are manifested in the future. The occurrence policy must be offered in the form of a long-term contract in order for it to be workable in the pollution liability market. Other options include creating assigned risk pools, encouraging relevant industries to develop their own mutual insurance pools, and establishing an insurance program through the federal government. If all of these actions fail, it might become necessary to separate the problems of deterrence and victim compensation and develop a government compensation mechanism (analogous to workers compensation). There is a chance, however, that the decline of the market represents a temporary readjustment to prevailing conditions in the industry. If this is the case, the most prudent course of action is to adopt a wait-and-see position.[28]

Education, Information Disclosure, and the Media

A number of studies illuminate the value of education and information in the implementation process.[29] Wilms reports that the California Energy Commission in 1977–1978 sponsored training and information programs attended by nearly 7,000 architects, builders, and building officials.[30] When these individuals were interviewed, virtually everyone thought that education or training opportunities were abundant. Pettus's evaluation of the efforts to implement the Occupational Safety and Health Act (OSHA) underscores the importance of consultation and educational assistance to industry in the regulatory process.[31] Researchers believe that the more ambiguous and complex the regulations are, the greater the need is for formal education and information programs.[32]

Information disclosure has been used successfully by Congress and government agencies to modify behavior. The Department of Agriculture grading standards for meats and dairy products, for instance, inform consumers about the overall quality of the products they purchase. The Food and Drug Administration requires that ingredients and nutritional values be listed on a wide variety of foods. EPA's annual Toxic Release Inventory (TRI), first established in 1988, reports emissions of toxic and hazardous chemicals. Media attention and public access to the TRI probably has contributed to the reduction of such chemicals by industry over time. Congress has forced tobacco companies to place warning labels on cigarette packages. The Internet has recently become an important source of information for consumers and members of target groups. All of these steps are intended to educate consumers and affect their behavior. An important advantage of this device is that it is cost-effective and enduring. A disadvantage is that it could have a negative effect on business.

The media can be used to inform and educate industry and the public about regulations. A major advantage of the media, especially the electronic media and the Internet, is that a large number of people can be reached at one time. In addition, the electronic media and the Internet are easily accessible by the public. Unfortunately, media use is often expensive. A one-minute spot on television, for example, can cost thousands of dollars, and "free" public service advertising does not provide adequate coverage. Persuading newspaper and television reporters to cover attempts to implement new environmental regulations, however, would be less costly and could increase compliance. Reaching members of target groups through closed-circuit television while they are attending association meetings is more cost-effective than purchasing advertising space.

The media can play a vital role in the regulatory process by reporting on violators of government statutes. The threat of public stigma associated with prosecution for pollution, for instance, can be an effective force in controlling behavior. Hawkins thinks media coverage is a powerful incentive for compliance in suburban and rural areas where good reputations are valued and adverse publicity is readily transmitted.[33] Companies will go to considerable lengths, he argues, to keep their names out of newspapers and off television. The concern about reputation can be exploited by ensuring that maximum publicity is generated during litigation proceedings. Sabatier and Mazmanian agree that media coverage can have a beneficial impact on the regulatory process.[34]

Taxes and Fees

Taxes and fees can be used as negative incentives to achieve compliance. Weidenbaum, for instance, recommends that government levy substantial taxes on pollution discharges by industry.[35] Such taxation could be "progressive" to the degree that the tax rates would increase faster than the amount of pollution emitted by an individual polluter. Taxes and fees would provide an incentive for industry to concentrate on removing or reducing the most serious instances of pollution.

In 1978, Congress imposed a tax on fuel-inefficient cars to discourage the manufacture and purchase of what were referred to as gas-guzzlers. Starting with 1980 models, the tax was supposed to increase every year. Stone criticizes the use of this device in this and other cases because of the high cost of collecting the necessary information, the high cost of supervision, and the difficulty of determining levels for the taxes.[36]

Furthermore, in many instances, it will be hard for all concerned parties to agree on an acceptable level of pollution.

Freeman believes pollution taxes can make a significant contribution to achieving cost-effectiveness.[37] He explains:

> If several sources are discharging into the environment, they will be induced to minimize the total cost of achieving any given reduction in pollution. This is because each discharger will control discharges up to the point where its marginal or incremental cost of control is equated to the tax or permit price. If all dischargers face the same tax or price, their marginal costs of pollution control will be equal. This is the condition of cost-effectiveness. Low-cost sources will control relatively more, thus leading to a cost-effective allocation of cleanup responsibilities. There is no reallocation of responsibilities for reducing discharges that will achieve the same total reduction at a lower total cost.[38]

Policymakers must be able to calculate what the charge should be before implementing a pollution-charge system. Of course, charges can be adjusted if they are initially set too high or too low.

Rabe reports that an increasing number of states are revising their tax policies to protect the environment.[39] Iowa, for instance, exempts from taxation all pollution-control equipment bought for use in the state, Maryland provides significant tax incentives to purchasers of low-emission vehicles, and Minnesota levies sizable sales taxes on nonrecycled municipal solid waste. In New Jersey, new taxes on gasoline and rental car use are being appropriated for the purchase of about half of remaining undeveloped land to curtail development and deter sprawl. Finally, about ten states representing 30 percent of the U.S. population charge refundable taxes on beverage containers.[40]

Reporting and Formal Compliance Tracking

According to Weidenbaum, regulations impose an unacceptably high cost of paperwork for agencies and small businesses.[41] Congress tried to correct this problem in 1980 with passage of the Regulatory Flexibility Act and the Paperwork Reduction Act. Nonetheless, some agencies have moved toward greater reliance on paperwork and less reliance on formal inspection to ensure compliance.[42]

Advances in data storage and computer design now make it possible for federal, state, and local agencies to establish sophisticated electronic record-keeping and retrieval systems. Improvements in computers and software allow regulators to track compliance effectively and efficiently. Personal computers allow members of target populations to send data and other information electronically to oversight agencies. Electronic submissions by private parties facilitate data collection, cross-referencing, and trend analysis. Policymakers, for example, could adopt a network system in which data reported by inspectors in different regions of the country can be stored and cross-checked for possible violators. However, given the difficulty that government has had in developing and implementing information systems, such an approach should be adopted with some caution.

Bardach finds that in the overall system of protective regulation, paperwork functions as an enforcement mechanism in very much the same way as do inspectors who look directly into matters under their jurisdiction.[43] Paperwork enforcement has several advantages: it increases regulatory surveillance at less cost to the taxpayer than inspectors; regulated parties rather than agencies pay for filling out and submitting forms; the time and transportation cost of site visits are saved while postal and electronic submission costs in comparison are minimal; it can be easily combined, if necessary, with on-site visits (as has been done in California's regulation of nursing homes); through paperwork, an agency can monitor many more things inspectors cannot keep track of accurately over time; and filling out forms continuously reminds target group members of their responsibilities and therefore aids compliance.

This device also possesses several weaknesses. For one thing, the agency must pay for printing, collecting, storing, and auditing paperwork. Also, owners of small businesses generally do not like paperwork; they feel that they already have too many forms to complete. Because forms are self-administered, they are open to human error. Moreover, those subject to regulation must be able to read and write English well. Finally, the process is subject to dishonesty and cheating.

Following a discussion of these problems, Bardach observes how the Internal Revenue Service (IRS) relies heavily on regulatory and compliance paperwork to achieve its goals.[44] Of course, because of the huge number of people and businesses the IRS tracks, it has become more dependent on the computer than ever before. Millions of taxpayers now submit their tax returns electronically, making it easier for the IRS to transfer and store data. Despite the unpopularity and difficulties of paperwork, the ability of the agency to audit taxpayers (or convince the public that audits are inevitable) and impose stiff fines and penalties has persuaded most businesses and citizens to obey the law.

Licensing

Licensing is usually required when consumers on their own are unable to judge the qualifications of the persons offering the service (e.g., doctors, lawyers, and electricians). A license also may be required in order to perform a certain activity (e.g., driving a motor vehicle or generating nuclear power). Excessive licensing, however, has adverse economic effects and reduces consumer choice unnecessarily. Most members of professions, once licensed, are licensed for life unless they violate standards or commit a crime. Firms can be licensed for a limited term with recertification requirements.

There are two alternatives to reliance on this device. In those cases that do not present an overwhelming danger to the public, the government can establish a certification process that would provide citizens with information about the competence of professionals or firms. Customers would be free to seek out those who were certified, but unlike mandatory licensing, there would be no requirement that all practitioners be certified.

Registration, a second form of licensing, also can prevent fraud. When this device is used, individuals and firms are required to list themselves in an official register if they intend to undertake a certain activity (e.g., operate a gasoline station). The government cannot deny them the right to pursue that activity, but failure to register can result in civil or criminal sanctions. Stores that sell firearms, for example, are registered, along with each firearm sold. The registration of motor vehicles by the states helps combat automobile theft and crime.

Permits

The EPA has used permit systems to control pollution. Under the National Pollution Discharge Elimination System (NPDES) mandated by the Clean Water Act, for example, each state is required to submit a water quality plan for the state and, if approved, is allowed to issue permits regulating pollution discharge to individual polluters. The EPA issues permits in states that have not yet been approved. Like most other federal water pollution control regulations, the NPDES grants the states some latitude in designating water pollution standards.

The NPDES and similar types of permit programs (e.g., in RCRA) have disadvantages and advantages. Many observers believe that permit systems have not been cost-effective, have led to a huge amount of burdensome paperwork, and have resulted in long delays in the implementation process. In addition to the high costs of monitoring compliance and tracking permits, firms can lie at any point in the permit process.[45] An obvious advantage of this technique is that it allows EPA to determine the contents and the quantity of the harmful wastes being discarded. Furthermore, the permit system requires industry to pay the costs of investigation and the reporting of necessary information. It also provides government with a measure of certainty: firms that meet permit requirements are in compliance.

Rabe analyzes how four diverse states—Colorado, New Jersey, Oklahoma, and Pennsylvania—use permitting as a regulatory tool in environmental protection programs.[46] His study produces mixed results. All four states have substantially improved permit efficiency, as evident in various methods to systematize permit issuance and provide clearer expectations for regulated groups. New Jersey, however, is the only state attempting to link core regulatory techniques, including permitting, with pollution prevention and reduction of cross-media pollutant transfers. In Rabe's opinion, this highly integrated approach suggests what the "next generation" of environmental programs might entail.[47]

Standard Setting

When full information cannot be supplied to consumers briefly or easily or the severity of the risk involved is great and the potential harm irreversible (e.g., as in the transportation of airline passengers), the government may impose compliance standards. Such standards mandate that the manufacturing process, the product itself, or the service offered meet a minimum level of achievement. Currently, environmental pollution, safety and health, product quality, employment practices, and other business behaviors are regulated by mandatory standards.[48]

There are two basic types of standards: performance standards, which require that certain minimum goals be met without specifying the means the industry must use to comply, and specification standards, which spell out exactly what the company must do to conform to the regulation. Thus, a performance standard would require a firm to reduce to a minimum level the amount of a hazardous material to which its workers are exposed; a specification standard would tell that company exactly what equipment it must use to reach that minimum level.

Those being regulated generally prefer performance rather than specification standards.[49] Performance guidelines allow companies to find the most cost-effective way of complying with the guidelines and encourage technical innovation. Standards that stipulate what technology must be used tend to discourage innovation. Specification standards, however, are easier to measure, monitor, and enforce.[50]

Setting Penalties

The nature and size of penalties have an impact on compliance. McKean contends that "the larger the penalty, the greater the deterrence of violations—if the probability of conviction remains constant."[51] Thus, the perception of the probability of getting caught and convicted for avoiding regulations needs to be considered when setting penalties. Mitnick, Breyer, and Hawkins hold this view, too.[52] Also, the enforcement of each regulation has spillover effects on law-abidingness in most cases. This is the ripple effect that the IRS stresses in requests for larger auditing and enforcement budgets.[53] Moreover, McKean maintains that "if the penalty is deemed to be 'unreasonable,' however, regulators may be less eager to charge, police may be less willing to arrest, and courts may be more reluctant to convict."[54] In addition, higher penalties can lead to increased avoidance, possibly through litigation. This may be less of a concern in the regulation of small businesses, many of which cannot afford expensive and lengthy battles in court.

A simplistic reaction to avoidance is for policymakers to raise penalties and fines as a way of showing the target group that the regulations are serious. In some cases, this may be necessary, but such a strategy can backfire on policymakers.[55] The imposition of extremely severe penalties can lead to even more opposition and avoidance by angering the target group and its supporters.[56] The objective therefore is to specify a level of retribution that induces firms to comply but does not appear completely unreasonable to them or to their allies. Possessing accurate information about the perceptions and attitudes of the regulated parties can help policymakers determine this level.

The Connecticut Enforcement Plan, tried first in that state and later by EPA, attempts to deal with the problem of setting penalties for violation of environmental rules.[57] In the past, polluters almost routinely avoided compliance because they felt it was cheaper to do so. More often than not, the cost of purchasing and operating new antipollution equipment was much greater than the fines levied and the money spent in court to delay compliance. Policymakers therefore believed something had to be done to make noncompliance expensive. Under the Connecticut Enforcement Plan, noncompliant companies are subject to fines equal to the amount they gained through noncompliance over the period of noncompliance. In other words, fines are equal to the cost of installing and operating antipollution equipment plus interest during the period of avoidance. The incentive for refusing or delaying compliance is thus reduced.

Inspections

The debate is heated over whether delegating authority to state and local agencies to conduct inspections of firms is an effective regulatory approach.[58] Roland and Marz contend that delegation of discretion over environmental regulation to the states may trigger a process analogous to Gresham's law, in which lax regulation in one state drives out stringent regulation in neighboring states.[59] They cite the regulation of pesticides in five midwestern agricultural states as an example. Thompson and Scicchitano's comparative study of federal and state enforcement of OSHA standards, however, yields contrary results.[60] Using four measures of "enforcement vigor," they find that most state agencies are busier conducting more inspections and citing more violations than federal officials, though the state agencies are less inclined to issue citations assessing large penalties. They conclude that most states are doing a better job than the federal government in enforcing OSHA standards.

Policymakers who must regulate a large and diverse population with a limited budget and staff often find it necessary to devise sampling strategies for inspections. Benveniste and Pettus feel that this is a prudent approach under these circumstances.[61] According to Eads and Fix, because of the vast number of workplaces in the country and the limited number of OSHA inspectors, targeting is used to limit general scheduled inspections to the categories found to be more hazardous than the norm for all industries.[62] In the past, firms that fell within the "high hazard class" were subject to regular, thorough inspections. A highly controversial OSHA directive, issued in the early 1980s, required only a simple examination of records. If injuries were high, then full programmed inspections were conducted.

In most cases, OSHA inspectors take a company's word that violations will be brought into compliance. From Eads and Fix's standpoint, this could lead to an underreporting of disease and injury to escape physical review.[63] The sharp decline in follow-up inspections and failure-to-abate penalties provides little incentive for violators to comply with agency orders. Nevertheless, this practice fosters a cooperative posture and encourages efficient resource management in designing a rational and flexible regulatory policy.

Studies of the Office of Surface Mining by Mitnick and Hedge and Menzel reveal that the attitudes and behavior of inspectors should be considered in the development of an enforcement program.[64] In Hawkins's opinion, the behavior of field staff can directly affect compliance.[65] There is likely to be greater compliance if staff are perceived to be tough. He uses the police as an example in this regard. Danaceau, in contrast, maintains that adversary relationships should be avoided and that inspectors should emphasize prevention in carrying out their enforcement duties.[66] He also adds that inspectors must meet the following criteria: be knowledgeable about the underlying social goals of the program and how their work contributes to meeting these goals, be able to respond to the concerns and anxieties of industry, be aware of the financial positions of firms, be consistent in their inspections, and meet occasionally with one another to discuss their work and problems.

Heffron and McFeeley point out several difficulties in using inspections as a device to encourage compliance.[67] They argue that inspections are intrusive and sometimes conflict with privacy rights. Moreover, inspections are frequently ineffective because of confusing standards and the pressure from labor, industry, and even agency superiors to ignore violations. These problems are most significant when voluntary compliance is the chief regulatory activity. Collusion between inspectors and company employees also occurs. Heffron and McFeeley cite the Federal Aviation Administration and the DC–10 incident resulting from safety problems in the late 1970s, previous reviews of safety standards at nuclear power plants, and bribery in the U.S. Department of Agriculture meat inspection program as instances where such collusion has taken place.[68]

Adjudication

Adjudication involves a limited number of parties and is judicial in nature.[69] Formal adjudication involves either a formal trial in which the agency charges an individual or business with violating a regulation or a proceeding to set rates or decide which of several parties will receive some benefit (e.g., a license or permit to enter a market). The threat of going to court is generally considered an effective device for promoting compliant behavior.[70]

The Administrative Procedure Act of 1946 established a strict format of notice, hearings, procedures, evidence, oral argument, and formal judicial decision that adjudication proceedings are required to follow.[71] As a result, adjudication is usually a time-consuming and cumbersome process.

Enforcement proceedings begin when a possible violation has been brought to the attention of agency administrators. Officials of the agency initiate an investigation by notifying the individual or firm under investigation. Agency investigators assigned to the case collect information by interviewing those involved, subpoenaing documents and other materials, and conducting preliminary hearings. The director of the investigation then assesses the record and files a report recommending disposition of the case.

At this point, the case may be closed if the chief investigator finds that the evidence does not support the complaint, or it may be settled through a consent order. A consent order may be issued by the agency when a firm states that it is willing to cease the practice allegedly in violation of the law without admitting any wrongdoing.

When such an agreement is reached, the agency writes a proposed order that stipulates any corrective action that the firm must take. At the federal level, the order must appear in the *Federal Register* and is open for public comment (normally for sixty days). Reactions become a part of the record and are considered by agency hearing officers in deciding whether to issue the consent order in final form. At this juncture, the hearing officers may decide that the case should go to adjudication or that the order should be modified before it is issued in final form. If a case is not dismissed or settled through a consent order, the agency can initiate adjudicatory proceedings by issuing a formal complaint against the alleged violators. A formal trial begins after the case has been narrowed to the substantive issues involved.

Summary

This chapter analyzed a wide variety of regulatory devices, some of which could be employed in a strategic regulatory plan for achieving compliance with provisions involving gasoline additives, such as MTBE, and USTs. Each device has strengths and weaknesses that must be considered in the light of the theoretical issues examined in the last chapter. Choosing a combination of regulatory activities rather than just one might offset the negative effects of each activity on efforts to achieve compliance. Establishing an effective policy feedback and evaluation system can also help in this regard.

As can be seen in the discussion of the possible adoption of self-regulation and on-site inspections, for example, regulators are in the difficult position of having to weigh the costs and benefits of alternative techniques and make a decision based on their computations. The absence, presence, and salience of certain conditions make such computations very complex. Moreover, some of the variables can be hard to operationalize and quantify. This is why it is extremely important for policymakers to minimize uncertainty by collecting the greatest amount of accurate data on conditions in the regulated community, regulating agency, and outside arena that is possible before selecting regulatory devices. Otherwise, the information presented in this chapter, as well as the conceptual framework outlined in this study, is almost useless. The next part of this book analyzes the extent to which this was done in the decision to use MTBE as a gasoline additive.

II

Regulation without Strategy: The Case of Methyl Tertiary Butyl Ether

5

MTBE and Clean Air Regulation

The 1990 Clean Air Act Amendments introduced a variety of new approaches to clean air management, reflecting improvements in technology and the recognition that traditional command-and-control mechanisms were inadequate.[1] A major new element of the amendments was the introduction of technology forcing rules, chief among them the requirement that cleaner-burning reformulated gasoline (RFG) be developed for use in those regions with serious ground-level ozone. The RFG requirement mandated that oxygenates be added to gasoline in order to reduce carbon monoxide emissions, a precursor to ozone. Oxygenates cause gasoline to burn completely and displace aromatics and sulfur.[2]

Under the Administrative Procedures Act (APA), agencies must demonstrate the efficacy of proposed rules prior to adoption. This has increasingly resulted in a science-based assessment of potential regulatory approaches. Rather than replace the traditional interest-based politics of regulation, the result is a hybrid process where political interests are constrained by science-based options. At the same time, the science itself—or at least the scientific questions asked—has become constrained by the political concerns that are present.

Strategic regulatory planning relies on finding a meaningful equilibrium between scientific efficacy and interest-based political bargaining. By the end of the 1980s, oxygenates appeared to provide a large piece of that balance. They had been demonstrated to reduce tailpipe emissions and, though not free of costs, had found a coalescence of support among disparate stakeholders. The impact of significantly increasing the release of MTBE into the environment, however, had not been assessed systematically.

The chapters in Part II examine the RFG requirements mandated by the 1990 Clean Air Act as an example of nonstrategic regulation. Viewing MTBE contamination as an unintended consequence, this study shows that even science-based policy can be problematic if broader strategic objectives are not clearly understood. This chapter examines the environmental impacts of MTBE and its prevalence as a groundwater pollutant.

The Emergence of MTBE as a Gasoline Additive

Methyl tertiary butyl ether is a blend of methanol and isobutylene and is used as a motor fuel additive. It is an oxygenate that is used to increase the oxygen content of gasoline in order to improve combustion. MTBE is the most common of several oxygenates that are used to reduce emissions in areas that do not meet federal air quality standards under either the federal wintertime oxyfuels or RFG programs. About 30 percent of gasoline sold in the United States falls under the RFG standards, and approximately 87 percent of RFG gasoline contains MTBE.[3] Oxygenates contain organic molecules that contain oxygen. Both alcohols (including ethanol) and ethers (like MTBE) are commonly used. Oxygenates are helpful for promoting better combustion under adverse conditions and minimizing the release of unburned fuel. In addition, they help convert carbon monoxide (CO) into carbon dioxide (CO_2).[4]

Gasoline additives have been around for much of the previous century. Considering the limited efficiency of internal combustion engines, various additives have been used to improve performance. Tetra-ethyl lead was a common additive used to increase octane and minimize engine knocking. The 1970 Clean Air Act phased lead out of gasoline. Lead is a neurotoxin, accumulating in fatty tissue and has been linked to learning disabilities in young children. It is also incompatible with catalytic converters required for automobiles to meet new emission standards. In 1979, the EPA approved the use of MTBE, first patented in 1948, as an octane booster to replace lead.[5] The approval came in the form of a waiver under Section 211(f) of the 1970 Clean Air Act, which allowed EPA to grant exceptions for fuel additives after considering their potential for interfering with emissions systems or vehicle performance. The statutory language is narrow and has been interpreted as preventing the agency from considering health effects in granting waivers. MTBE appeared to be an ideal replacement for lead because it has a high octane rating and is comparatively clean burning. In addition, MTBE emissions are not as toxic as lead or other components of gasoline. The EPA's original waiver approved the use of MTBE at levels up to 7 percent by volume in gasoline, though most uses were in the range of 2 to 3 percent by volume.[6]

The use of MTBE increased through the 1980s as it was found to reduce significantly wintertime CO emissions. In 1984, EPA approved MTBE levels of 11 percent by volume, and in 1988 this was increased to 15 percent by volume. Rather than a systematic regulatory decision, this was implemented through the granting of waivers. Fuel companies were required only to submit data on MTBE's compatibility with gasoline, fuel economy, emissions, and toxicity in animals.[7] MTBE's effectiveness at reducing wintertime CO levels increased demand, particularly in cold weather cities such as Denver. In 1989, ARCO introduced what they termed "a cleaner-burning" reformulated gasoline with 11 percent volume MTBE in southern California.

Problems with MTBE emerged as early as 1984. Since MTBE is water soluble, it spreads rapidly through water tables. It is resistant to biological degradation and therefore does not break down as it travels through soil. In a state like Maine where the water table is shallow and most of the geology consists of a thin layer of soil over impermeable stone, a small quantity of gasoline spilled in an automobile accident can spread rapidly and contaminate water wells over a significant area.[8] In 1986, Maine officials presented a paper detailing their findings concerning MTBE at a national conference sponsored by the American Petroleum Institute (API). They also met with EPA officials to discuss their findings. In 1987, EPA's Office of Pollution Prevention and Toxic Substances distributed an internal memo reporting that MTBE had been found to contaminate drinking water in four states. The report noted that 20,000 people had been affected and that "this problem could rapidly mushroom due to leaking underground storage tanks."[9]

MTBE Use

MTBE has been used in U.S. gasoline at low levels since 1979 to replace lead as an octane enhancer, primarily in premium grades of gasoline at levels of 2 to 3 percent by volume.[10] Some premium blends contain as much as 9 percent by volume.[11] In 1992 its use expanded to include oxygenating fuels. Regulations resulting from the 1990 Clean Air Act Amendments established two programs that involve the use of oxygenated fuels. The Wintertime Oxyfuel Program, initiated in 1992, requires that oxygenated fuel (2.7 percent oxygen by weight) be used in cities that experience elevated levels of carbon monoxide during the winter or other specified months. The RFG program initiated in 1995 requires that RFG be used year-round in cities with the worst ground-level ozone levels. This program requires a minimum content of 2 percent oxygen by weight (11 percent by volume). Due to the severity of California's ozone problem, the state has developed its own alternative fuel program with more stringent requirements.[12] California is exempt from the wintertime oxyfuels program because of concerns that the increased oxygen content would lead to higher NOx (nitrogen oxides) emissions. It is required, however, to maintain the RFG standards (2 percent by weight minimum).[13]

As of February 2003, RFG use was mandated by the EPA in a number of areas, including Baltimore, Chicago, greater Connecticut, Houston, Los Angeles, Milwaukee, New York, Philadelphia, Sacramento, San Diego, and California's San Joaquin Valley. In addition, seventeen states and the District of Columbia decided to opt in to the program in designated areas. These states are California, Connecticut, Delaware, Illinois, Indiana, Kentucky, Maryland, Massachusetts, Missouri, New Hampshire, New Jersey, New York, Pennsylvania, Rhode Island, Texas, Virginia, and Wisconsin.[14]

MTBE contains an oxygen content of 19 percent. To fulfill the winter oxyfuel requirement gasoline with 2.7 percent by weight, oxygen must contain about 15 percent MTBE by volume; at 2.0 percent by weight, gasoline must contain about 11 percent by volume of MTBE.[15] This equates to approximately two and a half cups of MTBE for every gallon of wintertime oxyfuel gasoline. Because MTBE is water soluble, it travels farther and faster than other fuel constituents.[16] The EPA reports that MTBE in groundwater moves at nearly the same velocity as the groundwater itself.[17] MTBE breaks down slowly, so residual MTBE persists in soil and groundwater.[18]

MTBE dominates the oxygenate market for two reasons. The volatility of MTBE is lower than ethanol, making it easier to achieve the emissions standards. Also, MTBE can be shipped through existing pipelines.[19] Because ethanol raises the vapor pressure of gasoline significantly, increasing evaporative emissions, it must be shipped separately from gasoline and blended near the distribution point. Furthermore, it is comparatively expensive to produce and transport, requiring substantial federal subsidies to make it viable.[20] Ethanol is the oxygenate of choice in urban areas near corn-growing regions in the Midwest, but without the federal subsidy, ethanol would not exist as an option.

Though controversial, the federal oxyfuels program has been successful at improving air quality. In areas of the Northeast where RFG is used, concentrations of benzene, one of the most toxic constituents of automotive emissions, have decreased by as much as 43 percent.[21] Use of RFG was attributed with reducing ground-level ozone by 18 percent during the 1996 smog season in Los Angeles.[22] Although there remain questions as to emission variations across the vehicle fleet and under varying weather conditions, oxyfuels are credited with reducing CO emissions by as much as 10 percent.[23]

MTBE Hazards

The benefits of MTBE use are mitigated by a variety of health concerns. If inhaled, MTBE metabolizes to tertiary butyl alcohol (TBA) and formaldehyde. MTBE exposure has been linked to an increase in lymphomas and leukemia in rats. Although the risk to humans has not yet been demonstrated, the fact that MTBE metabolizes into formaldehyde and TBA could indicate a possible route for MTBE's carcinogenicity.[24] Finally, the U.S. EPA concludes that while "available data are not adequate to estimate potential health risks of MTBE at low exposure levels in drinking water . . . MTBE is a potential human carcinogen at high doses."[25]

McCarthy and Tiemann point out that gasoline is a highly volatile, toxic compound.[26] Several of its components, and in particular benzene, are known to be carcinogenic and highly toxic chemicals. Yet, although MTBE is less toxic than the components of gasoline it displaces, MTBE is much more mobile and resistant to biological decomposition than the other elements of gasoline. Once in surface water or groundwater, MTBE is extraordinarily difficult and expensive to mitigate. In addition to toxicity at high exposure levels, MTBE presents problems at even low levels. MTBE has been found to leave an odor and a taste that has been characterized as "'objectionable', 'bitter', 'solvent-like' and 'nauseating.'"[27] EPA reports that individuals have detected odors and taste at MTBE concentrations as low as 2.5 parts per billion (ppb) for odor and 2 ppb for taste.[28] As a consequence, EPA issued a nonregulatory advisory that MTBE concentrations be kept within 20 to 40 ppb, while noting "that some people may detect the chemical below this concentration range."[29]

MTBE Contamination in the Environment

Approximately 63.6 million gallons of gasoline were used each day in the United States in 2002.[30] The EPA reports that approximately 9 million gallons of gasoline are released into the environment every year.[31] Almost 33 percent of that total is RFG, with almost 70 percent of RFG containing MTBE. Gasoline is distributed through thousands of miles of pipelines and is trucked on every highway in the nation, to some 10,000 distribution points, and on to more than 180,000 retail outlets and fleet storage facilities, or to the hundreds of thousands of farms, industrial sites, and homes.[32] As EPA concludes, "Gasoline is removed from bulk storage into individualized storage units associated with such products as cars, trucks, boats, planes, lawn mowers, brush cutters, and chain saws.... There are opportunities for leaks wherever gasoline ... is stored, and there are opportunities for spills whenever fuel is transported or transferred from one container to another.... No system involving so much product and so many individual handlers can be foolproof."[33]

Airborn Exposure

MTBE is released into the air during production and distribution and through motor vehicles emissions. Like other airborne pollutants, its concentrations are highest near the source of emission and can be as high as 1800 micrograms per cubic meter.[34] Primary areas of concern therefore are gasoline stations and congested streets.[35] Data suggest that service people who work in proximity to areas of evaporative emissions—including gasoline station staff, mechanics, and tanker truck drivers—are experiencing exposure levels of two to three times the rest of the population.[36] On the positive side, MTBE degrades in the air much more rapidly than in soil or water. The half-life of airborne MTBE is thought to be as short as three days.[37]

Airborne MTBE exposure is also a problem indoors. Indoor exposure is generally a result of MTBE evaporative emissions from contaminated tap water. Boiling water and hot showers may be the primary source of emissions as a consequence of the efficiency through which steam can disperse evaporative emissions around an enclosed space. While direct ingestion of contaminated water may occur, as much as 71 percent of indoor exposure is due to airborne MTBE.[38]

Groundwater Contamination

Almost half of the U.S. population uses groundwater as a source of drinking water.[39] The physical characteristics of MTBE make groundwater contamination a considerable problem. MTBE is highly water soluble and, though volatile in concentrated form, lacks volatility when dissolved in water. It is resistant to soil absorption and resists biodegradation. The primary source of MTBE contamination in groundwater is leaking USTs. The EPA estimates that there are approximately 760,000 USTs currently in use for gasoline products with a total capacity of some 6 billion gallons. There are an additional 3 to 4 million USTs in use that are not subject to regulation.[40] The Resource Conservation and Recovery Act (RCRA) excludes several categories of USTs from regulatory oversight, including farm and residential tanks with capacities of 1,100 gallons or holding fuel used for noncommercial purposes, tanks storing heating oil used on the premises where it is stored, any tank with a capacity of 110 gallons or less, and emergency spill and overfill tanks.[41]

The breadth of the problem is illustrated by California. EPA estimates that the state has a minimum of 10,000 MTBE point sources leaking from USTs.[42] In a study contracted by the California state legislature and governor's office, Keller and his colleagues found that as early as 1998, they could identify 5,738 active sites for monitoring. The study projects that 78 percent of existing leaking underground fuel tanks will lead to MTBE contamination of groundwater.[43] Over 50 percent of the sites were found to have MTBE concentrations exceeding 500 ppb, 20 percent had concentrations over 10,000 ppb, and 4.5 percent had concentrations over 100,000 ppb.[44]

The EPA sees similar problems throughout the nation. Since the UST monitoring program began, approximately 400,000 releases from USTs have been confirmed. Although not every state is testing for MTBE at UST sites, those that do have found MTBE at a majority of sites with leaking tanks.[45] As early as 1998, EPA reported that of the thirty-four states that test leaking UST sites for MTBE, twenty-seven found MTBE present in more than 20 percent of the sites, and ten states found MTBE to be present in more than 80 percent of the leaking UST sites. In addition, twenty-five states reported MTBE contamination of private drinking water wells and nineteen reported MTBE contamination of public drinking water wells.[46] A joint U.S. Geological Survey–EPA study of twelve northeastern states reports that "MTBE was detected in 7 percent of drinking water supplies, with 0.8 percent of those detections above 20 (ppb). . . . MTBE is detected five times more frequently in drinking water from community water systems in RFG or Winter Oxyfuel areas than in non-RFG or non-Winter Oxyfuel areas."[47]

A second major source of groundwater contamination is fuel spills. In one incident reported by EPA, a single automobile accident contaminated twenty-four wells: "In December 1997, a car accident in Standish, Maine, led to the release of 8 to 10 gallons of gasoline that contaminated 24 nearby private wells. Eleven wells were contaminated with MTBE to a level above 35 (ppb); two were contaminated at over 1,000 (ppb); and the well nearest the accident site contained the highest concentration of 6,500 (ppb). . . . The contamination extended to the top of the underlying bedrock at a depth of 9 feet below the surface."[48] Two other public wells in Maine were found to be contaminated at low levels by spillage from overfilling of nearby USTs. The tanks themselves were less than a year old; testing revealed no leakage into the ground or vapor leaks. It was estimated, however, that between 10 and 40 gallons had been spilled because of overfilling.[49]

Pipelines have also been identified as a source of contamination of groundwater and surface water. Approximately 525 billion gallons of crude oil and refined petroleum products pass through nearly 160,000 miles of pipelines in the United States every year. EPA reports that an average of twenty-nine gasoline spills occur annually from these pipelines, with a total average volume of 1.03 million gallons released into the environment every year.[50] Even home heating oil has been identified as a potential carrier. Although MTBE is not a component of home heating oil, heating oil is often transported in tanker trucks used to transport gasoline. In twenty-seven sites where heating oil releases resulted in MTBE contamination of groundwater, MTBE concentrations ranged as high as 4,100 ppb.[51]

Surface Water Contamination

Keller et al. identify five sources of surface water contamination by MTBE: fallout associated with precipitation, urban runoff, groundwater flow, fuel spills, and emissions from motorized watercraft. Small boat engines and personal watercraft with two-stroke engines are especially significant sources. A 15 horsepower two-stroke carbureted outboard engine releases nearly 34 milligrams of MTBE per meter traveled.[52] Still, due to its volatility, MTBE evaporates fairly quickly from surface waters, while its resistance to biodegradation makes it extremely persistent in groundwater.

Cleanup and Remediation Issues

MTBE mitigation options vary depending on the location of contamination. Since MTBE does not absorb readily into soil, soil contamination is comparatively easy to mitigate. EPA recommends soil vapor extraction as an in situ treatment procedure and low-temperature thermal desorption as an ex situ measure. EPA considers both methods effective as long as mitigation occurs before MTBE migrates into groundwater.[53] Because MTBE dissipates rapidly from surface water, surface water remediation is unnecessary. EPA reports that "unless frozen, MTBE will volatilize and find its way into the atmosphere."[54] Keller et al. estimate that "more than 80% of the MTBE mass [is] expected to volatilize with[in] 2–3 weeks of cessation of MTBE discharge."[55] The volatilization rate in streams and rivers is considerably higher, with a half-life on the order of hours to days.[56]

Groundwater is a different issue. Because MTBE is frequently found with benzene and because benzene is frequently the contaminant of concern, EPA compares MTBE to benzene in discussing cleanup issues:

> MTBE is about 30 times more soluble than benzene in water. Pure MTBE can reach an equilibrium concentration in water of approximately 5 percent (i.e., 48,000 mg/L). . . . When moving from the liquid phase (i.e., free product) to the vapor phase, MTBE is three times more volatile than benzene. . . . When moving from the dissolved phase (in water) to the vapor phase, MTBE is about ten times less volatile than benzene. . . . MTBE is much less likely than benzene to adsorb to soil or organic carbon. . . . MTBE is more resistant to biodegradation than benzene. When MTBE is in the soil as the result of a petroleum release, it may separate from the rest of the petroleum, reaching the groundwater first and dissolving rapidly. Once in the groundwater, MTBE travels at about the same rate as the groundwater whereas benzene and other petroleum constituents tend to biodegrade and adsorb to soil particles.[57]

As a consequence, measures that are primarily geared toward mitigating benzene contamination will be insufficient to reduce MTBE contamination effectively.

Keller et al. point out that remediation success is "highly site specific," dependent on "the location of the site, the depth to groundwater, the extent of the vertical and horizontal migration of the groundwater plume, contaminant characteristics and the subsurface geology."[58] Cost estimates for remediation range from $250,000 to $430,000.[59] And sites with "a complex hydrogeological environment or large gasoline/MTBE source zones" can see costs increase up to $2.5 million.[60]

Prevalence of MTBE Contamination

EPA has concluded that MTBE is a national problem, though the agency acknowledges that there are insufficient data on the magnitude of the contamination. The U.S. Geological Survey reports that MTBE was detected in about 5 percent of groundwater samples collected nationally by the National Water-Quality Assessment. Less than 1 percent of samples exceeded the EPA consumer advisory standard of 20 ppb.[61] EPA has issued a draft health advisory for drinking water with MTBE levels ranging from 20 to 200 parts per billion (ppb).[62]

The extent of MTBE contamination varies across the nation. Oxyfuel program participation has emerged as a key indicator of potential contamination, with California, the northeastern states, and cold-weather states having the greatest problems. However, contamination is not limited to these states. Florida, for example, does not participate in the oxyfuel programs, yet 76 percent of gasoline station sites sampled showed MTBE contamination.[63] MTBE was detected in 70 percent of gasoline samples taken from over 200 sites in Indiana, Illinois, and Michigan. Though not required as part of the federal oxyfuel program, MTBE has been used in these states as an octane enhancer. The contamination, however, is thought to be a result of the Midwest's vast gasoline distribution systems, including tankers, storage tanks, and pipelines.[64]

MTBE across the Nation

The New England Interstate Water Pollution Control Commission conducted an EPA-funded survey of all fifty states to determine the level of MTBE contamination at leaking underground storage tank sites. The data are revealing: fourty-three states require monitoring groundwater for MTBE at leaking UST sites. When surveyed on the frequency of MTBE detection in gasoline-contaminated leaking UST sites, eight states reported 0 to 20 percent of sites; seven states reported 20 to 40 percent of sites; one state reported 40 to 60 percent of sites; eleven states reported 60 to 80 percent of sites; and 4 states reported 80 to 100 percent of sites. MTBE levels exceeding the lower EPA threshold of 20 ppb were found by seven states 0 to 20 percent of the time; four states 20 to 40 percent of the time; seven states 40 to 60 percent of the time; 10 states 60 to 80 percent of the time; and ten states 80 to 100 percent of the time.[65] Several states, including Alaska, California, Illinois, and New York, responded that they were unable to report due to insufficient data. Tables 5.1 and 5.2 report the frequency of detection of MTBE at UST sites around the nation.

Several states have particular experiences with MTBE that are worth noting. Alabama, for example, proclaims "no significant detections" of

Table 5.1
Frequency of MTBE detection in soil/groundwater at gasoline-contaminated leaking UST sites

Frequency	Soil	Groundwater
0–20% of the time	CO, HI, MA, MS, NE, OH, WI, WY	CO, HI, IN, MA, MS, NE, ND, OH, OK, WI, WY
20–40%	AL, ID (est.), MI, NM, NJ, NY, UT	AR, NY, UT, WA
40–60%	MT	ID (hard), IA, MI, MT, SC, OR, SD
60–80%	DE, IA, LA, MN, MO, NH, MD, NC, RI, TN, WV	AL, AZ, DE, GA, LA, MN, MO, NH, ME, NJ, NM, NV, TN, TX, WV
80–100%	FL, NH—new sites; CT, VT—when looked for;	FL, KS, NH—new sites; CT, MD, NC, RI, VT, VA,

Notes: Alaska, California, and Mississippi reported insufficient statewide data at time of the survey for either soil or groundwater. Illinois and Kentucky do not analyze for MTBE. New York soil data are estimated, and groundwater data are from a snapshot survey of state fund projects through October 1998.
Source: New England Interstate Water Pollution Control Commission, *Survey of State Experiences with MTBE Contamination at Leaking UST Sites* (August 2000).

Table 5.2
Frequency with which MTBE levels exceeded 20 ppb at groundwater sites

Frequency	States exceeding 20 ppb
0–20% of the time	HI, ND, OH, OK, WA, WI, WY
20–40%	AR, MN, OR, TX
40–60%	AZ, AL, IA, ME, MT, NM, TN
60–80%	ID, IN, MO, NE, NV, NH, NY, SC, VA, NJ
80–100%	CT, DE, FL, KS, LA, MD, MA, NC, RI, VT
Don't know	CA, CO, GA, MI, MS, PA, SD, UT, WV

Note: At the time of the survey, Montana had not reviewed all data from MTBE-affected sites or conducted a complete survey to determine number of MTBE-affected sites.
Source: New England Interstate Water Pollution Control Commission, *Survey of State Experiences with MTBE Contamination at Leaking UST Sites* (August 2000).

the gas additive. The state sampled 939 wells, 27 springs, and 87 surface water sources. Five wells were found to contain MTBE with detection levels between 0.79 and 8.39 ppb.[66] Though this was below the health threshold of 20 to 40 ppb, concern among residents was rife. In Alaska, MTBE was introduced in the Fairbanks and Anchorage areas in fall 1992. Complaints about health effects from its use were so intense that the governor suspended use of MTBE in December 1992. MTBE was detected in groundwater at half of fifteen service station sites in Anchorage and was confirmed to be in groundwater at four of them.[67]

Arizona opted in to the federal RFG program in 1997. MTBE has been used in RFG programs in the Phoenix and Tucson areas. In addition, several southern Arizona areas receive gasoline from California distributors that include MTBE as a regular additive for the California market. Maricopa County has used both MTBE and ethanol, but by 1996 nearly all of the wintertime gasoline sold in Tucson contained ethanol. However, regulations regarding volatility are difficult to meet with ethanol in Arizona's summer heat, so MTBE is used as the summertime oxygenate. Arizona has been relatively free of problems of groundwater contamination, although four wells in Phoenix were closed because of a leaking UST at a gasoline station nearby.[68]

California has some of the most serious incidences of groundwater contamination. In addition to the UST problem, California has experienced significant contamination of surface waters from recreational activities. Two-stroke engines, commonly found in outboard motors and personal watercraft (such as Jet Skis and Wave Runners), release approximately 25 percent of their raw fuel directly into the water as a function of their design. Although manufacturers are introducing more efficient four-stroke models, the vast majority of recreational watercraft continues to use two-stroke propulsion.

The Lake Tahoe area has had a particularly notable problem. The Tahoe Research Group study based at the University of California at Davis reported a significant increase in MTBE detected in Donner Lake over the summer boating season: "During March and April (1997), before boating activity increased on the lake, it was calculated that Donner Lake contained 45–65 pounds of MTBE. By July 1st this had increased to 250 pounds with a sharp increase to the maximum of 815 pounds shortly after the July 4th holiday. Over the September 1st Labor Day weekend MTBE also increased but much less dramatically (i.e., approximately a 100 pound increase)."[69]

Colorado was one of the first states to implement an MTBE program when it introduced RFG in the Denver area in 1988. Colorado was also one of the first to experience environmental problems. By 1991 distinct odors and a reduction in fuel economy were among the primary complaints cited by consumers.[70] Groundwater contamination was also an issue. The state reports MTBE contamination in 0 to 20 percent of gasoline-leaking UST sites, though Colorado does not report how often these levels exceed 20 ppb.[71]

Iowa is one of the primary producers of ethanol. Nonetheless, in a 1999 study of leaking USTs, the state Department of Natural Resources reported that nearly 32 percent of the 2,569 groundwater samples collected contained MTBE levels above 15 ppb. One site reported an MTBE concentration of 99,400 ppb.[72] Just under 30 percent of the sites had MTBE levels above the EPA health advisory level of 20 ppb.

MTBE has been used in Kansas as an octane booster for several years. Data from 818 monitoring sites show MTBE to be present in 88 percent of the sites. In one community, the public water source had an MTBE concentration of 1,050 ppb. Like Iowa, Kansas is a corn-producing state that could use ethanol exclusively.[73]

New Jersey, like California, has had a long and difficult experience with MTBE. Sampling of public water wells conducted as early as 1985–1986 detected MTBE concentrations up to 81 ppb. As a consequence, New Jersey was one of the first states to implement a maximum contaminant level for MTBE.[74] The state reports MTBE contamination in 60 to 80 percent of leaking UST sites, with MTBE levels exceeding the EPA threshold in 60 to 80 percent of the cases.[75] Between 1989 and 2000, the New Jersey Department of Environmental Protection (NJDEP) registered over 84,000 USTs; 34,000 of these contained gasoline, with a combined storage capacity of 170 million gallons. NJDEP estimates that these tanks store up to 1.7 billion gallons of gasoline on an annual basis. With MTBE representing 11 percent of volume, NJDEP estimates throughput of up to 187 million gallons of MTBE in New Jersey's USTs.[76]

New Mexico's Department of the Environment reports that groundwater at two-thirds of its sites may be contaminated by MTBE.[77] New Mexico reports MTBE contamination in groundwater at 60 to 80 percent of gasoline-contaminated leaking UST sites, with MTBE levels exceeding the EPA threshold in 40 to 60 percent of the cases.[78]

Rhode Island reports MTBE contamination in groundwater at 80 to 100 percent of leaking UST sites, with MTBE levels exceeding the EPA threshold in 80 to 100 percent of the cases.[79] The Association of State and Territorial Solid Waste Management Officials *MTBE and Fuel Oxygenates Workgroup Newsletter* reported the following incident in Rhode Island:

> At the beginning of September [2001], the general manager of the Pascoag Utility District sat down to write a letter to his customers: 'Do not drink your water.' . . . About 5000 people have been unable to drink or use their water since September 1st. The Rhode Island Department of Health advised residents to neither drink nor cook with their water, and to limit their shower time because of high MTBE levels. . . . The Rhode Island Health Department issued an advisory at the beginning of November [warning] residents against using the water to bathe children less than 6 years old. The contaminant levels had gone from 620 ppb to 1100 ppb. The Health department's maximum level is 40 ppb.[80]

The source of the contamination was traced in part to a Mobil gasoline station.[81]

Texas produces most of the nation's MTBE. In random monitoring, Chevron detected MTBE in groundwater in 96 percent of the service stations tested. MTBE levels of 1000 ppb were found in 63 percent of the sites.[82] Texas reports MTBE contamination in groundwater at 60 to 80 percent of leaking UST sites, with MTBE levels exceeding the EPA threshold in 20 to 40 percent of the cases.[83]

In 2000, the state of Washington Department of Ecology tested sixty-two groundwater sites, finding MTBE in thirty of them. The state reports MTBE contamination in groundwater at 20 to 40 percent of leaking UST sites, with MTBE levels exceeding the EPA threshold in 0 to 20 percent of the cases.[84] This was a surprise to regulators because MTBE was not being used by any refineries in the state. Ultimately, the state found that as other states began to ban MTBE, distributors were dumping MTBE-laden gasoline in Washington.[85]

Summary

MTBE contamination is a serious problem around the nation, with particularly serious impacts in states participating in the oxyfuel and RFG programs. MTBE has been detected in groundwater in all states, though the extent of contamination varies widely. MTBE was first introduced as a gasoline additive, finding its way into USTs in the 1970s. It was initially used as an octane enhancer to replace lead, which was banned in the 1970 Clean Air Act Amendments. Early MTBE concentrations in gasoline ranged from 4 to 7 percent by volume. Currently, MTBE concentrations range between 11 and 15 percent by volume. The EPA initiated the Federal Wintertime Oxyfuel program in 1992 and the RFG program in 1995 to meet the oxygenate requirements of the 1990 Clean Air Act Amendments.[86]

With the integration of gasoline distribution resources across the nation EPA considers MTBE to be potentially present in any UST in the country. MTBE therefore presents a contamination threat in all areas of the country, not just regions participating in the Oxyfuel or RFG programs. The U.S. Geological Survey has detected MTBE in 5 percent of groundwater samples collected through the National Water-Quality Assessment Program, with 1 percent of samples exceeding the EPA's consumer advisory of 20 ppb. MTBE is more likely to be found in much higher concentrations in areas participating in the Oxyfuel or RFG programs. The 1990 Clean Air Act designates the ten largest metropolitan areas with the most severe summer ozone problems as RFG participants and those areas that have not met the National Ambient Air Quality Standards for carbon monoxide as Oxyfuel participants.[87] MTBE contamination is ubiquitous and will cost huge sums of money to abate.

6

Failure in Regulatory Planning

While policy is always made within an environment of some uncertainty, politics is least rational when issue ambiguity is greatest. The interplay among legislators, policymakers, environmentalists, consumer groups, industry groups, and the public at large reflects a constantly changing constellation of interests and concerns. The 1990 Clean Air Act represents a package of statutes that emerged between these interests and concerns for at least a decade. The result was a package that pleased no one and offered only limited improvement to the air pollution management regime.

Statutes emerge in a politically competitive environment, while regulations emerge in an environment that is simultaneously political and constrained by organizational culture and capacity, the mandates of the Administrative Procedures Act, and a variety of executive orders on rule making, which require rational assessment.[1] Thus, if statutes reflect competing objectives or regulatory options that are constrained by administrative or economic conditions, the ability of regulators to act rationally is greatly inhibited. The oxygenate requirements of the Clean Air Act provide an important case in point. The Clean Air statutes simply required an oxygenate fuel additive; they did not mandate MTBE.[2] In fact, the oxygenate requirement could not have survived without extensive lobbying by agricultural interests that saw the opportunity to expand the corn-based ethanol market. Nonetheless, the economic difficulty in transporting sufficient quantities of ethanol from corn-producing states to the western cities and states (Denver and California, for example) made MTBE the only realistic alternative.

This chapter demonstrates how the implementation of the oxygenate requirements of the Clean Air Act is an example of nonstrategic regulatory planning. The chapter begins with an examination of the regulatory pressures that led to the oxygenate requirement, assesses how MTBE emerged despite its potential hazards, and examines the failures of nonstrategic regulatory planning.

The Politics of the Oxygenate Requirements of the 1990 Clean Air Act

The Clean Air Act Amendments of 1990 were adopted after a decade of political battles framed by the legacy of the 1970 amendments and Republican control of the White House. In 1981, the National Commission on Air Quality, itself created by the 1977 Clean Air Act Amendments, recommended that in the wake of the energy crises of the previous decade and the resulting economic reverberations, emission standards be lowered and attainment deadlines extended. The Reagan administration later submitted a Clean Air Act reauthorization proposal that was weaker yet.[3] With little executive leadership and a Congress deeply split over the question of rigorous environmental regulation, reauthorization languished.

Still, by the end of the Reagan presidency, environmental quality reemerged as a salient issue among the public. Public opinion polls through the late 1980s demonstrated that a growing proportion of Americans felt that environmental quality should be pursued regardless of cost.[4] Vice President George H. W. Bush ran in part on a promise of providing responsible environmental leadership. By 1989 a New York Times/CBS Evening News Poll found that 75 percent of Americans agreed with the statement: "Protecting the environment is so important that requirements and standards cannot be too high, and continuing environmental improvements must be made regardless of cost." Only 19 percent disagreed.[5] With a moderate Republican in the White House, change in the majority leadership of the U.S. Senate (the replacement of Democratic senator Robert Byrd with Senator George Mitchell), and strong environmental support among the public, Congress again took up clean air reauthorization.

In the context of the political battles leading up to the 1990 amendments, reformulated gasoline was a nonissue. Ethanol producers and oil companies were battling over the alternative fuels section, environmentalists and automakers were locked in the traditional battle over tailpipe emissions standards and time frames, and high- and low-sulfur states were battling over the acid rain provisions.[6] ARCO changed the dynamic by announcing that it would release a reformulated gasoline that would burn cleaner than conventional fuel and run in both older automobiles without catalytic converters and newer automobiles with contemporary smog equipment. ARCO's market share immediately increased, though Bryner suggests that the company's announcement was more an effort to negotiate a lighter alternatives fuel requirement.[7] ARCO's longstanding use of MTBE as an octane enhancer made it a natural distributor for reformulated gasoline (RFG).

Against the backdrop of existing political concerns, RFG became immediately important. Although it had not been sought by regulators or environmentalists, once on the table, RFG became the starting point for any later negotiations. Oxygenated gasoline was preferred by automotive manufacturers, which were concerned about the impact of methanol-based alternative fuels on automotive performance and on components that might be vulnerable to methanol-related corrosion. Oil companies, worried that methanol mandates would threaten gasoline's dominance as an automotive fuel, strongly favored oxygenates, which could be blended with existing fuel. Although ethanol would remain a small part of the oxygenate market, corn state lobbyists and agribusiness, including multinational corporations such as Archer Daniels Midland, had a strong interest in seeing an oxygenate requirement. Regulators and environmentalists were on board because of the potential for easy emission reductions. The primary regulatory parties, then, included an alliance of oil, automobile, and agriculture interests fighting on behalf of the oxygenate program.[8] Unlike all other aspects of clean air legislation, RFG seemed to provide a technical win to all sides.

The RFG Regulation Negotiation

The consensus-based regulation negotiation (reg-neg) that EPA convened in 1991 underscores the coalescence of interests around the RFG question. In promulgating RFG regulations, EPA sought broad involvement from all stakeholders. In complying with the Federal Advisory Committee Act, EPA put out a request for participation in the *Federal Register* in February 1991. The agency first convened the negotiating committee for RFG on March 14, 1991. It included representatives from federal, state, and local regulatory agencies; the American Petroleum Institute and refiners' associations; corn growers; ethanol and methanol trade groups; gasoline producers and distributors; motor vehicle manufacturers; and large environmental organizations including the Sierra Club and National Resources Defense Council.[9] The reg-neg was able to achieve an Agreement-in-Principle within five months, releasing a formal agreement on August 16, 1991. Philip Harter, the process mediator, summarized the outcome as "a full consensus: all parties signed the agreement in a ceremony that was aired on the nightly news of all the major networks. It was a big deal."[10]

The Agreement-in-Principle did not deal with whether MTBE should be preferred or whether MTBE or other oxygenates were a potential risk to the environment. Rather, the agreement sought to find a balance in implementation methodology, including how to model and thus certify oxygenate content and how to test emissions against 1990 baselines.[11] The broad assumption by all stakeholders at the time was that oxygenates, on balance, were a good thing for the environment. Although the process was political rather than scientific, participants did rely on the best available science to answer the questions they were asking. In retrospect, however, those involved in the process—both inside and outside the regulatory negotiation—may have been asking the wrong questions.

Regulatory Failure I: Asking the Wrong Questions

With the momentum that RFG had acquired, EPA moved forward with the data that were available. Up to this point in 1991, virtually all research on MTBE was conducted by producers, which focused on its compatibility with gasoline, its emissions, and acute toxicity. No consideration was given to the potential for other environmental impacts. section 211(b) allows EPA to require manufacturers to provide information regarding health effects of fuels and fuel additives as a condition for commercial registration. Also, EPA can regulate or ban fuels based on the health effects of their emissions or for interfering with vehicle emission control equipment under section 211(c). Section 211(f) requires

EPA to consider the emission control system and vehicle performance and drivability impacts, as well as materials compatibility of fuels and fuel additives. Formal assessments of the public health impacts or impacts on environmental quality are not required.[12]

The Clean Air Act provides no authority to EPA to consider environmental contamination, and although the Clean Water Act does, the organizational structure of EPA is media specific. Regulatory development and enforcement of the Clean Air Act take place within the Office of Air and Radiation, and Clean Water Act management occurs within the Office of Water. The lack of coordination between EPA research teams was cited by the agency itself as the primary failure in identifying the emergent environmental problems associated with MTBE use as an additive in gasoline.[13] During the 1980s and early 1990s when MTBE was under consideration, the relationship between program offices and EPA's Office of Research and Development was strained.[14] This was a result of the residual tension between staff regulators and EPA's upper administration under the Reagan administration.[15]

Congress consulted with EPA in developing the specifications for RFG included in the 1990 amendments to the Clean Air Act. EPA, in turn, based its recommendations on preliminary data collected through the Auto-Oil Air Quality Improvement Research Program. This program, also known as the Auto/Oil study, was a $40 million research effort funded by fourteen oil companies and three U.S. automobile manufacturers. The Auto/Oil study data were integrated with EPA's own emission models developed in the EPA Office of Mobile Sources.[16] The studies were reported in a series of publications between 1991 and 1997. Since these studies represented the primary data and considering the relatively short time frame for implementing the 1990 Clean Air Act Amendments, EPA was highly dependent on industry data during the reg-neg process.

The Auto/Oil studies would later be criticized for establishing a methodology that sought to demonstrate MTBE's superiority over methanol and for failing to take into account real-world conditions.[17] The evaluation of the impact of oxygenated fuel on vehicle emissions in the laboratory ignored the critical intervening variables of road conditions, weather, and the varying mechanical conditions of actual automobiles. The utility of MTBE was later brought into question by the

California study, which suggested that RFG without MTBE met the emission standards for new model automobiles.[18] But at the time, the Auto/Oil study provided the best available data. In short, the question of discrete contamination effects was not on anybody's mind during the regulatory planning process.

Regulatory Failure II: Resistance to the Evidence of MTBE Contamination

When anecdotal data began to emerge about the consequences of MTBE use in reformulated fuels, EPA was unprepared. When the Wintertime Oxyfuel program went into effect in 1992, there were almost immediate complaints of inhalation effects from exposure at gasoline stations. These complaints were most frequent in colder areas such as Alaska, Colorado, and Minnesota. In commenting on the extent to which EPA was caught off guard, a senior official from EPA's Office of Air and Radiation said, "MTBE was a non-issue until 1992. . . . Given that MTBE is in gasoline, which in and of itself is not a good thing for you, how much data do you really need for an additive? On that basis, the information we had on MTBE was seen as quite adequate. . . . We had done two bioassays—that's considered a lot. That's more information than we have on many chemicals. It didn't seem very toxic. . . . We're adding this to gasoline, not Cheerios!"[19]

EPA was skeptical about the inhalation complaints because they were anecdotal, and EPA culture, like scientific culture generally, prefers laboratory confirmation. Nonetheless, EPA did hold public hearings on the issue and initiated a research program into MTBE inhalation effects in January 1993 to determine whether MTBE presented a health risk in advance of the fall 1993 oxyfuel season. The agency initiated an Office of Research and Development study in 1993 to assess the early complaints of inhalation effects such as nausea and dizziness. The study concluded that the anecdotal and self-selected nature of the complaints left the agency unable to draw any substantive conclusions.[20] Regulators responded to continued public complaints with several additional studies jointly funded by EPA and several industry groups, including the American Petroleum Institute, the Oxygenated Fuels Association, and the

Synthetic Organic Chemical Manufacturers Association. Several of the studies included the Centers for Disease Control.[21] The results were similarly inconclusive. EPA initiated an Office of Research and Development study in 1994 to further review the data, leaving the agency to conclude that MTBE appeared to be no more of a health risk than nonoxygenated gasoline.[22]

EPA reported that some individuals were sensitive to MTBE's odor and might present symptoms not observed in a healthy person. This finding was later criticized by the National Research Council, which led to a review by the Health Effects Institute (HEI), a partnership between EPA and industry.[23] In 1996 HEI reported that adding oxygenates to fuel is "unlikely to substantially increase the health risks associated with fuel used in motor vehicles" and declined to recommend any reduction in its use.[24] The HEI also acknowledged that a failure to anticipate the potential health impacts from a new substance was problematic. The institute said, "Although we can never have full knowledge about a new substance, we would be well served to anticipate better and plan for such health questions before they occur."[25] Despite the emerging concerns about MTBE, EPA implemented the RFG program in 1995.

In April 1996, California initiated the second phase of the RFG program, introducing reformulated fuels with 11 percent by volume of MTBE. Almost immediately, leaking USTs contaminated two municipal aquifers in Santa Monica.[26] EPA's response was to publish a nonbinding water advisory focusing on taste and odor, since MTBE is detectable at levels lower than those thought to present health risks.

By 1998 EPA convened a Blue Ribbon Panel to assess the MTBE problem. The panel included many of the same organizations as the earlier RFG regulation negotiation committee. However, unlike the earlier reg-neg, the panel did not reach a consensus. Indeed, Lyondell Chemical Company, a panel participant and Houston-based MTBE producer, published its own dissenting conclusion. Panel members represented the HEI, local water districts, the Natural Resources Defense Council, the American Petroleum Institute, the American Lung Association, MTBE producers, ethanol producers, and an assortment of university-based scientists and federal and state environmental regulators.[27]

In July 1999 the panel published its recommendations. Specific recommendations for preventing further pollution included significantly enhancing the UST regulatory program; accelerating the planned implementation of the improved water testing provisions of the Clean Water Act, particularly in areas where RFG is used; and restricting the use of two-stroke engines in lakes and reservoirs that serve as drinking water resources. In the area of remediation, panel recommendations included congressional expansion of available resources for up-front funding of treatment for drinking water systems that are known to be contaminated with MTBE. The panel's report stated that the panel "agreed broadly that, in order to minimize current and future threats to drinking water, the use of MTBE should be reduced substantially. Several members believed that the use of MTBE should be phased out completely. The Panel recommends that Congress act quickly to clarify federal and state authority to regulate and/or eliminate the use of gasoline additives that pose a threat to drinking water supplies."[28] Finally, the panel recognized the need to test any new compound better before introduction into widespread use: "The introduction of reformulated gasoline has had substantial air quality benefits, but has at the same time raised significant issues about the questions that should be asked before widespread introduction of a new, broadly-used product. The unanticipated effects of RFG on groundwater highlight the importance of exploring the potential for adverse effects in all media (air, soil, and water), and on human and ecosystem health, before widespread introduction of any new, broadly-used, product."[29]

The politics concerning the abatement of MTBE has been quite contentious. As Franklin observes, "The politics of removing the oxygenate requirement, or even granting an oxygenate waiver to California, are particularly treacherous, because the fuel provisions of the [Clean Air Act] were some of the most hard-fought battles during the entire Amendment debates. . . . The oxygen requirement was crucial to securing the agreement of the farm lobby and corn-ethanol coalition states, and removing it could unravel the delicate balance of power in support of the Amendments. . . . Environmentalists are concerned [about a] domino-like effect that would ultimately emasculate the Act."[30] The coalition that emerged to oppose a ban included both the Sierra Club and Natural Resources Defense Council (NRDC). Environmental groups were concerned that a significant reduction in MTBE use would result in reduced progress on air pollution reduction.

The Northeast States for Coordinated Air Use Management (NESCAUM) recommended a phased reduction of MTBE. NESCAUM argued that MTBE in RFG could be reduced significantly without a drop in air quality.[31] However, there remained concern that banning MTBE altogether would, on balance, be unproductive. NESCAUM reported that "gasoline refiners that supply the Northeast have overcomplied with RFG toxic performance standards by more than 75 percent, in part due to the presence of MTBE. This substantial margin of overcompliance may be lost if MTBE is reduced or eliminated from RFG. In addition, toxic air emissions from conventional gasoline sold in the Northeast have declined 13 percent since 1990, and those emission benefits may also be diminished or lost if MTBE is phased out of RFG."[32] In short, they argued that a substantial reduction in MTBE, combined with aggressive enforcement of existing UST standards, would mitigate the water pollution problem.[33]

Other analysts saw it differently. The 1998 California study recommended a complete phase-out of MTBE.[34] By 2000, both the Sierra Club and NRDC published press releases stating that phasing out MTBE was now appropriate, though both issued the caveat that an MTBE phase-out would not result in any net loss of air quality improvements.[35]

In 2002 California Governor Gray Davis announced a statewide ban on MTBE. Initially targeted for enforcement on December 31, 2002, the ban was pushed back to 2003 following California's electricity shortage in 2000 and 2001, intense industry lobbying by the Oxygenate Fuels Association (an MTBE trade group), and a California Energy Commission study that recommended postponing the ban for fears that gasoline prices would rise by 50 to 100 percent.[36] Davis also requested a waiver from the oxygenate requirement altogether, citing authority under section 211(c)(4)(B) of the Clean Air Act to opt out of the requirement if nonoxygenated fuel would meet federal emissions standards. EPA denied the request, citing "uncertainty" over the impact of a waiver on emissions. Farm state senators lobbied EPA to deny the waiver, as did oil companies and automobile makers, which voiced concern about the impact of state by state differences in fuel standards.[37]

Regulatory Failure III: Confusing Chemical Contamination and Mechanical Failure

The single most significant regulatory failure may have been EPA's tendency to view MTBE contamination as a UST issue: if tanks are leaking, they should be fixed or replaced. Franklin argues that by framing the issue as a mechanical failure, EPA focused more on deficient infrastructure than on deficient rule making.[38] EPA did not see the potential for sustained environmental risk emanating from MTBE as a fuel additive. The agency failed to anticipate any added hazard of introducing a new chemical into an already dangerous compound (gasoline). The agency failed to respond effectively to early reports of emerging contamination. Finally, when data demonstrating the extent of MTBE contamination in groundwater were reported, the agency failed to address the core cause (the presence of MTBE in gasoline), preferring instead to focus on leaking USTs.

The Lack of Strategic Regulatory Planning in Implementing the Reformulated Gasoline Provisions

Chapter 2 outlines a strategic approach to regulatory planning, which suggests a strategic, step-by-step approach to problem mitigation. By using the steps of the model as evaluative criteria, it is possible to analyze how and where the oxygenate requirements suffered policy failure. This section analyzes policymaking related to the oxygenate requirement through the lens of each of these steps.

Step 1: Problem Recognition

The problem that the Clean Air Act seeks to mitigate is air pollution. Although not intended to mitigate other environmental conditions, there was an expectation that the act would not exacerbate other environmental problems. All policy begets unintended consequences. We can anticipate many of the consequences, but a policy's unintended consequences can quickly ricochet out of control. That noted, it is reasonable to predict what the likely unintended consequences of a policy might be as part of a problem definition. This is frequently done with economic filters. President Reagan initiated executive order 12291 requiring that all regulations administered by executive agencies be implemented only when "potential benefits to society outweigh potential costs to society." President George H. W. Bush demanded that economic growth not be significantly affected by environmental regulation that he would be asked to sign. It is clear that with regard to unintended environmental effects, however, the 1990 Clean Air Act failed to cast its problem net wide enough.

Implementing agencies are constrained by the mandates they are given. Yet agency staff may exacerbate these constraints by performing in a nonstrategic, overly narrow way. Rather than evaluate the broad goals of the air management regime they were tasked with creating, EPA simply accepted a narrow list of program objectives focused on emissions reduction. While strategic thinking may not have resulted in the broadening effect one might hope for, its absence virtually guaranteed that regulators failed to ask the right questions. So in spite of the fact that EPA scientists recognized that MTBE presented an environmental hazard and that section 112 of the Clean Air Act includes MTBE in the list of hazardous air pollutants, the agency did not see the potential of groundwater contamination as an emerging concern. Even the HEI, an industry-EPA research partnership, acknowledged that the failure to anticipate the potential health impacts from introducing MTBE into the environment was a significant oversight.[39] The recognition and articulation of the problem defines the boundaries within which a policy response may emerge. MTBE as a groundwater contaminant was simply outside those boundaries.

Step 2: Identification of Parties

The lack of anticipation of an MTBE contamination problem, and the consequential lack of preparation on the agency's part, made EPA particularly reliant on industry data and vulnerable to an inadequate definition of the problem. The strategic analysis of who is involved, what their concerns are, and with what resources they are coming to the table is an inoculative device. The importance of strategic knowledge as one enters into a regulatory discussion is underscored by the speed with which regulators become overburdened by mounting industry and political pressures.

The primary alliance of petrochemical companies, automotive manufacturers, multinational farming concerns, legislators who represent areas heavily affected by these concerns, and a handful of environmental organizations that saw the oxygenate issue as an opportunity to make substantive improvements in air emissions presented regulators with a heady set of interlocking constituencies. Although this set of participants could be a positive force in a regulatory planning process, the absence of other information sources and opposing parties allowed these groups to dominate policy discussions. Had a strategic analysis of the players been initiated earlier, regulators may have been able to facilitate across a broader set of response alternatives. In the end, the MTBE groundwater contamination question was limited to fixing leaking USTs rather than reducing MTBE prevalence as a consequence of the need to balance a strong coalition in favor of the oxygenate programs and the urgency caused by the UST releases.

Step 3: Historical Analysis

A lack of experience with MTBE at all levels of government combined with a lack of scientific information, rather than a strategic failure, was more than likely the problem. Still, there was sufficient indication of an emerging MTBE problem in the Northeast to justify a formal assessment. The Maine Department of Environmental Protection reported MTBE was a groundwater contaminant associated with gasoline spills as early as 1984. These releases were associated with leaking underground and above-ground storage tanks. MTBE was found to be the first gasoline constituent to reach drinking water supplies, followed by benzene, toluene, ethylbenzene, and xylenes.[40] Further, the extent to which MTBE persists in the environment was known to producers in the early 1980s. In an industry slide presentation reviewing a contamination incident in Rockaway, New Jersey, a Shell scientist wrote that in 1981, the joke inside Shell was that "MTBE really stands for 'Most Things Biodegrade Easier.'"[41]

Still, what industry knew and what regulators knew were not necessarily identical. A 1987 memorandum between executives at ARCO and CITGO Petroleum describes an industry-wide effort to discredit Maine's Department of Environmental Protection report on MTBE contamination in groundwater.[42] Federal regulators did not come to the MTBE issue until 1991 and did not begin receiving complaints until the 1992–1993 winter oxyfuel season. Although several states recognized potential environmental hazards with MTBE early on, there were no independent national studies conducted until 1993, and these were limited in scope and quality.

Step 4: Situational Analysis

MTBE contamination presents the obvious challenge of mitigating groundwater pollution and controlling inhalation exposure. Yet the question of whether environmental contamination can effectively be contained by replacing leaking USTs remains a contested terrain. All sides agree that leaking USTs need to be replaced and that the scope of regulation over USTs needs to be expanded. Yet there is growing sentiment that MTBE itself ought to be minimized or banned outright. EPA continues to struggle with this issue, and considering the interests involved, it is unlikely to resolve this any time soon. The odd partnering of petrochemical companies and agribusiness, centrist environmental lobbies and automobile manufacturers, and corn state legislators and fuel distributors has created a momentum that will be difficult to slow through traditionally incremental approaches.

The MTBE issue unfolded under the radar of environmental regulators and as a consequence of incremental policy choices driven by political compromise, scientific uncertainty, and economic self-interest. It is not likely to resolve itself through similar processes without a fundamental shift in the definition of the MTBE problem. Now that MTBE contamination has become defined as a discrete environmental problem, it is possible that a thorough strategic regulatory plan can emerge. If, however, MTBE contamination continues to be seen through the lens of leaking USTs or through the trade-off between clean air and clean water, regulatory difficulties are likely to continue.

Step 5: Strategic Regulation Formulation

The MTBE response is a case study of Lindblom's notion of muddling through.[43] Since the core problem was mitigating air pollution, all regulatory devices were directed at emissions reduction. As the auxiliary problem of water contamination emerged, it was treated as a limited mechanical failure in gasoline distribution systems. Since these systems, from USTs to trucking and pipelines, are already regulated, there seemed to be no need to revisit or revise regulatory devices. As a consequence, MTBE mitigation efforts have been implemented on a state-by-state basis with very different assumptions underlying approaches in each state.

Step 6: Ex Ante Review

The incremental nature of the MTBE issue precluded a formal preimplementation analysis of what impacts were likely to result from adding significantly greater amounts of oxygenates into the gasoline distribution system. The RFG regulation negotiation in 1991 brought different stakeholders together, each with vastly different interests. Through a coalescence of interest and lack of data on contamination impacts, they found that oxygenated gasoline met overlapping preferences. The momentum that ensued made pausing to assess unintended consequences extraordinarily difficult. Moreover, since all of the stakeholders were well aware of the toxicity of traditional gasoline components, the question of discrete environmental impacts from MTBE seemed redundant.

Bardach summarizes a common approach to rational, preimplementation analysis of policy alternatives that mirrors the National Environmental Policy Act (NEPA)-defined environmental impact statement process.[44] This approach suggests a formal step-by-step process of assessment:

1. Define problem statement with focus and specificity.
2. Identify the empirical state of the science on the specific problem, and review how it has been addressed in the past.
3. Construct alternatives that link to mitigation of core problem.
4. Select explicit evaluative criteria for use in projecting probable outcomes.
5. Project the outcomes in an empirical and transparent manner.
6. Confront the trade-offs that inevitably emerge in complex problem mitigation.
7. Select the preferred alternative.

Through such a process, Bardach assumes that policy analysts will be better able to assess fit and feasibility. This model is inherently empirical and fits well within the broader strategic regulatory planning model. It is focused, requiring specificity at each step in the analysis, particularly in the areas of transparency, explicitness in evaluative criteria, and confronting trade-offs. Many critics have characterized the primary regulatory failure as a lack of preimplementation testing of impacts of introducing MTBE into the general environment.[45] A rigorous preimplementation review would have precluded this omission.

Step 7: Ex Post Review/Revision

The MTBE issue is unique in that it emerged as a result of the success of the oxyfuel and RFG program. The effort to provide an additional technical fix to the emissions problem succeeded. The problem, of course, is that the emergence of the MTBE contamination problem is the consequence of successfully integrating oxygenates into gasoline across the country.

The ex post review is important because it requires analysts to refine the problem statement—to temper the understanding of the primary problem with a sober accounting of unanticipated consequences. The Ingram framework discussed in chapter 2 is relevant to consider in the context of ex post review.[46] Ingram argues that implementation itself will contribute toward an understanding of more tractable problems. The implementation of the oxygenate regulations demonstrated that mitigating air pollution was only part of the problem.

The studies that have been conducted since the HEI investigation in 1996 fulfill the functions of the ex post review and are instrumental in redefining the primary problem statement. In particular, the HEI study (1996), the California study (1998), and the Blue Ribbon Panel recommendations (1999) each provide a meaningful ex post review with similar results: MTBE should have been tested for discrete contamination effects before widespread introduction in the oxyfuel and RFG programs. Each study has recommended that MTBE be phased out.

Summary

This chapter evaluated the regulatory process leading to the introduction of reformulated gasoline. It identified several areas of strategic failure in regulatory planning that allowed MTBE to emerge as a significant environmental contaminant and public health issue. These failures include bureaucratic insulation between regulators working on air quality and regulators working on water quality, a failure to assess the discrete impacts of introducing MTBE into the environment, resistance to emerging evidence of MTBE contamination, and confusion over the unique chemical properties of MTBE contamination with the continuing problem of leaking underground storage tanks. The MTBE experience illustrates the problems of disjointed incrementalism and poor alignment between policy formulation and implementation efforts.

The introduction of MTBE as an oxygenate in gasoline changed the nature of the politics of clean air. As an off-the-shelf chemical that has been used to enhance octane since 1979, MTBE emerged as an ideal candidate for improving tailpipe emissions in 1989. ARCO's success as an industry leader in the clean gasoline market brought other, perhaps reluctant, gasoline producers to the oxygenate table. The air quality improvements that oxygenates promised also attracted support from EPA and state regulators, as well as environmentalists such as the Sierra Club and NRDC. The emerging market for MTBE led to the involvement of large chemical producers such as Houston-based Lyondell Chemical. The potential market for ethanol also led to the inclusion of corn state legislators and large corporate players such as Illinois-based Archer Daniels Midland. These stakeholders did not view clean air policy options through the same lens, yet on the question of oxygenated gasoline their interests coalesced.

The MTBE experience was unusual because different stakeholders agreed to an alternative that lacked substantial data. Stakeholders who ordinarily disagree vociferously shared a common interest in seeing the adoption of oxygenates. The result was simultaneously a regulatory success in lowering emissions and a regulatory failure in groundwater contamination. This complex result is a failure of regulatory planning, as a consequence of both the contamination issue and the continuing difficulty regulators now face in mitigating the deleterious effects of MTBE while maintaining air quality improvements. Although the problem was unanticipated, it could have been identified early in the process and mitigated far sooner than it was.

While it is clear that strategic regulatory formulation was not used in this issue area, there is no 100 percent guarantee that if such a strategy was used, it would have changed the outcome. The issue of MTBE contamination was not widely understood or studied prior to its adoption as a gasoline additive. If the information was not available, a strategic planning process might have identified the data deficiency, but there is no assurance that this problem would have been highlighted. Strategic thinking increases the probability that additional factors will be considered, but in no way does it guarantee rational comprehensive analysis. The costs of such a rational comprehensive analysis are typically too high for noncrisis decision-making processes, and we should neither expect such a process nor criticize decision makers for its absence. Nevertheless, strategic thinking is feasible in public policymaking. The failure to include an assessment of the environmental impacts of MTBE in the regulatory process might have been remedied by a strategic planning process.

Chapter 7 reviews the ongoing mitigation efforts across the nation and offers a possible strategic regulatory approach for mitigating MTBE contamination. As the earlier chapters have illustrated, the development of a strategic regulatory plan is a process for addressing policymaking. In this sense, chapter 7 makes a process recommendation rather than a policy recommendation. The strategic policy itself is dynamic and can emerge only from the regulatory planning process.

7

A Strategic Approach to MTBE Regulation

This chapter examines how a strategic regulatory planning process may add greater effectiveness to the MTBE mitigation effort. The chapter offers a strategic model that may enhance regulatory focus and direction of MTBE abatement. Strategic regulatory planning is a process model that, if successful, may allow regulators and stakeholders a better outcome. The strategic regulatory model is not, however, a policy or outcome in and of itself. It is the vehicle, not the destination. The chapter examines the current efforts to resolve MTBE contamination on both the state and federal levels. The chapter then revisits the seven-step model defined earlier in the book in an effort to determine what regulators can do to respond to the MTBE problem effectively. The chapter addresses the central questions of whether a unified strategic approach would be beneficial and whether such an approach is practical.

Current Status of MTBE Mitigation Efforts

The current status of MTBE mitigation varies across the nation. In the absence of federal leadership, states have moved independently to respond to the problem. As table 7.1 illustrates, several states have banned MTBE entirely, and several others are in the process of phasing in bans.[1] In most cases, states are switching to ethanol. In some instances, however, states that voluntarily opted into the reformulated gasoline (RFG) program are now opting out. Many states and some multistate regions have created commissions and task forces to address the MTBE issue. We review several mitigation efforts around the country in an effort to summarize the disparate but nationwide concern for mitigating MTBE

Table 7.1
State MTBE bans and phase-outs

State	MTBE phase-out Date
MTBE bans enacted	
California	Jan. 1, 2004
Connecticut[a]	Jan. 1, 2004
Kentucky[b]	Jan. 1, 2006
Missouri[b]	Jul. 1, 2005
New York	Jan. 1, 2004
Illinois[b,c]	Jul. 24, 2004
Colorado	May 1, 2002
Indiana[b]	Jul. 24, 2004
Iowa[b]	May 11, 2000
Kansas[b,d]	Jul. 1, 2004
Michigan	Jun. 1, 2003
Minnesota[e]	Jul. 1, 2005
Nebraska[f]	Jan. 1, 2001
Nevada[g]	Jan. 1, 2004
Ohio[d]	Jul. 1, 2005
South Dakota[h]	July 1, 2000
Washington[i]	Jan. 1, 2004
No MTBE bans enacted	
Arizona[j]	
Delaware	
District of Columbia	
Maine[k]	
Maryland	
Massachusetts	
New Hampshire	
New Jersey	
North Carolina	
Pennsylvania	
Rhode Island	
Texas	
Utah	
Virginia	

Table 7.1
(continued)

[a]This bill passed and the ban took effect Jan 1, 2004, to make it consistent with New York State's scheduled ban. Senate Bill 840 passed the Joint House-Senate Environment Committee on March 17, 2003, and is awaiting State Senate and House action.
[b]Maximum 0.5 volume percent MTBE.
[c]MTBE banned in Chicago beginning December 2000.
[d]This provision will take effect only if EPA grants the state a waiver to control or prohibit MTBE in gasoline.
[e]Year-round statewide oxygenated gasoline requirement with ethers limited to 0.33 volume percent after July 1, 2000, and banned after July 1, 2005.
[f]Maximum 1.0 volume percent MTBE.
[g]This is not a statewide ban. The Washoe County (Reno) MTBE maximum limit of 0.3 volume percent was effective the same date as the California ban. Clark County (Las Vegas) adopted a 10 volume percent ethanol requirement in 1999 for gasoline sold from October through March.
[h]MTBE limited to 2.0 volume percent beginning February 2000.
[i]Maximum 0.6 volume percent MTBE effective July 22, 2001.
[j]Arizona Senate Bill 1504, approved by the governor on April 28, 2000, states that it is the "policy" of the state that MTBE be phased out as soon as possible, but no later than 180 days after the effective date of the California ban if feasible.
[k]Maine Public Law Chapter 709 established a "goal" to eliminate MTBE in gasoline sold in the state by January 1, 2003.
Source: U.S. Department of Energy, Energy Information Administration, "Motor Gasoline Outlook and State MTBE Bans," April 6, 2003, <http://www.eia.doe.gov/emeu/steo/pub/special/mtbeban.html.>, retrieved April 7, 2004.

problems. In general, states are moving away from MTBE but toward what is as of yet unknown. The experiences set out in this chapter illustrate this ambivalence and provide testimony for the need to establish a nationwide regulatory planning process.

State Actions

In December 1992, Alaska became the first state to ban MTBE outright.[2] The state's Department of Environmental Conservation notes, however, fuel stations were "not required to remove the blended fuel from their tanks nor were they required to discontinue its use."[3] MTBE continues to be an important concern in Alaska.

In California a phased-in ban on MTBE went into effect January 1, 2004. In addition to banning MTBE, all other oxygenates other than ethanol—including methanol, ethyl tertiary butyl ether, and tertiary amyl methyl ether—are also banned, "unless a multimedia evaluation of [its] use in California gasoline has been conducted and the California Environmental Policy council . . . has determined that such use will not cause a significant adverse impact on the public health or the environment."[4] California also banned the use of two-stroke engines on Lake Tahoe, significantly reducing MTBE concentrations in the lake and establishing an important precedent for preventing surface water contamination in other areas.[5]

Illinois banned MTBE effective July 2004. A few years earlier, in December 2000, Chicago became the first city to ban the chemical because of concerns that MTBE-treated gasoline would be diverted to Chicago as it was being banned elsewhere.[6] Ethanol is readily available in Illinois, a farm state, as an oxygenate replacement.

Indiana banned MTBE effective July 2004. Prior to this, the state developed voluntary MTBE cleanup standards. Although Indiana does not participate in the RFG program, the Indiana Department of Environmental Management states that MTBE is found in the state's gasoline supply as a result of either low volume use (3 percent volume) as an octane enhancer or of fuel mixing during transportation and distribution.[7]

The Iowa legislature requested the testing of soil and groundwater for MTBE at leaking UST sites in 1999.[8] After receiving the test data, the legislature banned MTBE in the state.[9] The legislation required ongoing monitoring at underground storage tank sites.[10]

Maine became the first state to apply for EPA approval to opt out of the federal RFG program in 1998.[11] It had opted in to the RFG program in 1991.

Maryland was one of the first states to experience MTBE contamination and has been testing water systems since 1995. However, it did not form a state task force until 2000, well after many other states had already produced reports on the issue. The conclusions of the task force are in line with other analyses and include a recommendation to "give careful consideration to eventually reducing or phasing out the use of MTBE."[12]

Other states have acted as well. Missouri requires that pumps dispensing gasoline containing MTBE be labeled after August 2001.[13] New Hampshire has requested EPA permission to opt out of the RFG program. It opted in in 1991.[14] New York banned MTBE effective January 1, 2004.[15] North Carolina moved to ban MTBE after classifying it as a probable carcinogen.[16] Ohio moved to phase out MTBE in May 2002, with a ban effective in 2005.[17] In an unusual display of unity, both houses of the Washington State legislature voted unanimously to ban MTBE as of January 1, 2004.[18] Finally, Colorado's Senate bill 00–190, signed into law by the governor on May 23, 2000, prohibited the sale of gasoline fuels "containing or treated with MTBE" as of April 30, 2002.

NESCAUM: A Regional Response

The Northeast States for Coordinated Air Use Management (NESCAUM) represents New York, New Jersey, Massachusetts, New Hampshire, Vermont, Rhode Island, Connecticut, and Maine. In 1999 it produced a report that recommended repealing the 2 percent oxygen mandate for RFG, as well as a phase-down and cap on MTBE content in all gasoline.[19] The report also called for regulating consistency in fuel specifications and recommended clarification of state and federal authority to regulate or eliminate MTBE and other oxygenates. Like other MTBE reports, NESCAUM recommended finding a way to maintain the toxic-emission-reduction benefits achieved thus far by the federal RFG program and moving slowly to "provide adequate lead-time for the petroleum infrastructure to adjust in order to ensure adequate fuel supply and price stability."[20]

The NESCAUM report led to the creation of a Northeast Regional Fuels Task Force, which includes the NESCAUM states, as well as Pennsylvania, Delaware, Virginia, West Virginia, and Washington, D.C. The task force endorsed a balance between the effort to maximize air quality and protect public health while simultaneously recommending that the region reduce the volume of MTBE in gasoline to protect water resources. Further, the task force recommended that this be done in a manner that minimizes impacts on gasoline price and supply.[21] This action is not unusual in MTBE mitigation. States battling significant urban smog are resistant to relinquish the benefits of MTBE, while everyone agrees that there is a clear need to mitigate contamination.

Federal Efforts

As table 7.2 reveals, federal efforts to mitigate MTBE contamination have been limited. Under the Clinton administration, EPA ordered all large public water systems to sample for MTBE in surface water and groundwater sources. Under authority of the Safe Drinking Water Act, EPA placed MTBE on the Drinking Water Contaminant Candidate List (CCL) in 1997 and the final list in 1998.[22] The Contaminant Candidate List is EPA's priority listing of contaminants for evaluation by EPA's drinking water program.[23] In addition, EPA continued efforts to increase compliance with existing UST regulations, particularly the sections regarding spill prevention, overfilling, corrosion, and leak detection systems. The agency conducted an evaluation of UST system performance to determine whether UST regulations needed revision, and it recommended that state UST officials monitor and report spills involving MTBE. Finally, EPA funded demonstration projects on MTBE remediation and additional research on MTBE and oxygenates in general.[24]

In 2000, following recommendations of the agency's Blue Ribbon Panel on MTBE, EPA published an Advance Notice of Proposed Rulemaking (ANPR) in the *Federal Register* to limit or eliminate the use of MTBE as a fuel additive in gasoline.[25] Section 6 of the Toxic Substances Control Act "provides EPA with broad authority to issue rules to regulate the manufacture, processing, distribution in commerce, use and/or disposal of chemical substances in the United States where such regulation is necessary to prevent unreasonable risks to health or the environment."[26] The ANPR states that "EPA's review of existing information on contamination of drinking water resources by MTBE indicates substantial evidence of a significant risk to the nation's drinking water supply."[27] As a result, the ANPR recommends either banning or greatly reducing the use of MTBE in gasoline.

In addition to a complete ban, alternatives under consideration include capping the amount of MTBE that could be used in gasoline, limiting use of MTBE in particular geographic areas or during particular times

Table 7.2
MTBE time line

1970	Clean Air Act initiates phase-out of lead in gasoline to meet new emission standards. Automobile manufacturers install catalytic converters on all new cars starting in 1975, and unleaded gasoline is introduced for motor vehicles equipped with catalytic converters. EPA banned the use of leaded gasoline in highway vehicles in December 1995.
1979	MTBE approved by EPA as an octane enhancer to replace lead.
1984	MTBE contamination in groundwater discovered in Maine.
1988	Reformulated gasoline (RFG) introduced in the Denver metropolitan area as a pilot study.
1989	Based on Denver area success in reducing cold weather emissions, ARCO introduces MTBE-based "clean" fuel in California.
1990	Clean Air Act Amendments require oxygenates in gasoline.
1991	Auto/oil study initiated to study impacts of MTBE on fuel performance, automobile engine wear, and emissions.
	RFG regulation negotiation convened to develop alternatives for implementing oxygenate requirements of the Clean Air Act.
1992	Winter oxyfuel program initiated.
	After introducing MTBE in Fairbanks and Anchorage in fall 1992, complaints about MTBE-related health effects were so intense that the governor of Alaska suspended its use in December, after only four months.
1995	Year-round RFG program initiated.
1996	Health Effects Institute Study released, acknowledging that the failure to anticipate the potential health impacts from introducing MTBE was problematic.
1998	California Study released, questioning the utility of MTBE and recommending a phase-out.
	EPA puts MTBE on drinking water Contaminant Candidate List (CCL)
1999	EPA's Blue Ribbon Panel study released, recommending a phase-out of MTBE.
1996–2000	Widespread evidence of contamination documented across the nation.
2000–2004	State bans begin to go into effect. (See table 7.1.)
	Congressional bans on MTBE debated but no resolution passed.

Table 7.2
(continued)

2000	EPA under the Clinton administration initiates draft regulations banning MTBE.
2001	Incoming Bush administration sends all pending regulations back to agencies.
2003	EPA under the Bush Administration suggests a MTBE ban.
2003–2004	House passes Resolution 6, the Energy Bill, which provides "safe harbor" liability protection for MTBE producers. Fails to pass in the Senate.
2004	California, the nation's largest market for MTBE, bans MTBE, effective January 1.
	Bush administration quietly kills EPA proposal to ban MTBE.

of the year, and limiting the types and manner of facilities in which MTBE can be stored and transported.[28] EPA concluded in 2000 that:

> dealing with the problem before MTBE is added to gasoline may be the best solution for mitigating any unreasonable risks associated with MTBE. . . . it may not be practicable to prevent significant quantities of MTBE from getting into surface water or groundwater once the chemical is added to gasoline. . . . A risk-mitigation strategy centering on cleaning up water may not be the preferred strategy . . . for mitigating any unreasonable risks associated with MTBE. Consequently, EPA believes that a comprehensive approach must include consideration of either reducing or eliminating the use of MTBE as a gasoline additive.[29]

Although EPA has issued several reports identifying the health risks posed by MTBE and has initiated a proposed regulation to ban MTBE, and although EPA's 1999 Blue Ribbon Panel recommended phasing out and ultimately banning MTBE, the federal government has yet to take any substantive step toward comprehensive MTBE mitigation.

Congress started taking up the issue in 2001, when seven bills addressing MTBE contamination were introduced. Several of them sought to remove the oxygenate requirement and ban the use of MTBE. Others sought funding for research and remediation. There continues to be strong opposition to removing the oxygenate requirement from the various proponents, including farm state legislators and industry groups such as the Renewable Fuels Association.[30]

In 2001 the incoming Bush administration returned the proposed MTBE regulations to their respective agencies for reconsideration, effectively killing them. These included a national secondary drinking water proposed regulation,[31] a proposed rule controlling MTBE as a gasoline additive,[32] proposed rules adjusting RFG,[33] and the EPA's proposed phase-out of MTBE under the Toxic Substances Control Act. The administration also raised concerns that the variety of fuel blends potentially required by changes in state regulations would create undue burdens to industry. The Bush administration's Energy Task Force report cites the issues of such "boutique fuels" as "presenting major production and distribution challenges for refiners." Former EPA administrator Christie Todd Whitman said that the EPA "is considering limiting states to three of four formulas of gasoline instead of the dozen or more currently in use."[34] She emphasized, however, that this approach has problems: "It is very much a states' rights issue. Boutique fuels are a result of states making independent decisions about [meeting] their clean-air requirements."[35] Several oil companies have stopped producing gasoline with MTBE, including Unocal and BP. As part of their concern with the boutique fuels issue, the American Petroleum Institute has called for the elimination of the oxygenate mandate.[36]

The most significant congressional discussion of MTBE unfolded during the 2003–2004 legislative session—not on the question of a federal ban but rather on the question of liability protection for MTBE producers. The so-called safe-harbor section of Energy Bill HR 6 would have provided liability immunity to gasoline producers.[37] HR 6 passed in the House but failed in the Senate. Still, the Bush administration would not ban MTBE, and in February 2004, it quietly killed a second EPA-proposed draft regulation banning MTBE.[38] A comprehensive resolution of MTBE contamination continues to be elusive.

Applying the Seven-Step Model for Strategic Regulatory Planning

There is a clear move toward banning MTBE at the state level, and both Congress and the EPA continue to debate the merits of an outright ban. Still, there continues to be a lack of continuity within the existing mitigation efforts and a lack of consensus on what might be done to move toward greater mitigation of MTBE-related environmental contamination. Linking the strategic model to the MTBE issue is necessarily a fluid process. The model for strategic regulatory planning may provide a useful path for finding an appropriate accommodation between mitigating contamination and maintaining the air quality benefits that MTBE achieves. While the model can be implemented in any number of ways, the complex nature of the MTBE problem, the discrete number of identifiable stakeholder constituencies, and the collaborative nature of the RFG rule-making process that initiated the oxygenate rules make a collaborative strategic response most appropriate.

The Negotiated Rulemaking Act (1996) identifies several preconditions that are necessary for successful collaborative processes: common agreement that a problem exists; a limited number of identifiable affected constituencies exist; there is a reasonable likelihood that a balanced and representative committee can be convened that will agree to negotiate in good faith toward a consensus recommendation; and there is an appropriate agency with adequate resources to convene and support a collaborative process.[39] The MTBE problem meets these conditions. More important, a collaborative process may enhance the likelihood that the MTBE issue can be effectively addressed by the strategic model. At each stage of the model, a comprehensive engagement of the facts as viewed through multiple lenses is necessary and appropriate. Collaborative processes are uniquely suited to engage discrete issues and facts from different perspectives, while maintaining an alignment with core values and objectives. While consensus may be the desired outcome, collaborative processes are effective in achieving broader participation and clarification even when they fall short of consensus. The sections below revisit several steps of the model in an effort to identify where the model can generate greater utility in the regulatory process.

Step 1: Problem Recognition

On the one hand, defining the problem is easy: MTBE contamination of the nation's groundwater presents a known threat to public health. On the other hand, MTBE use as an oxygenate has brought measurable improvements in air quality and has reduced ozone levels in key smog prone areas such as Denver and Los Angeles, as well as a significant drop in airborne benzene concentrations in the Northeast.[40] Clearly, the improvements in air quality have meaningful public health consequences. Therefore, any articulation of a strategic problem definition must include both the mitigation of MTBE contamination and the simultaneous protection of air quality gains since the oxyfuel and RFG programs went into effect.

Such a problem definition is important. It is necessary to link MTBE mitigation with the maintenance of air quality gains. It is also necessary to define the problem as narrowly as possible so as to avoid constraining later fact finding, analysis, or response formulation. For example, some have argued that the production and use of MTBE is the problem. In fact, the problem is narrower: MTBE contamination should be the focus of any strategic effort. Banning the production and use of MTBE may be an appropriate response, but it is not the only response.

Step 2: Identification of Parties

The parties consist of all of the stakeholder constituencies that were present early on (e.g., corporate and independent liquid fuel distributors and retailers and the American Lung Association), including those that participated in the 1991 RFG regulation negotiation, as well as constituencies that have emerged as stakeholders in the ensuing years—particularly state and local water managers and environmental regulators.[41] It might be helpful to expand the stakeholder base to include water resource managers and state and local environmental advocacy organizations.

In addition, it is appropriate to convene a science advisory committee, along the model of existing EPA Science Advisory Committees, to work with the stakeholder group as technical advisers. According to EPA guidelines, Science Advisory Committees work as subgroups of the EPA Science Advisory Board, which serves as a technical peer review panel. Members are appointed in compliance with the Federal Advisory Committee Act and operate according to an approved charter, which is renewed biennially.[42] All meetings are announced in the *Federal Register* and open to the public, and opportunities for public comment before the Science Advisory Board are required. The board is a technical peer review panel, with agency data, processes, and procedures subjected to critical assessment and evaluation by recognized experts in the relevant technical fields (such as scientists and chemical engineers from universities).[43] An MTBE Science Advisory Committee does not supersede or displace the stakeholder group, but rather aligns and validates stakeholder processes with known science.

Steps 3 and 4: Historical Analysis and Situational Analysis

The evolution of the MTBE problem, as it currently exists, must be taken into account by policymakers. As the discussion has shown, there have been several approaches to mitigating the most severe elements of MTBE contamination. Since the earlier efforts at MTBE mitigation focused on narrow mechanistic approaches such as replacing leaking USTs, a comprehensive historical analysis was never done. It is appropriate that a strategic and comprehensive approach take into account the full context of the MTBE problem as it is now understood. The collaborative approach suggested would allow regulators to assess the emergence of MTBE contamination more broadly and therefore establish an appropriate baseline for moving through the situational analysis. Since the goal of the strategic regulatory model is to enhance the effectiveness of regulatory strategies, the collaborative process may allow a meaningful situational analysis to evolve. Stakeholders can address the motivations, goals, positions, and resources of each party to either comply with, ignore, or fight the desired behavioral changes. Since these motivations will change with regulatory pressure, the engagement of the collaborative effort during regulatory analysis will maximize the likelihood that stakeholder motivations align toward a commonly defined set of objectives.

Step 5: Strategic Regulatory Formulation

Strategic regulatory formulation is based on a clear-eyed assessment of the regulated community, the regulating agencies, and external environmental conditions affecting cost and level of coerciveness of potential regulatory devices. Two important factors may make strategic regulatory formulation more attainable now than in earlier regulatory efforts. First, if a collaborative framework is used, an effort to define a common problem statement will be in place, as well as an effort to endorse collaboratively the evidence surrounding that problem definition (joint fact finding). This is an essential advantage because it allows stakeholders and regulators to focus on problem solving rather than political posturing. Second, the availability of several major studies that cohere around recommendations for responding to the MTBE problem provides an immediate and substantive starting point. The Health Effects Institute (HEI) study, the California study, and EPA's Blue Ribbon Panel collectively provide a meaningful road map for mitigating the MTBE problem.

Health Effects Institute HEI released a report in 1996 acknowledging that the failure to anticipate the potential health impacts from introducing MTBE into the environment was a significant oversight.[44] HEI's committee on oxygenates evaluation identified several areas of concern regarding potential health effects of MTBE:

Headache, nausea, and sensory irritation in some (possibly sensitive) individuals, based on studies in communities where oxyfuel was being used;

Acute, reversible, neurotoxic effects, based on changes in motor activity observed in rats exposed to MTBE; and

Cancer, based on increases in the frequency of tumors at multiple organ sites in rats and mice after exposure to MTBE.[45]

The HEI committee went on to note that these conclusions were based on "limited information" and that questions still remained "about how to interpret the observed effects for humans. . . . Nevertheless, the Committee concluded that these effects point to potential human health risks."[46] The HEI study was an early warning for both regulators and industry.

The California Study Keller et al. concluded that MTBE contamination presented a significant public health risk and observed that although RFG has resulted in reduced tailpipe emissions when compared to traditional gasoline, MTBE and other oxygenates were found to have more significant reductions in older vehicles.[47] The benefit to newer technology vehicles was less, and in some cases indistinguishable from nonoxygenated RFG. The California study recognized that an immediate MTBE ban, however, would cause severe disruption of fuel supplies, with significant associated economic impacts. Keller and his colleagues recommended a phase-out, with several intermediary policies suggested for the transition period. The most relevant to a national strategy include the following:

Restrict the use of . . . MTBE to ozone non-attainment areas during the summer months.

Promote the accelerated removal of older, high emitting motor vehicles through the use of industrial emissions offsets or a fund created by an appropriate tax.

Maintain the Underground Storage Cleanup Fund Program, possibly beyond the year 2005 to cover the costs of MTBE cleanup, with a review in 3 years to determine the effectiveness of upgraded underground storage tank systems in reducing the rate of failures, and thus the potential to reduce the annual fees.

Where contamination of groundwater is known or suspected, evaluation of plume extent and potential threats to drinking-water supply wells should be carried out immediately. Plume containment, remediation, or other corrective actions should then proceed as soon as possible to reduce risk and costs.

Require the adoption of Best Management Practices for surface water reservoirs.

Establish specific emissions requirements for motor boat engines, in particular with respect to emissions of unburned fuel. Promote legislation with incentives to phase out motor boat engines that do not meet emissions requirements.

Invest in a long-term research program, using the enormous base of expertise available in . . . universities and professional organizations, to determine the toxicological effects of untested industrial products that will be used in large amounts. Such research should, for example, examine effective alternatives for motor vehicle fuels, and develop more cost-effective remediation and treatment technologies. The current structure of . . . [regulatory] Agencies, which focus on specific media (land, air, water), leads to fragmented and incomplete environmental impact assessments. Any new large scale programs . . . should be preceded by an independent Environmental Impact Assessment, rather than an a posteriori evaluation of the consequences.[48]

These recommendations establish an important baseline for a cautious regulatory response.

The Blue Ribbon Panel The findings and recommendations of the EPA's Blue Ribbon Panel on MTBE established the most comprehensive road map for responding to MTBE. The panel's findings included the following key points, which continue to reflect the need to balance emissions benefits against the risks associated with soil and water contamination. As such, the panel's recommendations provide the most substantive ideas for abating MTBE. The panel found that:

The distribution, use, and combustion of gasoline poses risks to our environment and public health.

RFG provides considerable air quality improvements and benefits for millions of US citizens.

The use of MTBE has raised the issue of the effects of both MTBE alone and MTBE in gasoline. . . . What seems clear . . . is that MTBE, due to its persistence and mobility in water, is more likely to contaminate ground and surface water than the other components of gasoline.

MTBE has been found in a number of water supplies nationwide. . . . The Panel believes that the occurrence of MTBE in drinking water supplies can and should be substantially reduced.

MTBE is currently an integral component of the US gasoline supply both in terms of volume and octane. As such, changes in its use, with the attendant capital construction and infrastructure modifications, must be implemented with sufficient time, certainty, and flexibility to maintain the stability of both the complex U.S. fuel supply system and gasoline prices.[49]

Based on these findings, the panel made several recommendations, which were released as a "single package of actions" that could be implemented by federal and state regulators within the existing statutory environment.[50] The panel went on to "urge their rapid implementation."[51] The primary recommendations for water protection included:

Accelerating the replacement of existing tank systems including prohibiting deliveries to non-upgraded tanks.

Evaluating and improving technology related to USTs and leak detection systems.

Require monitoring and reporting of MTBE releases.

Encourage consideration of "proximity to drinking water supplies" in land-use planning.

Improve training and licensing programs for UST operators, and expand the "universe of regulated tanks."

Increase assessment of drinking water supplies and implementation of protection for drinking water supplies, and increase funding for treatment of contaminated supplies.

Restrict use of recreational watercraft.

Expand protections of private wells.[52]

The "key elements" of the panel's recommendations for the RFG program included:

Action agreed to broadly by the panel to reduce the use of MTBE substantially (with some members supporting its complete phase out), and action by Congress to clarify federal and state authority to regulate and/or eliminate the use of gasoline additives that threaten water supplies.

Action by Congress to remove the current 2% oxygen requirement . . . while quickly reducing usage of MTBE.

Action by EPA to ensure that there is no loss of current air quality benefits.[53]

Taken collectively, these recommendations provide concrete examples of the types of interventions that are possible to meet the MTBE contamination problem. They are not necessarily the only steps or the most appropriate ones. They illustrate, however, that sufficient data exist to demonstrate the substance and depth of the MTBE problem and the emerging agreement among diverse stakeholders that MTBE mitigation is necessary. The collaborative process suggested here would have an important starting point in formulating recommendations, but the process would still require a significant and sustained effort to reach an integrated and collaborative regulatory approach at the federal level.

Steps 6 and 7: Ex Ante Review and Ex Post Review/Revision

As with any other regulatory process, it is appropriate to engage in a preimplementation policy analysis to evaluate the fit and feasibility of potential regulatory tools. The ex post review (postimplementation evaluation) will be effective if explicit regulatory objectives are defined and clear evaluative criteria are established. Since these stages of the strategic regulatory model are later in the process, little preliminary work is necessary at this time. However, it is appropriate to establish a placeholder for both preimplementation analysis and postimplementation review—remembering the importance of the preconditions of successful evaluation research: explicit problem definition, regulatory objectives, and evaluative criteria.

Summary

This chapter reviewed the current status of MTBE mitigation at the state and federal levels. The chapter revisited the seven-step model of strategic regulatory planning in an effort to identify what can be done at this stage in the regulatory process to respond effectively to MTBE contamination. The chapter argues that a collaborative response will optimize the likelihood that an effective strategic response will emerge.

A strategic analysis of the issue provides an indication of the difficulty of developing a uniform national policy regulating MTBE. It also illuminates the benefit of MTBE in producing clean air. MTBE should be seen as a technological fix to an air pollution problem that has costs as well as benefits. One example of a potentially valuable strategic direction resulting from this analysis is the need to develop a substitute for MTBE that has less impact on groundwater. In the past, it has been easier to ban toxic substances when a cost-effective substitute was available.

The larger issue for policy design is the question of the efficacy of the type of strategic analysis used in the UST program and presented for MTBE in this chapter. Can such an analysis lead to more comprehensive policymaking? The interconnection of environmental policy problems and proposed solutions leads us to wish to graft a rational element onto a typically incremental, interest-driven policymaking process. The question is, Can it be done?

The argument against strategic planning is that it is a waste of time and resources in a system that cannot absorb and use this information. As difficult as it is (in Aaron Wildavsky's words) to "speak truth to power," it is worth the effort.[54] An honest attempt at strategic thinking will open decision makers to new information and concepts. These data and concepts may be rejected, but that they are different from traditional options adds value to the process overall. There are many plans that governmental agencies present as "strategies." However, simply because an agency labels an approach as strategic does not make it an example of strategic thinking.

The absence of strategy in the MTBE case did not lead to nondecision making. As this chapter showed, many states have banned or are in the process of phasing out MTBE. The policy process has worked in its normal, imperfect, and meandering way. Our hope is that the damage done by MTBE in groundwater is not irreversible. The question that remains unanswerable is whether this damage could have been avoided in the first place had a strategic regulatory planning process been pursued prior to the implementation of the oxygenate rules in the early 1990s, or even after MTBE contamination was widely noted after the winter oxyfuel program went into effect.

III

Regulation with Strategy: The Case of Underground Storage Tanks

8

The Problem of Leaking Underground Storage Tanks

Part III of this book applies the model introduced in part I to the case of USTs. It presents the UST regulatory program developed by the National Academy of Public Administration (NAPA) and senior management in the EPA's Office of Solid Waste and Emergency Response in the mid-1980s. Although the plan was never an official government document, it was the first effort to design a UST regulatory program, and elements of its strategic approach were used by the EPA's Office of Underground Storage Tanks. Some of the program's success in reducing the number of leaking underground tanks may be attributable to the early use of strategic thinking by EPA.

This chapter presents a detailed analysis of USTs and the statutes that regulate their use. It begins by discussing why leaking USTs are a potential threat to natural resources and humans. This deals with step 1 of the strategic regulatory planning process, problem recognition. It presents a historical view of the problem recognition phase from the mid-1980s when underground tanks were first regulated. The next part of the chapter examines the politics surrounding tank regulation before and after passage of tank regulation in the mid-1980s. These are steps 2 and 3 of the planning process: identification of involved parties and historical analysis. This section of the chapter identifies who was involved in the UST issue at the time that the strategic regulatory plan was developed in the mid-1980s and discusses the nature of their past involvement. In so doing, it also begins step 4, the situational analysis. The final section reviews the provisions involving USTs. This also provides a portion of the situational analysis. It identifies the objectives of the regulatory program and specifies the program's desired outcomes. In summary, the data and information reported in this chapter concern steps 1 through 4 of the regulatory planning process, the background work needed to develop a strategic plan for regulating underground tanks.

Step 1: Problem Recognition

Petroleum and chemicals have increasingly been stored in USTs. USTs save space and reduce the risk of fire and explosion. However, just as metal barrels with hazardous waste have corroded and leaked, so too have USTs. In contrast to hazardous and toxic waste sites, the underground tanks regulated by Title I of the 1984 Hazardous and Solid Waste Amendments (HSWA) to the Solid Waste Disposal Act of 1976 contain commercial products rather than waste. Again, this distinction is important to keep in mind. Prior to the promulgation of HSWA's new tank standards, the EPA estimated that over one-fourth of the nation's underground tanks were leaking and posed risks to the environment and public health.[1] The toxic *product* regulation under discussion here is not addressed by the Toxic Substances Control Act (TSCA) but by the HSWA. Hence, the focus of the discussion is not on the production of these materials (a TSCA issue), but rather on the *storage* of these materials.

Groundwater contamination became a major environmental issue in the 1980s. Environmental regulation in the 1970s dealt largely with pollutants that could be seen or smelled in surface water or in the air. Recognition of the importance of groundwater as a natural resource has grown substantially, especially in communities dependent on it. In the United States, when tank regulation began in the 1980s, groundwater provided 20 percent of all water used for any purpose. Approximately 83 billion gallons of groundwater (of a total water draw of 440 billion gallons) were used each day, primarily for irrigation and drinking water. Data from 1995 indicate that groundwater usage had dropped to 76.4 billion gallons per day, of a total water usage of 402 billion gallons per day (19 percent).[2] Nevertheless, in many areas of the country today, groundwater remains the sole source of drinking water. In fact, in the 1980s, groundwater provided drinking water for over 116 million people, or about half of the nation's population.[3] According to EPA in 2002, 11,746 water systems in the United States relied on surface water, serving 183.7 million people, while 41,691 systems relied on groundwater, serving 84 million people.[4] Ninety-five percent of the nation's rural population relies on groundwater for most of their drinking water.[5]

Releases of petroleum or chemical substances from an underground tank may, under certain circumstances, move through soil into an aquifer. Since gasoline, for example, is less dense than water, it floats to the top of the water table when groundwater contamination occurs. Since the gasoline sits on the surface, it has a high probability of entering the water supply in a concentrated form. Once in a drinking water supply, traces as small as one part per million of gasoline can be detected by taste and smell. If the leak is large enough and the water is not treated to reduce the contamination, health problems will develop in the populations exposed. Benzene and ethyl dibromide, two components of gasoline, are suspected carcinogens.

Leaking USTs present a threat to more than just groundwater. Releases can contaminate surface water, and certain volatile substances may cause fires and explosions. In addition, toxic fumes can seep into homes through basements, posing significant indoor air pollution problems. Thus, tank leaks can result in personal injury, loss of property, and danger to the environment.

As of September 30, 2001, the EPA estimated that there were 704,717 federally regulated underground storage tanks at over 269,000 locations throughout the country.[6] When tank regulation began, there was an absence of stringent standards for the construction of these containers. Many tanks at that time were old, unprotected against corrosion, and very susceptible to leaking. It was precisely these dangers that persuaded Congress to enact regulations concerning underground storage containers.

Why Tanks Leak

A large portion of the tank population was installed in the 1950s and 1960s. As the country's population grew and people migrated to suburban areas, the need for commercial and retail establishments such as gasoline stations increased. Hundreds of thousands of tanks installed during this period of expansion were not protected against the corrosion that would inevitably result from being underground for such a long period of time. Gasoline tanks were not protected because it was not known that gasoline additives were corrosive, and the product stored was so inexpensive at the time that slow leaks were not worth preventing or stopping. When tank regulation began in the 1980s, the Congressional Research Service estimated that there were 1.4 million gasoline tanks, and of those, over 1.2 million were believed to be constructed of steel with little or no corrosion protection. Only 25,000 tanks were manufactured with steel cathodically protected, and only 100,000 were made of fiberglass treated with resin to provide chemical resistance.[7]

One of the most significant effects of the underground tank program was that a large number of old tanks were drained and taken out of service to avoid the need to comply with the new rules. Many of these tanks were in mom-and-pop grocery stores that had a gasoline pump out front. There were over 500,000 fewer underground tanks in the United States in 2002 than there were in the mid-1980s.

In 1986, the EPA investigated the problem of leaking USTs by conducting an extensive study of 12,444 reported leaks in the fifty states.[8] According to this study, nearly three-fourths of the leaks were in tanks over thirteen years old, with almost one-fourth being in tanks above twenty-seven years old. Moreover, when leaks were located in piping, nearly three-fourths of the leaks were in pipes less than thirteen years old and almost one-fifth were in pipes less than one year old. Piping is considered part of the tank system regulated under HSWA, and thus an important component of the UST problem. Corrosion and structural failure are the most common causes of tank leaks.

In a 1986 survey of its members conducted by the American Petroleum Institute, 93 percent of the 1,700 reported cases of leakages occurred in steel tanks and piping.[9] In this subgroup, 82 percent of the leaks were caused by corrosion. Given the age and unprotected nature of many tank systems, it was not surprising that corrosion and structural failure were primary causes of leaks. In general, EPA studies indicate that between 50 and 80 percent of leaks are caused by faulty piping alone. Other causes of UST leakage are faulty installation, spills during tank filling, and incompatibility with fuel additives, such as MTBE.[10]

Corrosion of tanks and piping is not the only reason that tank contents are discharged into the soil. Poor installation may cause leaks in new and even corrosion-resistant tanks. For example, fiberglass tanks, which do not have the structural strength of steel, can be easily damaged if they are not installed properly. If the coating of a fiberglass tank is marred during installation, leaks can develop. In addition, natural phenomena, such as earthquakes, extreme temperatures, and moisture, may damage tank structure, resulting in product discharge into the surrounding soil.

Leaks are not the sole source of releases. Operator errors may occur when tanks are being filled and result in spills and overfills, which may seep into the soil surrounding tanks. Before a tank is filled, the level of fuel stored must be measured. If this measurement is incorrectly calculated and more fuel than the tank can hold is pumped, a spill will occur.

Findings from EPA's study of tank releases across the nation indicated that around the time of HSWA's passage, at least 30 percent of the petroleum tanks tested were leaking.[11] An American Petroleum Institute study concluded that 40 percent of the tanks it tested were leaking at that time.[12] These results suggest that up to half a million petroleum tanks in the mid-1980s were discharging hazardous materials.[13]

A 1986 study by EPA's Office of Underground Storage Tanks (OUST) indicated that leaking tanks were prevalent in the Northeast, particularly in New York, New Jersey, and Pennsylvania. To a lesser extent, release incidents occurred in the Midwest and the Southwest. States in the Deep South, such as Alabama, Georgia, and Mississippi, reported comparatively few problems with leaking tanks. Among the states in the West, California and Colorado had the highest number of leaking USTs. In general, however, the number of release incidents in the West was relatively small at the start of the UST program. Overall, the 12,444 documented releases involved contamination of over 700 private wells; contamination of 40 municipal wells; 100 incidents of human illness; 155 cases of fire or explosion, resulting in two deaths; 202 cases of aquatic, plant, or wildlife damage; and 908 cases of combustible fumes in confined areas.

The 1986 EPA study showed that tanks were twice as prone to leak as pipes (41 percent compared with 21 percent). Overfills during delivery of a product were also an important cause of releases (13 percent). Additional data about release incidents from this EPA study indicated that over 90 percent of reported releases occurred in operating facilities.

Furthermore, small leaks (less than 100 gallons) were most likely to develop in abandoned tanks, whereas large leaks (2,501 gallons or more) were most likely to take place in operating tanks.

This does not mean that leaks from abandoned tanks posed a minor problem at the start of the underground tank program. According to the 1986 EPA study, most releases were first detected by physical inspection (i.e., by sight or smell). Another significant method of detection was through inventory control. Leaks in some abandoned tanks were discovered only when the tanks were pulled out of the ground. By that time, of course, it was too late to correct the situation. A program in Vermont in the early 1980s identified and removed abandoned underground tanks. About 10 percent of the tanks excavated in Vermont's "yank-a-tank" program were found to be leaking.[14]

Step 2: Identification of Parties

According to a study published in 1985 by the Congressional Research Service, more than 3 million active and abandoned gasoline storage tanks were buried underground in the United States.[15] By 2000, the EPA estimated that this had been reduced to about 2 million regulated USTs and about 400,000 unregulated tanks.[16] In the 1980s, between 600,000 and 700,000 tanks were located at over 200,000 retail gasoline outlets across the country. The CRS study estimated that about 50 percent of these tanks were owned by major oil companies. Determining ownership status for the other half was difficult. For example, one individual may own a particular portion of land that is leased out on a long-term basis. The lessee might choose to use the land as a gasoline retail facility. A third party, a wholesaler, may own the tanks at the facility, and a fourth party may lease the concession itself and run the day-to-day operations. In very few situations did one individual own and operate an active facility. One impact of the 1984 act was to drive many mom-and-pop gasoline stations and their tanks out of business. This accounts for the reduction in tanks from the mid-1980s to the present.

Of the gasoline tanks not located at retail outlets, some belonged to automobile and truck rental companies and automobile, truck, and taxi fleets. Others were owned by the federal government. Government tanks are located in various places, such as military bases, General Services Administration service centers, U.S. Postal Service facilities, and federal buildings, including the U.S. Capitol. In the 1980s many state, county, and municipal governments owned fuel tanks to supply their police and fire departments, highway departments, and boards of education. Hospitals owned underground containers to store fuel for both emergency power generation and heat. During the energy crisis of the 1970s, many individuals and firms installed tanks with emergency fuel needed for their operations.

Two studies initiated by the EPA were designed to produce more detailed knowledge of the petroleum tank universe. A national survey of underground motor fuel storage tanks was undertaken by the Office of Toxic Substances to determine the number of USTs nationwide and by geographic region.[17] That survey estimated that 600,000 motor fuel tank systems were located at 270,000 establishments nationwide. (A tank system is either one tank or a set of tanks connected by a pipeline.) Fully half of the nation's petroleum tank systems were located in the Northeast and Midwest; only 30 percent were located in the Central, Mountain, and Pacific regions. The remaining 20 percent were in the South. The survey also indicated that gasoline stations composed 47 percent and government facilities 20 percent of all establishments with underground tank systems; the other third were fuel-related facilities or large industrial establishments. Gasoline stations averaged three tank systems per establishment, and other facilities averaged under two.

A second major tank study was conducted in 1986 by EPA's OUST.[18] In an effort to gather information and to support the development of regulation, OUST conducted a project to assess the risks posed by USTs and to model the economic impact of various regulatory devices. Results from that study estimated the number of petroleum tanks to be between 1.3 and 1.4 million.

In contrast to our understanding of the petroleum tank situation at that time, very little information was available in the mid-1980s on the number of chemical tanks. A 1986 OUST study estimated the number of chemical tanks nationwide at over 100,000. However, this estimate was considered to be rough.[19] In September 2002, EPA indicated that there were an estimated 54,000 underground chemical tanks in the

United States. It is unclear if the early estimate was incorrect or if half of the nation's underground chemical tanks were taken out of service between 1986 and 2002.

Step 3: Historical Analysis

Prior to 1984, federal legislation did not adequately regulate USTs. The Resource Conservation and Recovery Act of 1976 (RCRA) regulates tanks that contain hazardous *wastes* but not tanks with petroleum or hazardous *products*. The Clean Water Act of 1972 required owners of very large underground tanks (those with a capacity greater than 42,000 gallons) to take certain measures to prevent corrosion and to test tanks periodically. These requirements, however, applied only to tanks that may serve as a direct source of pollution into navigable waters. Since underground containers generally damage groundwater and affect only surface water as a nonpoint source of pollution, the Clean Water Act has not been used to regulate most of them. The Superfund act authorizes EPA to respond whenever hazardous substances are released into the environment. It has not been used to respond to leaks from oil tanks because petroleum is not considered a hazardous substance under the act. In addition, it has not been used to prevent most leaks or to set tank standards since its sole purpose is environmental cleanup. The Safe Drinking Water Act of 1974 ensures that contaminants entering public water systems do not endanger human health. EPA has set maximum levels for contaminants in drinking water, but such standards pertain to tank leaks only when drinking water is directly affected.[20]

The Passage of UST Legislation in 1984

Groundwater contamination became a major environmental issue in the early 1980s. Some state and local governments, recognizing the gap in federal regulations, began developing their own standards addressing the problem of leaking USTs. The state of California, Miami-Dade County, Florida (Miami), Suffolk County, New York (Long Island), and Barnstable County, Massachusetts (Cape Cod)—all areas heavily dependent on groundwater—developed programs to clean up and prevent leaks from both petroleum and chemical tanks prior to November 1984.

National attention was focused on USTs as a result of a Senate Environmental Subcommittee hearing in November 1983 at which time EPA officials suggested that leaking tanks, particularly gasoline tanks, represented a major unaddressed source of groundwater contamination. Nationally televised reports of tank leaks in Rhode Island and Pennsylvania by *60 Minutes* and *Good Morning America* also pointed out the possible severity of the problem.

In 1984 Congress was primed to pass environmental legislation, especially in the area of hazardous waste management. The controversy surrounding the reign of EPA administrator Anne Gorsuch-Burford and the extremely slow expenditure of Superfund money by the EPA assistant administrator Rita Lavelle had angered many lawmakers in both the House and Senate. In particular, many legislators felt that Congress had appeared ineffective in addressing hazardous waste issues and that it seemed unaware of major environmental problems until it was too late. These legislators were determined to be out in front on the issue of groundwater contamination. Hence, when the issue came up, Congress was set to move quickly.[21] In February 1984, Senator David Durenberger of Minnesota (a state in which groundwater is an important resource) and Congressman Don Ritter of Pennsylvania (in whose district a leak had contaminated wells for over three years) each introduced a bill to address the problem of leaking USTs. Both bills sought to establish a comprehensive federal regulatory program containing the following elements:

- Owners and operators of USTs were to notify EPA or a designated state agency of their existence. This information was to be compiled into a comprehensive inventory. Furthermore, tanks for which notices were received were to be certified by EPA.
- EPA was to promulgate new tank standards within nine months after the bill was passed. The standards were to include guidelines for design, construction, and installation and to prohibit bare steel tanks. Also, EPA was to be notified within thirty days of the installation of a new tank.
- No statutory standards for the development of EPA regulations for leak detection, reporting, and prevention for existing tanks were given.

- Only releases, and not corrective actions (i.e., cleanups), were to be reported. Every owner, however, was required to take "appropriate" corrective action in response to leaks.
- EPA could inspect facilities only for the development or enforcement of regulations. Inspectors could not be used to conduct a study or to monitor or test a facility.
- A state could be authorized to run the UST program if it met the requirements of the federal program, including adequate enforcement programs.
- Owners and operators were required to maintain evidence of financial responsibility for bodily injury and property damage to third parties caused by sudden and nonsudden accidental occurrences.

The Durenberger and Ritter bills, which would have regulated over one million tanks, brought swift responses from the many individuals and organizations potentially affected and widened the debate to include alternative solutions to the problem. One possible legislative vehicle for tank regulation was the Superfund toxic waste cleanup laws, then under revision by Congress. Under Superfund, oil was not considered a toxic substance subject to the law's liability provisions. One proposal was to repeal this petroleum exclusion as a means of regulating leaking underground gasoline tanks. The American Petroleum Institute, representing the major oil companies, opposed being subject to the joint, strict, and several liability provisions of Superfund if the petroleum exclusion was lifted. Oil companies opposed Superfund liability provisions because joint, strict, and several liability assigns liability regardless of fault. Even if a company acts in accordance with current standards, it can be held liable if a problem develops. Furthermore, joint and several liability allows the assignment of total liability for a problem to any company whose actions contributed to the problem.[22] Oil companies, because of the size of their assets, feared that they would be targeted for cleanup at any leak sites where their products were sold. In addition, small retailers were concerned that regulations could drive them out of business. If retrofitting of existing tanks with expensive technology or the replacement of bare steel tanks was required, small operators would have a difficult time raising the necessary capital. Also, the Steel Tank Institute feared that the prohibition on unprotected steel tanks would hurt the reputation of their product. Specifically, it wished to have the legislation allow the installation of unprotected steel tanks in certain areas that were considered low risk because of their soil structure or distance from groundwater supplies.

In general, target groups in the 1980s insisted that not enough was known about the relationship between leaking tanks and groundwater contamination to warrant the immediate development of regulations. As Congress intensified deliberations, an ad hoc tank coalition—consisting of the American Petroleum Institute, the Steel Tank Institute, the National Oil Jobbers Council, and the Society of Independent Gasoline Marketers—was formed. At hearings on the proposed legislation held by Senator Durenberger in March 1984, members of the coalition put forward their positions and proposed that the problem be studied in more detail before Congress continued. Their objections, together with political difficulties surrounding the two potential legislative vehicles (Superfund reauthorization and RCRA amendments) for underground tank regulations, stalled the progress of the bills.

As the summer of 1984 approached, Congress became increasingly anxious to pass environmental legislation before the upcoming elections. The Tank Coalition, realizing that tank regulation was inevitable, began to negotiate a compromise bill. In October 1984 a final version of HSWA, which followed the Durenberger and Ritter proposals, was passed by both houses of Congress. In November 1984 President Reagan, perhaps wishing to deflect criticism of his environmental policies and problems at EPA, signed the amendments into law. Title VI of the amendments added subtitle I (s.9000), "Regulation of Underground Storage Tanks,"—to the Solid Waste Disposal Act of 1976.

Since the passage of these amendments, there has been a long and gradual process of developing and implementing tank regulations. The law required EPA to set standards for new tank design and installation, leak detection, spill control, leak cleanup, and tank closure. According to the Congressional Research Service, "Regulations have been phased in since 1988, and the last of these regulations (which requires that all tanks be upgraded, replaced, or closed) entered into effect on December 22, 1998."[23] In 1986 the federal government enacted a program to help ensure that funds were available to clean up leaks from underground storage tanks. The Leaking Underground Storage Tank (LUST) trust fund was part of the Superfund Amendments and Reauthorization Act of 1986 (PL 99–499). It provided government resources to clean up leaks when tank owners refused to act and provided funds for the cleanup of abandoned tanks when owners could not be found. It also required that tank owners demonstrate that they had the resources to clean up leaks and pay for damages resulting from tank leaks.[24]

Step 4: Situational Analysis

Regulatory Objectives and Desired Outcomes

The first part of the situational analysis is a description of the regulatory objectives and a discussion of desired outcomes. The following discussion identifies the tank regulation objectives established by Congress in 1984 and the additions made with enactment of the LUST trust fund in 1986. Subtitle I of HSWA requires EPA to develop a comprehensive program for the regulation of USTs "as may be necessary to protect human health and the environment" (s.9003 (a)). Specific provisions of HSWA concern notification, interim prohibition, new tank standards, monitoring and reporting standards for existing tanks, corrective actions, financial responsibility, inspection and enforcement, and state authorization.

Notification Under section 9002(b), state governors were required to designate an agency to receive notification forms from tank owners by May 1985. By November 1985, EPA was required to issue those forms (or guidelines for state forms) and instructions for their use. By May 1986, owners of regulated storage tanks currently in use or taken out of use since January 1, 1974, were to submit a form to the designated agency.

Interim Prohibition Since May 7, 1985, section 9003(g) has prohibited the installation of any new USTs unless:

- It prevents releases caused by corrosion or structural failure for the operational life of the tank.

- It is cathodically protected against corrosion, constructed of noncorrosive material, or designed in a manner to prevent the release or threatened release of any stored substance.
- The material used in the construction or lining of the tank is compatible with the substance to be stored.

The only exception to this standard is for tanks installed in soil where tests indicate that the likelihood of corrosivity is low. The interim prohibition terminated when EPA promulgated final tank standards in spring 1988.

New Tank Standards EPA was required to issue performance standards covering all elements of a UST system: its design, construction, installation, release direction, and compatibility with stored materials. EPA had broad discretion in the development of standards and was asked to consider factors such as type of tank, its location, soil and climate conditions, position of water table, and the technical capability of owners and operators. Standards for new petroleum and chemical tanks were finalized in spring 1988.

Monitoring and Reporting Standards for Existing Tanks Under section 9003(c)(1) and (2), tank owners were required to implement a leak detection system and maintain the records it produces. EPA had great flexibility, however, to choose among various release-detection technologies. For example, either observation wells or inventory control together with tank testing could be required. As with new tank standards, EPA was allowed to consider a number of factors (e.g., tank type and location) in order to make distinctions in the regulations. Tank owners also must report any detected releases (under section 9003(c)).

Corrective Actions Under section 9003(c)(4), regulations require that corrective actions be taken once a release is detected; section 9003(c)(3) requires that such actions be reported. The legislation did not define "corrective action," nor did it specify what triggered such an action, how long it must continue, and what would make it acceptable. These determinations were left to EPA as part of the rule-making process. These standards were to be promulgated by February 1987. They were issued one year late, in spring 1988.

In October 1986, Superfund was amended with the Superfund Amendments and Reauthorization Act. Superfund established a $100 million a year trust fund to clean up leaking tanks when responsible parties were unable to pay for a cleanup. The EPA administrator or state may use the resources of the trust fund to undertake actions with respect to a release from a UST. Priority for corrective actions was given to USTs that presented the greatest threat to human health and the environment. Specifically, the fund would be used in the following circumstances: there was no solvent owner or operator; it was necessary to take immediate action to protect human health and the environment and only the fund was available to provide the resources; an owner or operator refused to cooperate in a cleanup or comply with an order by the administrator or state; and expenditures at locations apart from the facility were necessary to protect human health or the environment. In addition, there would be a limited number of cases for which there is an identifiable and solvent owner or operator who is willing to cooperate in the clean-up, but whose financial resources would not be adequate to pay the entire cost of a response. In those cases, the administrator or state was authorized to use the fund to pay the costs that exceed the level of financial responsibility required of the owner or operator as required by the administrator.

Financial Responsibility Section 9003(d)(1) of HSWA permitted EPA to promulgate rules on maintaining evidence of financial responsibility for taking corrective action and compensating third parties for bodily injury and property damage resulting from either sudden or nonsudden releases from a UST. Such responsibility could be established by insurance, guarantee, or the qualification of the tank owners to be self-insured. The 1986 Superfund Amendments modified HSWA and required EPA to promulgate financial responsibility or insurance regulations. These regulations were issued in 1988.

Inspection and Enforcement Under section 9005(a), EPA was permitted to enter facilities containing regulated USTs at reasonable times to inspect tanks, copy records, obtain samples, and monitor or test tanks.

In addition, EPA could require a tank owner or operator to furnish information relating to the tank, its associated equipment, or its contents and to conduct monitoring and testing. These authorities could be used to develop a rule, conduct a study, or enforce the provisions of the legislation.

Section 9006 provided EPA with the authority to enforce the provisions of the legislation through administrative compliance orders and civil judicial actions. If a violator failed to comply with an administrative compliance order, a fine of up to $25,000 a day could be assessed. Failure to notify the designated agency of an existing or a recently retired tank carried a fine of up to $10,000. (The exact fine is determined by EPA.) These limits are considerable since many firms that owned USTs are small businesses.

State Authorization Section 9004 of HSWA allowed states to apply to operate their program in place of the federal program. EPA could approve the application if it determined that the state program was no less stringent than the federal one and that there were provisions for adequate enforcement of compliance. To be approved, a state program needed to promulgate requirements for installing new tanks, implementing leak detection systems, and maintaining records of product inventory. States needed to require reporting of releases from tanks, develop standards for taking and reporting corrective actions, and adopt standards for closing tanks to prevent future releases. State programs also needed to demonstrate that they required tank owners to possess the capacity to pay the cost of environmental cleanup of leaks from tanks. These requirements could not be less stringent than federal rules, although section 9008 allowed states to implement more stringent regulations. Section 9004(b), however, allowed state rules to be temporarily approved if one or more of their requirements were less stringent than federal requirements.

Positions and Possible Activities of Affected Parties

The second part of the situational analysis is the party analysis. This phase seeks to identify the predisposition of policymakers and the regulated parties to comply with regulation. Again, the discussion presents the perspective of the affected parties at the inception of the program in the mid-1980s. This segment of the chapter presents the party analysis used by the National Academy of Public Administration (NAPA) and EPA during the development of a strategic regulatory plan for USTs. The study reviews the positions and potential actions of tank manufacturers, small businesses, major oil companies, trade associations, the insurance industry, and state and local governments. The party analysis was conducted in 1985 in the early stages of the development of an UST regulatory program.

Tank Manufacturers During the debate about the underground storage tank legislation, manufacturers of steel tanks expressed concern that bare steel tanks would be prohibited in all circumstances. The interim prohibition was changed to reflect this concern: it allowed tanks without corrosion protection in areas with high-resistivity soil. In addition, it was perceived that tank manufacturers in general would be anxious to cooperate in the development of methods for evaluating new tanks and leak detection systems. Undoubtedly, manufacturers of specific kinds of tanks and detection systems would push for regulations that favored their product.

Incentives for tank manufacturers to assist in the notification program were not great. However, the Steel Tank Institute (which represented 80 percent of the steel tank manufacturers) participated in efforts to inform tank purchasers of the interim prohibition requirements.

Small Businesses Small businesses were deeply concerned about the economic impact of UST regulations. Some leak detection systems were fairly expensive, especially relative to the profit margins of many of these small businesses. Requirements for retrofitting existing tanks with these systems could significantly affect profit margins or even business viability. Required tank testing, which would force a tank out of operation for one or two days, would disrupt many small businesses. Moreover, many small businesses feared they would have difficulty raising the capital necessary to comply with new regulations, as new tank standards could dramatically increase the cost of replacing tanks.

The financial impact and potential liability associated with corrective action could be even more burdensome. Abatement of releases from underground storage tanks ordinarily runs between $50,000 and $150,000, and some have cost several million dollars. In the mid-1980s it was unclear whether insurance against such risks would be available or affordable. It was conceivable that small firms would not be able to demonstrate financial responsibility and could be driven out of business by the new regulations.

Concerns about the financial implications of tank regulations were reflected in calls to the EPA Small Business ombudsman hot line in the mid-1980s. In addition to requests for additional information about the impending regulations, many callers expressed their dismay at the liability prospects. One distressed caller questioned the liability structure: "Why should we be jointly and severally liable? We have no negligence defenses if someone installs a tank improperly or if a supplier improperly fills a tank." A few particularly disgruntled callers, generally small, independent businesspeople, feared that the new regulations would "swallow them up." They accused EPA and the major corporations of being in collusion to drive the small retailers out of business.

Major Oil Companies Major oil companies, which own service stations across the nation, voluntarily began practices to upgrade the quality of their underground tanks. Motivated by the need to avoid product loss, many such companies started programs to replace old steel tanks with new corrosion-protected tanks and to monitor tanks to determine if they were leaking. With greater access to the capital necessary to embark on such projects, the oil companies were less unnerved by the impending regulations for new and existing tanks than their small business counterparts.

However, these large companies were concerned about the financial responsibility requirements of the HSWA legislation. They believed that they could become the deep pockets that pay for the cleanup costs for most leaking underground tanks because of the size of their assets and the principle of retroactive joint and several liability. Some companies sought to limit their exposure by requiring station operators to buy the tanks from the company for one dollar. Furthermore, because they operate in many states, large companies preferred uniform federal regulation to divergent state regulations. For example, a standard notification form required in all states would be less expensive and more convenient for a multistate operation than would different forms for each state.

Trade Associations Some trade associations favored tank regulations as a means of improving efficiency by reducing product loss. Others favored "reasonable" regulation as a means of avoiding "onerous" regulation. Some groups were more interested in fighting regulation than in participating in its implementation. In many cases, organizations take these actions in order to show their members that they fully understand government proposals concerning their industry, defend the interests of their members, and can influence what government eventually does.

Because of the need to foster their insider image, program planners thought that trade associations might be willing to act as conduits for information to tank owners and operators. If the views of trade associations were allowed to influence regulations, the resulting tank program would appear reasonable to them, and they would be likely to cooperate in its implementation. A high rate of compliance could be the result of such involvement.

Insurance Industry Insurers in the mid-1980s were increasingly reluctant to provide policies covering pollution liability. Due to a general financial crisis in the industry, the level of surplus for policyholders had sharply declined, reducing the industry's capacity to write policies. This shortage was addressed by dropping riskier coverages, such as environmental impairment liability insurance.

The industry felt that pollution insurance was particularly risky for two reasons. First, the amount of damage caused by a release into the environment is difficult to predict beforehand. As already mentioned, the abatement of petroleum releases can be quite expensive. When third-party injury and property damage must be compensated for, the cost can be particularly high. Second, the insurance industry recognized that judicial decisions were becoming less predictable. The principle of joint and several liability, insurers assert, makes it difficult to relate the risk associated with a policyholder's operation to the risk that a policyholder will face in court. A company that follows accepted practices and is only loosely connected with operations at a certain site can be held liable for all corrective actions that are required if a leak occurs on that site.[25]

Based on the prevailing climate, it seemed likely that insurers would be more motivated to participate in the program if tank regulation helped them limit their liability exposure and make risks measurable and predictable. Tank insurance could be profitable if insurers were supplied with data that would allow them to vary rates according to risk. To assist this process of data collection, state insurance regulators and EPA could ask tank insurers to require owners and operators to produce evidence of notification before issuing or renewing a policy. This would augment other notification initiatives and provide a critical check on the notification process.[26]

State and Local Governments A 1984 survey by NAPA assessed the status of underground tank regulations at the state level. This study evaluated the state and local regulatory environment at the start of the federal regulatory effort.[27] In 1984 only one state, California, had a comprehensive program with provisions to clean up and prevent leaks from tanks containing either petroleum or chemical products, although eight other states were developing comprehensive tank regulations at that time. Nine states fully regulated petroleum tanks but did not regulate chemical tanks. Twenty-four other states required tank registration, and many regulated tanks through nationally established fire codes. Examples of such standards are those published by the National Fire Protection Association (NFPA 30) and the Uniform Fire Code (UFC 79). These codes recommend practices for handling leaks of flammable and combustible liquids in order to prevent fire, explosion, or other public safety hazards. They were not designed, however, to prevent environmental contamination. Seventeen states did not regulate USTs at all, although three of these states were actively considering legislation.

Since 1984, in response to the federal initiative, many states have developed UST programs. This was predicted by EPA staff in 1984 and was considered an important factor in conditioning the pace with which new rules could be administered by the states. In 1985, NAPA's staff anticipated that "because of the size of the regulated community, the success of the federal tank program is dependent upon state participation. States with active and developing tank programs might cooperate to avoid disrupting their own programs while those states seeking to avoid tank regulations may participate in order to minimize their impact. On the other hand, active states may delay further development of their programs to see what shape the federal program takes, while states without programs may continue to ignore tank regulation."[28]

Since 1985 state programs have taken a variety of paths. A key strategy for states is to stimulate local governments to participate in tank regulation. Some local governments have already established their own programs, while others may know very little about the potential problems posed by leaking tanks. Yet local governments must be an important part of the federal program. They can use their records to identify tank owners and operators, work with tank suppliers to ensure tank owner compliance with notification requirements, identify institutions (public and private) that interact with tank owners, and be used to communicate the requirements of the new regulations.[29]

Summary

This chapter investigated the problems and politics concerning the regulation of USTs. The first part of the chapter discussed why leaking USTs are a possible threat to the environment and public health. This was followed by an examination of the politics surrounding efforts to regulate underground storage containers. The next section presented a review of the HSWA provisions involving USTs. The last section analyzed the parties involved in UST regulation. Overall, this chapter provided an example of the background material needed to develop a strategic regulatory plan.

Given the nature of the problem discussed at the beginning of the chapter and the legislative approach described at the end of the chapter, EPA had a predetermined set of options available for regulating tanks. This was not a case of Congress's simply saying to an agency: "Here is a problem. Solve it." Instead, a very specific policy structure was prescribed. Congress required EPA to develop quickly a state-run regulatory program. EPA would issue new tank rules, leak detection regulations, and cleanup (corrective action) guidelines. If EPA did not act quickly, the very strict standards of the interim prohibition would remain in effect. In addition, deviations from the standards set in HSWA's interim prohibition against certain tank owners would be seen as EPA retreating from the strict standards promulgated by Congress. Finally, and perhaps most significant, EPA was initially given little money and support to administer this massive regulatory effort.

Faced with these constraints, the agency took a number of decisive steps. First, it commissioned NAPA to work with senior managers in the Office of Solid Waste and Emergency Response and develop a regulatory plan for HSWA. Due to the magnitude of the UST problem, NAPA's study quickly focused on the tank issue. Second, EPA created a new office to address the tank problem exclusively, the Office of Underground Storage Tanks, which reported directly to the assistant administrator for solid waste and emergency response. That office began to expand, setting contracts, issuing grants to state governments, developing rules, and interacting with the regulated community. The $100 million a year trust fund created by Congress in 1986 has facilitated expansion of the regulatory program and has addressed the economic impact of the program on small businesses as identified in analyses by NAPA.

The remainder of this part of the book deals with EPA's initial effort to formulate a program for regulating USTs and assesses the results of these efforts over the second half of the 1980s until 2003. It is both a case study of environmental policy design and an analysis of one effort to develop and implement a strategic regulatory plan. The next chapter executes the fifth and sixth stages of the model, strategic regulation formulation and ex ante assessment.

9

A Strategic Regulatory Plan for Underground Storage Tanks

This chapter focuses on the application steps 5 and 6, strategic regulation formulation and ex ante assessment, of the strategic regulatory planning model for achieving compliance with the UST provisions of HSWA. A conceptual framework for selecting regulatory devices was outlined earlier in the book, and specific devices that might fit into such a framework were evaluated. The framework identified three general types of conditions (those in the regulating agency, regulated community, and outside arena) that can affect the cost and coerciveness of regulatory devices. The amount of money necessary for executing selected regulatory approaches and the restrictiveness of those approaches represent the overall government effort. The dependent variable was rate of compliance, and it ranged from avoidance behavior to compliant behavior. It is assumed that higher rates of compliance will lead to improvements in environmental quality.

Potential Obstacles to Achieving Compliance

As a result of executing step 4 (a situational analysis) in the strategic regulatory planning model, several potential obstacles to achieving compliance with UST rules were identified and considered prior to moving on to step 5. The potential obstacles tended to vary in significance and in the amount of control EPA had over them. Specifically, they involved the nature of the regulated community, political support, availability of liability insurance, inadequate information, and the legislation, the Hazardous and Solid Waste Amendments (HSWA). These obstacles were taken into account during the development of a strategic regulatory plan.

Step 5: Strategic Regulation Formulation

Developing a strategy for implementing a UST regulatory program, the National Academy of Public Administration (NAPA) and EPA planners adhered to four key assumptions while executing step 5 of the strategic regulatory planning model:[1]

1. Successful implementation depends on broad public support.
2. Due to resource constraints, implementation must rely on voluntary compliance and existing institutions.
3. Most regulated parties will comply with a reasonable program.
4. Successful implementation requires a credible enforcement presence.

Public Support

There was no outcry from the public to regulate operators of USTs. Nevertheless, the experience with environmental regulation in the 1970s and early 1980s demonstrated to the UST strategists that the public invariably supported legitimate efforts to protect the environment.[2] The key was to show the public that such regulation was warranted and reasonable. A central element of any plan to achieve these ends must be a meaningful public education program. The public must learn the true dimensions of the problems and potential threats. Government must stimulate the public to develop a sophisticated understanding of the problem, and it should seek to avoid the emotional tone of the hazardous waste debate of the late 1970s. Given the likelihood that federal resources would be limited for any new type of mass environmental regulation, public support would be essential in the appropriation of state and local funds for these programs.

Resource Constraints

During the strategic regulation formulation phase, it is important to determine the desired degree of compliance and the viability of self-regulation versus direct regulatory intervention. The amount of resources an agency has to administer a program clearly influences how much compliance can reasonably be expected and the level of government intervention possible. Where a legislative body has allocated sufficient money for policy formulation and implementation, the agency will have considerable latitude in selecting appropriate regulatory devices. Where a legislative body has allocated limited funds for such efforts, however, the regulatory alternatives open to the agency are more limited. At the time the tank program was established, congressional appropriations and resources for EPA to manage the program were quite constrained.

When underground tanks were regulated in 1984, there was a vast increase in the size of the regulated community. Since the increased size of the regulated community was not matched by a similar increase in resources, EPA and NAPA planners assumed that standard command-and-control regulation would not be possible.[3] Because resource constraints made such a regulatory approach unrealistic, an innovative method of inducing compliance was needed. To minimize resource constraints, EPA would rely on voluntary compliance and would use existing institutions to stimulate compliance. Existing units of state and local government (e.g., local health and fire protection agencies and state hazardous waste units), trade associations, tank and waste disposal service vendors, and environmental interest groups would be encouraged to play an active role in tank regulation.

The conceptual framework for selecting regulatory devices, introduced in chapter 3, is instructive here. Almost by default, the planners realized that the final regulatory devices chosen must be cost-effective. Scarce funds for government enforcement, coupled with the strong antiregulatory feelings shared by many small business proprietors, also suggested the selection of less coercive regulatory approaches if possible. While everyone who participated in the application of step 5 of the model idealistically hoped for 100 percent compliance, EPA officials probably would have been satisfied if the final plan had resulted in a level of compliance that significantly diminished releases from USTs into the environment. Failure to achieve this objective would have forced the agency to lobby Congress for additional money, something it wished to avoid in the mid–1980s period of mounting debt and budget cuts.

Planners faced a serious dilemma. On the one hand, they had assumed that voluntary self-regulation would be ineffective due to previous experiences by other regulatory agencies and due to the size and diversity of the target population. On the other hand, the limited financial resources of small businesses and the possible financial benefit of compliance to EPA made self-regulation an attractive option. EPA therefore decided that a low degree of coercion might be sufficient to achieve an acceptable level of compliance. Moreover, increasingly coercive techniques usually require greater government involvement and thus necessitate greater expenditures. Total reliance on traditional command-and-control type approaches to regulation seemed out of the question because of limited funds, forcing planners to consider new and innovative tactics. As a result, the application of step 5 was extremely complicated.

How Reasonable the Regulations Are Perceived to Be

The program's planners assumed that adequate levels of compliance could be achieved under certain conditions. First, regulatory requirements were clear. Second, the steps required for compliance were simple. Finally, compliance was affordable to members of target groups.[4]

The program's planners in the mid–1980s were acutely aware that many of the firms affected by HSWA were small businesses with little experience in meeting environmental standards. However, in order for regulations to be obeyed, target groups needed to: (1) know they were regulated, (2) understand the tasks required to comply with regulations, and (3) be able to afford the costs of compliance. In the case of improved tank management practices, whether small businesses would perceive the regulations to be reasonable hinged on several factors. First, was the competition required to incur similar costs, and would increased costs result in any competitive disadvantage? Second, could improvements be phased in gradually to allow income to retire debt? Third, could financing be obtained for required capital costs, especially for new tanks? If EPA designed its new regulatory requirements with these factors in mind, the agency believed that a satisfactory level of compliance might be achieved.

Credible Enforcement

EPA and NAPA planners felt that voluntary compliance alone would not suffice and that a credible enforcement program would be needed to stimulate voluntary compliance. Such an enforcement program would need to ensure that the costs of violating regulations significantly exceeded the costs of complying with regulations. This would need to be communicated to the regulated community and appear credible. In addition, because of the large and diverse nature of this regulated community, it was considered essential that enforcement be perceived as fair, especially by the general public. If violators were able to portray HSWA enforcers as government "bullies" that push around the "little guy," then public support for these regulations would never be developed.

An Emphasis on Induced Compliance

Following the execution of step 5, which included employment of the conceptual framework for selecting regulatory devices and an analysis of the strengths and weaknesses of each device, the program's planners developed a strategic regulatory program that emphasized "induced compliance."[5] This program contained three principal components: (1) stimulate voluntary compliance, (2) stimulate private enforcement by requiring liability insurance and/or financial assurance, and (3) implement strategic and selective high-visibility enforcement against violators.

By suggesting that EPA stimulate voluntary compliance, the program's planners in the 1980s were calling for the agency to do all it could to encourage regulated parties to learn about tank standards, understand how those standards apply to their operations, and take steps to comply voluntarily with the law's requirements. Clearly, owners of USTs have a stake in improving tank management: their desire to prevent the loss of valued products. The second component of "induced compliance was based on the expectation that voluntary compliance would never be total and that some degree of coercion would be necessary. Planners urged aggressive implementation of the requirement that the owners of USTs prove that they had the financial capability to clean up tank leaks and pay for associated damages. Planners hoped that the "insurance" requirement might stimulate a self-policing system based on insurance company interest in minimizing and stabilizing risk and tank owner interest in obtaining insurance at the least possible cost. If the system worked, complementing self-interest would result in improved tank management practices.

The third component of the induced compliance regulatory approach assumed that the other two components would not be comprehensive enough; violations of the law would occur. Voluntary, self-policed compliance could best be stimulated with a credible enforcement threat. Due to limited resources, such a threat would be credible only if it were selective and certain. Planners believed that the Internal Revenue Service (IRS) model of explicit, visible, and statistically selective inspection (or audit) was worth imitating in the regulation of USTs.[6] Although only a tiny portion of the nation's taxpayers are audited in a given year, most taxpayers believe that there is a real chance they may be selected. If a similar perception could also be nurtured among tank operators, the probability of regulatory compliance should be enhanced.

The recommended strategic regulatory plan was built on the understanding that government's regulatory activities can range from assisting voluntary compliance to active and vigorous enforcement. These are two ends of what can be termed a noncoercive-coercive continuum. Between these two extremes, government can employ a variety of regulatory techniques. It can, for example, require owners of USTs to provide "financial assurance." Advocates of such a strategy hoped that requiring insurance would limit government involvement and expenditures and encourage voluntary compliance. However, if insurance is not feasible, other methods could be adopted later to encourage respect for the law. The key was to develop a mix of coercive and noncoercive activities that were cost-effective, promoted compliance, and improved environmental quality.

In order to stimulate voluntary compliance, the underground tank program planners proposed three types of programs: education, technical assistance, and financial assistance.[7] Although it was considered advisable to direct resources to educational efforts aimed at the broad public, initially generating public support was not as important as educating the regulated community. Once again, resource constraints limited the type of educational campaign feasible. Rather than launching a mass media or direct mail campaign to reach the regulated community, planners advised that the program work through intermediaries, such as national trade associations, environmental groups, and organizations of state and local government officials. At the regional level, EPA offices would work with state governments, active local governments, trade associations, and environmental groups. Planners recommended that the messages disseminated through these intermediaries be tailored to regional and local audiences and that they should provide the following information:

- The rules and standards that must be followed
- How to find reliable vendors (e.g., tank suppliers, tank installers, tank monitors, and cleanup contractors)
- Technical information about assistance and other compliance advisory services available
- A listing of penalties for noncompliance
- Details about EPA's inspection and enforcement strategy
- A review of tort liability risks, which included the potential penalties faced by owners of USTs who damage other private parties.

Such an approach, as explained in chapter 10, could facilitate the establishment of integrated decision structures and demand patterns.

A major obstacle to compliance with tank regulation would be the technical capability of the regulated community to comply with standards. Planners recommended that EPA make available low-cost or free compliance assistance services. These services would provide general advice to the regulated community as well as site-specific consultation to individual firms. Site-specific consultation involved a review of applicable environmental rules, followed by an analysis of the steps required to ensure compliance. EPA's role would be to distribute handbooks and other informational materials to be used by those supplying technical assistance. The agency would also fund and evaluate pilot projects experimenting with different modes of delivering and funding technical assistance. EPA's new Office of Underground Storage Tanks (OUST) would probably not have the resources to fund these technical assistance services directly.

In fiscal year 1984, the Occupational Health and Safety Administration (OSHA) provided its highly regarded compliance assistance program with a budget of $23.5 million.[8] With this funding, approximately 600 OSHA consultants provided technical assistance to 30,000 firms and individuals. This $23.5 million was over three times as great as EPA's entire FY 1985 grant funding for the UST technical assistance program. Although the trust fund to clean up leaking USTs was funded at $100 million per year, it could be used only to clean up leaks, not to support technical assistance.

Tank replacement and environmental cleanup are substantial expenses for many newly regulated parties. The underground tank planners in the mid-1980s correctly predicted that small businesses would have difficulty raising the money required for tank replacement. Moreover, they would have even more trouble raising the money needed for any type of major environmental cleanup (potentially running well over $1 million). Although the 1984 and 1986 UST statutes did not enable EPA to provide significant financial aid, it could advise states and localities on low-cost strategies for easing small business financing difficulties and pooling resources. In fact, the state assurance funds that developed in the 1980s and 1990s were a direct result of this EPA initiative. The program's planners also thought that OUST could assist in funding pilot programs that could identify innovative financing techniques or novel methods of pooling risks and resources (e.g., insurance cooperatives).

As noted earlier, HSWA authorizes EPA to require owners and operators of USTs to demonstrate that they have the financial capability to clean up any damage that might result from a tank leak. Such financial assurance would typically be provided through an insurance policy covering such leaks. If the insurance requirement was feasible and affordable insurance were available, planners in the mid-1980s thought it might be possible to set in motion a market-based, self-sustaining system. Government's role would be to ensure that owners of USTs carried some type of insurance, investigate unabated tank leaks, and enforce the law when self-regulation failed.

Researchers at NAPA, in particular, supported a regulatory plan that relied on tort liability law as an incentive for improved tank management.[9] The risk of damage suits from private parties was thought to be a stronger incentive to good practice than EPA enforcement. In the budgetary climate of the mid-1980s, insurance companies were considered more capable than government of generating the resources required to monitor operator practices. With a risk-derived rate structure, insurance companies could also ensure that the costs of regulation were distributed

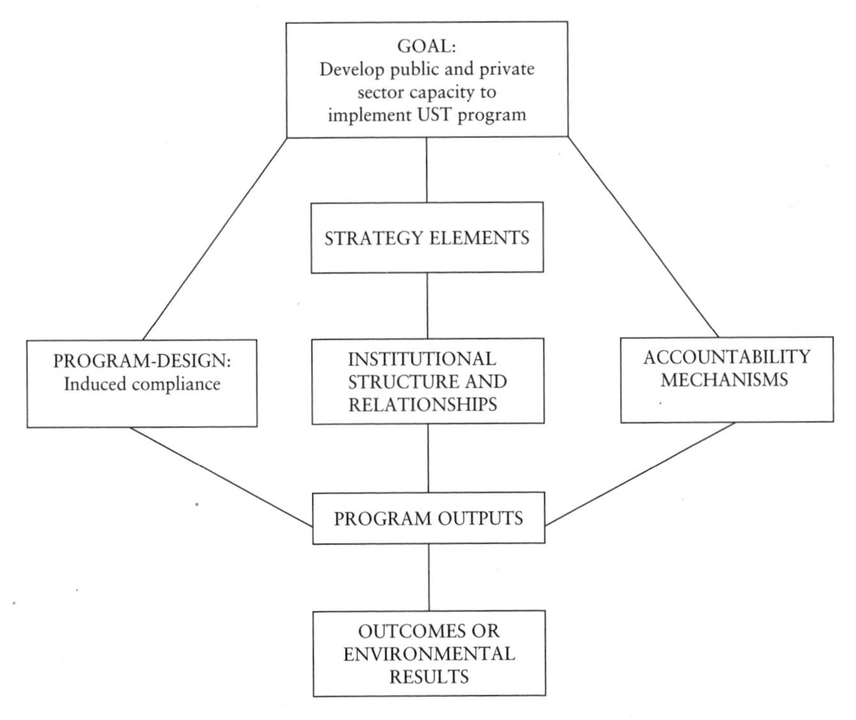

Figure 9.1
Basic components of the UST strategic regulatory plan

equitably among the regulated community. Such a rate structure would also generate financial incentives for compliance.

By focusing enforcement resources on major cases and implementing the insurance requirement, EPA could leverage scarce dollars to achieve significant results. Planners believed that efforts should be made to stimulate private tank insurance, while using public insurance if the private insurance market failed.[10] The private sector has greater flexibility in adjusting to risk and should be able to administer insurance programs more efficiently than government.

Figure 9.1 outlines the basic components of the strategic regulatory plan for managing USTs. Program outputs in the figure represent the final actions taken by EPA to ameliorate the UST problem. The outcomes or environmental results reflect rate of compliance and related changes in environmental quality.

Step 6: Ex Ante Analysis

The ex ante analysis addresses the feasibility of the selected regulatory approach before implementation. The purpose of this step is to avoid wasted effort, resources, and time spent in executing an ineffective regulatory program by identifying potential trouble spots and problem areas before it is too late. Although it is virtually impossible to anticipate every difficulty that might arise, ex ante assessment provides a good opportunity to double back and rethink specific elements of the proposed plan. Thus, this step was applied in the design of a strategic regulatory plan to ameliorate the UST problem. Most of this ex ante evaluation was written in the mid-1980s and is presented to represent the state of thinking at that stage of the implementation process. The ex ante analysis begins with a discussion of the potential complications that might occur in relying on insurance to achieve compliance.

Potential Complications Involving Insurance

Throughout the early 1980s, insurance companies reduced offerings or dramatically increased the price of certain types of liability insurance. As a result, municipalities, medical doctors, environmental facilities, and other organizations faced serious difficulties obtaining insurance. In 1985, environmental liability insurance became particularly difficult to purchase.

The scarcity of environmental insurance was attributed to several factors. The insurance industry in the United States was weak and under tremendous pressure because of intense competition (especially from foreign companies), the trend toward self-insurance among large enterprises, and the past practice of underpricing insurance to obtain cash for inflation-fueled investment. Moreover, judicial decisions allowed general liability insurance to be used to cover gradual pollution releases and discharges with long latency periods. Increasingly, juries began to assume that distant exposures had caused specific harm. Finally, there was a legitimate fear among insurance companies that interpretations of pollution liability were unpredictable and that policies might someday be asked to cover damages thought to be excluded. Consequently, a liability insurance crisis arose in the mid-1980s.

Clearly, it is beyond EPA's jurisdiction (or ability) to alleviate the liability insurance crisis. If insurance is unavailable, this particular component of the induced-compliance regulatory approach cannot be fully employed. Even if these insurance problems, which also exist in other sectors of society, can be resolved, it is difficult to insure many existing tanks. EPA's first comprehensive tank study indicated that up to 30 percent of the nation's tanks were leaking.[11] It is unlikely that a private insurance company would agree to cover these tanks.

Possible Solutions

These insurance problems need to be solved in order for EPA to implement this component of the strategic regulatory plan successfully. Researchers at NAPA, in particular, recommended that EPA work with Congress to address the issue of tort liability.[12] They advocated that either liability limits or some type of regulatory mechanism should be considered to ensure the availability of reasonably priced environmental insurance. The agency was also advised to work with the insurance industry to overcome technical uncertainties regarding risk prediction. EPA could help identify low-risk and high-risk tanks to facilitate risk-based insurance pricing. Furthermore, EPA was advised to back up the insurance requirement with a strong administrative mechanism for monitoring compliance.[13] For tanks that were uninsurable, planners suggested that EPA work with the states to develop assigned risk pools or Superfund-type fee systems to pay the cost of cleanup. Such a mixed public-private insurance system might ensure that all tank leak cleanups had a source of funding. The key challenge to EPA in implementing this approach was to keep insurance companies in the market and competitive. A second challenge was to induce these companies to monitor tank management practices and structure insurance rates according to risk.[14]

Tactical and Selective Enforcement

Early in the UST program, the major enforcement authority available under HSWA was the interim prohibition on installing new tanks that were unprotected against corrosion. As EPA promulgated new tank standards and corrective action regulations, new enforcement authorities became available. In 1988, states became eligible to apply for authorization from EPA to operate an underground tank program in lieu of the federal program. Until then, enforcement was a federal responsibility. However, program planners believed that in the long run, enforcement would be mainly a state and local activity. The federal government lacked the resources and awareness of local concerns to implement a thorough and effective tank enforcement program. Nevertheless, a credible federal enforcement presence would be needed to stimulate the voluntary compliance required for effective regulation.

EPA's Role

EPA's primary role was to prepare state and local governments for their lead role in enforcing underground tank regulations. In order to ensure that state and local governments assumed this function, the planners advised EPA to stimulate public support for enforcement efforts. They also suggested that EPA provide state and local governments with guidance on inspection and litigation procedures and with limited grant funding to seed state efforts. In addition, planners recommended that the agency play a clearinghouse role in exchanging case development lessons and emerging precedents. Finally, planners advised EPA to take the lead in publicizing enforcement efforts in order to build the regulated community's perception that violators would be punished. EPA's failure to play these roles could jeopardize the successful implementation of the overall strategic regulatory plan.

Approach to Enforcement

To regulate America's USTs, an enormous amount of private and voluntary effort would be required. It was questionable whether industry would be motivated to upgrade tank practices by pure altruism or even enlightened self-interest. A credible, visible enforcement program would need to accompany efforts at inducing voluntary compliance. Planners advised that a program begin to identify periodically several unambiguous and flagrant violators of the UST rules and take legal action against these offenders. News of these enforcement actions would then be communicated to tank owners and operators.

Enforcement must not only be credible; it also must be fair. If firms in compliance with UST regulations had no greater protection from liability judgments than firms not in compliance, there would be little incentive to comply with regulations. In fact, if compliance with federal standards did not reduce potential judgments, firms might be tempted to hide noncompliance and not register their tanks rather than improve tank management practices.

Still, enforcement remained a critical component of the induced-compliance regulatory approach. The approach recommended was a selective one, similar to the IRS audit policy. The IRS has an explicit and well-known strategy for auditing those with the highest probability of violation and with the potential to generate free media coverage of the audit. Although certain classes of taxpayers are more likely to be audited than others, all taxpayers have some chance of being audited. Although the odds of being selected are low for many taxpayers, most taxpayers act as if the odds are reasonably high. In addition, audits are not considered pleasant experiences. There are instances of tax cheating in the United States, but overall estimates of compliance levels are high, especially when compared to rates in other countries (e.g., France). The program's planners believed that EPA's UST program would do well if it could approach the success rate enjoyed by the IRS.

The UST program could develop and publicize a risk-based graduated inspection and enforcement policy. Owners of USTs would know that if they operated an old tank on a sole source aquifer, they had a relatively high probability of being inspected. Not only should the policy be widely publicized, but it also must be adhered to closely. Predictability of enforcement reinforces the policy's credibility. Owners of USTs should feel, for example, that even if they are not inspected in the next three years, the probability of inspection will be quite high by the fourth year.

Administering such an enforcement program through the states presented the EPA with a challenge that the IRS does not face. To succeed, the agency would need to leverage its scarce state grant resources and develop a network of state enforcement officials willing and able to adhere to national policy. Such a task would require an unusual degree of flexibility, coordination, and imagination.

Approach to Public Support

The EPA was advised to work actively to generate public support for the enforcement of UST regulations. Enforcement directed against small businesses run by average people entails political risks different from enforcement against larger, faceless corporations. It is easy for a federal regulatory agency to appear unreasonable when suing small businesses. It was important, therefore, to select initial enforcement targets carefully and to make certain that the agency's case against the violator was clearly communicated to the public. To increase the likelihood of clear communication, the EPA would need to work with other public agencies, environmental groups, trade associations, and service vendors in order to emphasize the health and environmental risks posed by leaking tanks; the fairness of the enforcement procedures; the seriousness of the particular violation; and the greater long-term costs of cleaning contaminated soil and water. Achieving adequate levels of public support for oversight efforts could help increase rates of compliance.

Summary

This chapter illustrated how steps 5 and 6, strategic regulation formulation and ex ante analysis, were applied in the mid-1980s in the development of a strategic regulatory plan to control the UST problem. Within the context of step 5, the framework for the selection of specific regulatory devices and the prior review of the strengths and weaknesses of alternative regulatory techniques proved useful in this study. The ex ante analysis pointed out a number of potential problems that might hinder the effectiveness of the overall strategic regulatory plan. Some of these difficulties were dealt with by modifying initial approaches, a midcourse correction that is quite common in environmental regulation (e.g., the Clean Water Act).[15] Step 7, the ex post review/revision phase of the model, is also relevant in this regard and is executed in the next chapter.

The work of the planners of EPA's underground tank program led to a number of principal conclusions. Owners of USTs represented a large and varied target population, primarily consisting of small businesses. At a time when the small business community was loudly voicing complaints about too much government regulation, the program was advised to be careful not to take actions that would lead to political backlash and further environmental degradation through the continued use of leaking USTs. Therefore, in the program's early years, planners suggested that the primary focus be on building public support and facilitating compliance. Enforcement would be an important but only secondary concern. It was also thought that the agency's long-term interest was to use the energies and resources of state and local governmental units, service vendors, trade associations, and environmental groups in communicating requirements and stimulating political support. Finally, EPA was advised to attempt to secure insurance industry cooperation and participation as a supplement to the public enforcement effort. These critical observations and recommendations were intended for incorporation into the strategic regulatory plan. The extent to which this was accomplished is analyzed in the next chapter.

10

Ex Post Review and Revision: Eighteen Years Later

The seventh and final step of the strategic regulatory planning model is ex post review and revision. This phase of the planning process takes place after implementation has begun and enough experience has been gained to gauge the success of the program. In essence, feedback and evaluation takes place here. The objectives of this review are to assess the degree to which implementation has conformed to the original design; to assess the adequacy, current relevance, and overall success of the original plan; and to suggest midcourse corrections, if necessary, in the regulatory program.

With these purposes in mind, this chapter conducts an ex post review and revision of the strategic regulatory plan developed for USTs in 1985. The chapter begins with a brief discussion of each of the objectives of ex post review and revision.

Objectives of Step 1: Ex Post Review and Revision

Assessing Conformity with the Plan

In order to assess the value of the strategic regulatory plan, it is important to know whether the plan was ever adopted and implemented. If the plan has not been adopted and implemented, it is crucial to understand why this happened. Failure to adopt and implement the program can occur because of faulty design, management perception that the design was faulty, misunderstanding or miscommunication of the program, changed conditions (e.g., a sudden loss of funds), a preference to pursue another path, or incompetent, ineffectual staff. In assessing conformity with the original design, one does not look for complete compliance, but for a general adherence to the program's central principles. Once it has been determined that the plan has been attempted, it is then possible to see whether the plan has accomplished its goals.

Assessing the Adequacy and Relevance of the Plan

With the passage of time, it is possible to assess the plan in the light of changing conditions and new experiences. Nonconformity with the original approach may be a logical reaction to new developments. After nearly twenty years of implementation, it is time to pause, reflect, and analyze the progress made under the prescribed program design. This reassessment of the plan is the starting point for revisions of the plan (if necessary), the third objective of ex post review and revision.

Midcourse Corrections in the Regulatory Program

It is difficult to predict private sector reaction to new governmental regulation, primarily because too many uncertainties often exist—for example:

- The vigor of enforcement
- The political will of governmental officials responsible for establishing the regulatory administrative structure
- The economic health of the regulated industry and the economy as a whole
- Industry's technical capability to understand and comply with regulation
- The degree to which compliance with actual regulatory provisions resulted in desired behavior
- Judicial and interest group interventions in the regulatory process
- Changes in technology

Each of these factors is difficult to gauge at the beginning of a regulatory program. After a period of time, however, it becomes possible to discern the effect of a given program on regulated parties. Unfortunately, many policymakers do not bother to perform an empirical analysis of their efforts.

As indicated in chapter 1, the formal, legalistic school of thought in regulation considers a concern for implementation illegitimate for administrators. Such concerns are believed to be the business of Congress, not the bureaucracy. If a statute calls for a given regulation, then its implementation must be pursued regardless of political feasibility. There are times when administrative discretion is so limited that a politically unrealistic regulation must be promulgated and implemented. In the 1970s, the bold and ambitious provisions of the Clean Air Act required EPA to reduce urban air pollution to a level that could be achieved only by limiting the amount of automobiles entering downtown districts.[1] Then EPA administrator Ruckelshaus attempted to persuade Congress to provide EPA with greater flexibility. When Congress refused, EPA required states and cities to develop transportation plans that were widely unpopular and ultimately never implemented. Such efforts at developing extremely restrictive standards often discredit a regulatory initiative and result in less pollution control. However, courts and environmental interest groups have attempted to hold EPA to literal interpretations of statutory provisions, and such efforts make it difficult to predict the success of a regulatory program.[2] The argument that a regulation is too stringent will usually fail to convince a judge that the regulation should be abandoned.

In the case of USTs, it is important to determine whether and, if so, to what extent members of the target population are complying with EPA guidelines. At the ex post phase in the planning process, it is time for policymakers to determine if the program has led to the type of behavior change intended. This is by necessity a fairly general inquiry, since most policymakers expect gradual change in the behavior of regulated parties. Policymakers will expect some variance in compliance as the plan is set in motion, with increasing compliance as time passes. If EPA officials conclude that greater conformity with UST provisions is not taking place, adjustments in the plan will be necessary. In the worst-case scenario, members of the target population will ignore government orders to modify their behavior, in which case policymakers might have to return to step 1 of the model and begin again. In the best-case scenario, everything will go according to schedule, compliance goals will be met or surpassed, environmental quality will continuously improve, and no midcourse corrections will be required. In all likelihood, program results will fall in between the worst- and best-case scenarios. Clearly, degree of compliance is a critical measure of program success, and it will help determine how much revision is necessary.

Before evaluating the overall results of the UST strategic regulatory plan, the subject of the final step, it is prudent to apply Ingram's framework for analyzing implementation success at this juncture.[3] By analyzing the UST plan with her framework now, the criteria she uses for assessing program success will be clearer later.

Ingram's Framework and the UST Plan

As table 2.1 showed, the nature of decision costs, the first variable in Ingram's framework, comprises negotiation costs and information costs. Since congressional support for cleaning up leaking USTs and preventing future spills was widespread, negotiation costs tended to be low. Information costs represent the "costs related to obtaining information about the operative causal connections between governmental actions and policy impacts and linkage among involved agencies" (e.g., EPA).[4] Such costs are high when one believes that certain governmental actions will have unpredictable results with unknown consequences, as in the case of the Hazardous and Solid Waste Amendments (HSWA). Under these conditions, Congress is likely to pass legislation with clear goals, giving little leeway to the agency in terms of timetables and deadlines, thereby limiting procedural flexibility (Ingram's second variable). Congress, however, may have to leave a certain amount of discretion to the agency in terms of setting standards. The application of step 4 of the strategic regulatory planning model indicates that these were the circumstances surrounding the enactment of the UST provisions of HSWA. Reading across the third row in table 2.1, policies that have low negotiation costs and high information costs should adopt an oversight and reformulation approach to implementation. Ingram points out that when "implementers are presented with ambitious goals and specific targets and deadlines, policy formulation and implementation become intermingled stages with continued legislative involvement in agency activities."[5] The National Academy of Public Administration (NAPA) plan, though conceived and implemented prior to the publication of her study, closely conforms to this scenario.

The latter portion of her framework involves the postimplementation issues concerning criteria for evaluation and the critical variables influencing program success. Again, reading across the third row in table 2.1, the UST type of policy should be evaluated by measuring the extent of policy learning that takes place. Given the complexity of HSWA's provisions regarding USTs, achievement of statutory goals may not be the only appropriate criterion to gauge success. The last component of her framework, which concerns the major variables that might affect the implementation of the four types of policies, indicates that the UST plan is most likely to be seriously affected by a lack of administrative capability. Thus, good administration of the UST program by EPA (and other responsible state and local agencies) should translate into successful implementation. Whether this and policy learning has occurred is addressed in the following sections.

Principal Changes since the UST Regulatory Plan Was Developed

In order to conduct a thorough expost review and revision, it is important to identify the conditions that have changed since the original program was developed. The strategic regulatory plan developed by NAPA and EPA planners was presented to EPA senior management in November 1985 and published in January 1986.[6] Since that time, five major changes have taken place:

1. The establishment of the $100 million a year trust fund program to clean up leaking USTs
2. The creation and institutionalization of EPA's Office of Underground Storage Tanks (OUST)
3. The promulgation of tank regulations and the development of a program design and direction by EPA
4. The development of state financial assurance and assistance funds
5. The creation of the UST Fields Initiative

Establishment of the Leaking Underground Storage Tank Trust Fund

Initially, NAPA and EPA planners argued that small businesses would have difficulty raising the funds needed to comply with HSWA's regulatory provisions. Two types of difficulties were identified by the program's planners. The first was raising the money needed to replace old, leaking tanks and install leak detection devices. This cost was considered high but potentially manageable as a normal cost of business. The second difficulty was far more serious: raising the funds needed to clean up tank leaks and paying damages from third-party lawsuits. As explained earlier, replacing tanks at a typical gasoline station and the cost of environmental cleanup and liability suits can be extremely high. These unpredictable and potentially devastating expenses led planners to recommend strongly that the agency require tank owners to carry cleanup and liability insurance. HSWA authorized but did not force EPA to require tank owners to carry insurance. When HSWA was enacted in 1984, it was very difficult to obtain liability insurance, and many tank owners were unable to obtain coverage.

In 1986 Congress created the Leaking Underground Storage Tank (LUST) Trust Fund to enforce corrective action by responsible parties and to clean up sites where the responsible party is not known or unable to respond. This fund, the result of an amendment to subtitle I of the Resource Conservation and Recovery Act (RCRA) was financed by a 0.1 cent tax on every gallon of gasoline sold nationwide. The tax raised about $150 million per year; over $1.6 billion was collected between 1987 and the fee's sunset in 1995. The tax was then reinstated in the Taxpayer Relief Act of 1997 and, under that statute, sunsets on March 31, 2005. As of 2001, its balance had swelled to approximately $2.6 billion, of which Congress appropriated $945 million to EPA through fiscal year 2001. At that time, EPA had given 85 percent, or $794 million, to state programs for administration, oversight, and cleanup. EPA has used the remaining 15 percent, or $151 million, to negotiate cooperative agreements, create programs on Indian lands, and further aid state and regional offices.[7] The legislation establishing the LUST Trust Fund significantly altered the statutory authority and financial resources devoted to tank regulation. Overall, it placed correction of leaking tanks on an equal and possibly superior footing with prevention of leaking tanks. With enactment of the UST Trust Fund, a high-priority federal effort to stimulate cleanup of tank leaks became a reality.

States must have a cooperative agreement with the federal government in order to receive LUST monies. These funds are divided among regional offices according to a formula using state-specific information. For fiscal year 2001, all fifty states had a cooperative agreement with EPA. By 2001, states had used one-third of LUST monies for administrative purposes, one-third for oversight and enforcement, and one-third for corrective action. Of all LUST cases, approximately 4 percent have been without a responsible party. On average, abatement actions at individual sites have cost $125,000.[8]

The idea of government funding for tank cleanup was originally discussed by the program's planners and rejected in favor of creating a situation where private insurance could be obtained at a reasonable cost. NAPA researchers in the mid–1980s encouraged EPA to enter into discussions with Congress on this issue. They thought that an aggressive EPA effort to require insurance would facilitate both leak prevention and cleanup. Insurance companies covering tank leaks could require adherence to EPA's new tank standards as a precondition for obtaining insurance. Similar to the role of state government in states where automobile insurance is required, EPA could focus its efforts on making certain that all tank owners carried insurance. An active EPA effort could create a large market for insurance and spread the risk among a large enough group of tank owners to lower the costs of coverage. The tank trust fund is essentially a form of government insurance. The initial underground tank strategy was formulated without knowing that such funds would be made available.

Creation of the Office of Underground Storage Tanks

In summer 1985, J. Winston Porter, then EPA's assistant administrator for the Office of Solid Waste and Emergency Response (OSWER) added a fourth branch to his organization, the Office of Underground Storage Tanks (OUST). Other offices already within OSWER included the Office of Emergency and Remedial Response (the hazardous waste Superfund program), the Office of Solid Waste (hazardous and solid waste regulation), and the Office of Waste Programs Enforcement (enforcement of Superfund and solid and hazardous waste regulation). Porter believed that the sheer scope of the tank regulation effort would require a new unit to oversee implementation and ensure compliance. While he could have easily divided responsibilities among his existing units, he and his advisers believed that these other units were already overburdened and, due to the size and complexity of the UST problem, a coordinated effort was required through a new office.

The designers of the strategic regulatory plan originally recommended that a new office be created. In fact, the organizational structure adopted by OUST adhered to the recommendation that a separate unit within a new office be devoted to implementing tank regulation. When OUST was created, it was divided into two branches: Standards and Regulation, and Implementation. Shortly after the Superfund Amendment and Reauthorization Act (SARA) was enacted, the UST Trust Fund program was assigned (by EPA senior management) to OUST. In autumn 1986 OUST established a third branch to oversee the trust-fund-financed cleanup program. This separate trust fund group was needed to allocate abatement funds quickly and facilitate rapid program start-up. Once the trust fund program was underway, OUST reorganized in spring 1987. The new organization included a policy division, an implementation division, and a new deputy director for program management. Overall, the institutionalization of OUST was a major development that followed the strategic regulatory plan submitted to EPA.

Development of Program Design and Direction

The establishment of OUST created organizational capabilities and limitations and gave the UST program a specific direction. This direction was derived from the combined expertise, attitudes, and energies of the people working in the program. Although a variety of planning documents were produced by OUST during its first eighteen months, its FY 1988 Program Guidance, submitted as part of EPA's Annual Agency Guidance, was probably the most accurate early statement of OUST's priorities.[9]

As might be expected in a regulatory agency, EPA's highest priority for the UST program in FY 1988 was to promulgate UST national standards and requirements. According to the guidance document, "Since a national regulatory program must be based first and foremost on a set of national standards and requirements, the completion of national standards continues to be the highest priority for OUST in FY 1988."[10]

A second important priority for OUST was to authorize state governments to implement the UST program. Although this task appears to be action-oriented, it is actually a fairly standard paper exercise of delegating federal authority to states. Many state governments are as far removed from hands-on tank management as the federal government. Due to the large size of the tank population, local governments tend to be the actual enforcers of underground tank regulation.

Establishing state programs was only the first link in a fairly long implementation chain. According to OUST, however, "States with approved programs . . . become the implementing arm of the national UST program, tailoring national requirements to reflect the unique environmental characteristics and governmental structure of each state."[11] OUST's position was that state delegation is a critical first step in establishing a functioning program. This is true. However, the reader should bear in mind that an approved state program is akin to an approved final regulation: it is a necessary but by no means sufficient condition for ensuring implementation. It may signify an active state program, or it may signify a state program that looks good on paper. The Program Guidance notes that

> in the long run, the success of a national program to regulate underground storage tanks depends on establishing strong local regulatory programs at the county or municipal government level. During FY 1987 and FY 1988, EPA will be working to assist local governments interested in regulating underground storage tanks. . . . However, this will not yet be a priority activity in FY 1988, since the first order of business is to assist states with developing state-level programs. As state programs become approved over the next couple of years, EPA will have more time to devote to the issue of local regulatory programs, and this will become one of EPA's priority efforts in FY 1989.[12]

The approach OUST adopted was to develop rules, then influence state policymaking, wait until FY 1989 to work with local governments, and only indirectly work with the very large regulated community.[13]

Another high-priority objective for the UST program was to implement the program directly in states unwilling to develop their own programs. (EPA also planned to develop UST programs directly with Indian tribes.) OUST's final high priority for FY 1988 was to administer the leaking UST trust fund program and distribute the $100 million allocated by Congress for cleanup. This involved reaching cooperative agreements with states to clean up leaking tanks.

By October 2000, the program priorities had evolved but were clearly related to the initial set of program objectives. In an October 23, 2000, memorandum on Underground Tank Program Initiatives, EPA assistant administrator Timothy Fields observed that "EPA and our state partners have made significant progress in protecting our nation's groundwater by ensuring that more than 1.4 million substandard underground storage tanks are no longer actively used. However, significant work remains to ensure that the 740,000 active underground storage tanks nationwide are operated properly and do not contaminate soil and groundwater. . . . As initial steps in addressing this remaining underground storage tank work EPA had identified [a] . . . framework of four priority initiatives."[14] The first of these initiatives was a pilot project program to redevelop brownfield sites in urban areas with abandoned or closed underground tanks. EPA estimated that there were approximately 200,000 of these out-of-service tanks in the United States, a significant proportion of the total remaining tank problem in the year 2000.

The UST Fields Initiative addresses brownfield sites contaminated by petroleum, sites not covered under Superfund law. Brownfields are abandoned or underused industrial and commercial properties that are perceived to be contaminated. In 2000, OUST estimated that of the 450,000 brownfield sites, approximately 200,000 contain USTs contaminated by petroleum. In October 2000, EPA selected ten pilot sites to receive up to $100,000 each from the LUST Trust Fund for cleanup. An additional forty sites were selected in June 2002 for petroleum cleanup in gasoline stations. Funding for the 2002 sites totaled $3.8 million in grants to twenty-six states and three tribes.[15]

The second priority program was an effort to improve compliance. The final underground tank regulations were not promulgated until 1998, but included well-defined new tank standards, upgrade or closure standards for existing tanks, and leak detection requirements. In 2000 EPA estimated that 85 percent of all tanks were in compliance with tank quality standards. However, in many states, only 60 percent of the tanks had acceptable leak detection systems.[16] To improve compliance, the updated UST implementation strategy called for improved data collection on compliance, specific state compliance targets, improved state-level inspection and enforcement programs, and continued provision of EPA technical assistance to states and tank owners.

The third priority program was to speed the pace of cleanup of petroleum releases from leaking tanks. In 2000, EPA estimated that there were 160,000 petroleum leaks requiring abatement throughout the nation. One area of particular concern (and of relevance to our book's other case study) was contamination due to MTBE releases. EPA would use a mix of programs such as national and regional cleanup targets, pilot projects, and technical assistance to improve cleanup rates.

The fourth priority was termed "evaluating UST system performance." According to EPA assistant administrator Fields, despite adherence to the 1998 regulations, "There is evidence of releases from compliant UST systems."[17] To execute this element of the tank implementation strategy, EPA would evaluate the performance of tanks in compliance to regulations and suggest improvements in requirements if necessary.

State Financial Assurance and Assistance Funds

Since OUST's creation, forty-three states developed State Financial Assurance Funds, providing a mechanism by which UST owners can comply with federal financial responsibility regulations. Funds are created by state legislation and are a supplement to or substitute for private insurance. Before a state fund can be used as a compliance mechanism, however, it must be approved by the EPA. These funds compensate owners and operators for the high cost of abatement and allow them to clean up past problems without going bankrupt in the process. From 1993 to 2003, states raised approximately $1 billion a year and expended more than $5 billion in cleanup funds. These state funds are an important funding source, as they represent twenty times more money than annual LUST fund appropriations.[18] Table 10.1 indicates which states had financial assurance funds in 2003.

In addition, financial assistance programs provide lenders with low interest loans or grants. Table 10.2 lists the sixteen states that offered this type of financial assistance in 2003.[19]

Table 10.1
State financial assurance funds

Approved[a]	Submitted[a]	Others
Alabama	Kentucky	Alaska—fund to reimburse cleanup costs
Arizona	Nebraska	Delaware—fund to reimburse cleanup costs
Arkansas	Pennsylvania	District of Columbia—no state fund
California	Virginia	Florida—no longer accepting requests
Colorado	Wisconsin	Hawaii—no state fund
Connecticut		Maryland—fund to reimburse cleanup
Georgia		Michigan—insolvent fund
Idaho		Oregon—no state fund
Illinois		Texas—no longer accepting claims
Indiana		Washington—state reinsurance program
Iowa		West Virginia—state subsidized insurance
Kansas		
Louisiana		
Maine		
Massachusetts		
Minnesota		
Mississippi		
Missouri		
Montana		
Nevada		
New Hampshire		
New Mexico		
New Jersey		
New York		
North Carolina		
North Dakota		
Ohio		
Oklahoma		
Rhode Island		
South Carolina		
South Dakota		
Tennessee		
Utah		
Vermont		
Wyoming		
35 states	5 states	10 states and District of Columbia

[a]State funds that have been approved or submitted to EPA and meet financial responsibility requirements.
Source: U.S. Environmental Protection Agency, "Status of State Funds," <http://www.epa.gov/oust/states/fndstatus.htm>, retrieved June 18, 2003.

Table 10.2
State financial assistance programs for USTs

California	Iowa	Massachusetts	Oregon
Delaware	Kentucky	Michigan	Pennsylvania
Hawaii	Maine	Minnesota	Utah
Idaho	Maryland	Ohio	Vermont

Source: U.S. Environmental Protection Agency, "Status of State Funds," <http://www.epa.gov/oust/states/fndstatus.htm>, retrieved June 18, 2003.

The Creation of the USTfields Initiative

The fifth change since the regulatory plan was developed was the UST fields program. According to EPA's Underground Tank Web site:

> To encourage the reuse of abandoned properties contaminated with petroleum from underground storage tanks [UST's], OUST created the USTfields Initiative in 2000. "USTfields" are abandoned or underused industrial and commercial properties where revitalization is complicated by real or perceived environmental contamination from underground storage tanks. The purpose of these pilots was to promote: the importance of public-private partnerships; the critical role of the state as the primary implementing agency; and the leveraging of private funds to maximize cleanups. A total of 50 USTfields Pilots were awarded up to $100,000 each from the LUST Trust Fund to assess, clean up and ready for reuse high-priority petroleum-impacted sites. (http:/www.epa.gov/oust/rags/ustfield.htm)

After the 50 UST fields pilots were awarded in July 2002, the program was discontinued and replaced by the Brownfields revolving loan fund, and was subsumed within that broader EPA program to reclaim urban land.

Conformity with the Original Plan

Enough time has passed to make an assessment of the overall success of the strategic regulatory plan. Although final conclusions cannot be reached, a meaningful evaluation of the success of the plan can certainly be presented. In following step 7 of the strategic regulatory planning model, Ingram's framework can be used to help evaluate the success of the UST program.

In determining success of implementation, it is also necessary to comment on whether the plan's recommendations were followed by the regulatory agency. An EPA focus on implementation, an effort to promote interest group interaction, the use of insurance requirements, and selective enforcement of compliance were the major components of the induced-compliance approach suggested by NAPA researchers. As we noted earlier, the primary distinguishing characteristic of these components was degree of coerciveness. Planners recommended that EPA involve state and local governments, interest groups, and industry in a systematic effort to encourage voluntary compliance. They recommended that EPA create a separate nonregulatory organizational unit to work with UST officials to stimulate and plan activities to improve tank management practices. They also suggested that the agency require tank owners to obtain insurance and focus government resources on enforcing compliance with the insurance requirement. Finally, planners suggested that EPA imitate the IRS by strategically selecting visible targets and enforcing HSWA's interim prohibition against installing new, unprotected USTs. Adherence by the EPA to these recommendations would suggest conformity to the basic structure of the NAPA plan and should lead to policy learning.

Organization Structure

The original organization structure of OUST closely adhered to the planners' recommendations. The function of implementing the regulatory aspects of the program would benefit by combining it with the resources and high-level attention generated by the trust fund. For that and other reasons, OUST was restructured. This reorganization allowed OUST to continue its effort to focus on implementation activities.

Approximately fifteen years later, the program had essentially the same structure, and after the National Performance Review of the Clinton administration, EPA had removed many branch-level and section-level organizations, creating a consolidated division structure. All of the functions performed in the late 1980s at the branch level continue to be performed in OUST in 2002—the development of policy, regulations, and guidance in all program areas is performed in the Policy and Standards Division—while relations with EPA's regional offices, states, local governments, and industry is coordinated by an Implementation Division. Office administrative functions, cross-cutting issues, and directives from above are handled in the immediate office of the director or deputy director.

Program Budget

From July through October 1986, OUST developed a program budget for FY 1987.[20] The OUST program budget described the organization's objectives and activities for FY 1987 and summarized spending and personnel allocations for each of seventy-five proposed projects. More than half of OUST's contract funding (53.2 percent) and over one-third of its staff time (35.8 percent) were allocated to implementation. Regulation development received about a quarter of the organization's personnel (25.4 percent) and contract (29.1 percent) funding. These figures were particularly striking in a new regulatory organization, where presumably a number of new requirements must be promulgated before implementation can even begin. This early program budget was an indication of OUST's intention to focus on implementation, a key recommendation of the strategic regulatory plan.

This emphasis on implementation continues today. The heavy field orientation is maintained by a small headquarters organization of thirty-three full-time staff. As in the early days, it is a program that focuses the vast majority of its human and financial resources on technical assistance to the states and compliance assistance to the regulated community. In part, this emphasis is possible because the material for which EPA is encouraging best management practices is a product (generally gasoline) and not a waste.

Organizational Behavior

If budgets and organization structures determine organization behavior, one can conclude that OUST has adhered to one of the basic principles of the strategic regulatory plan: the emphasis on inducing compliance. However, the plan was not simply an admonishment to emphasize such compliance. The strategic regulatory plan suggested that the new UST organization work with interest groups to encourage compliance, require tank insurance, and enforce tank laws.

Interest Group Relations

The plan suggested that the new UST organization convene an organized working group of UST policymakers from various levels of government and representatives of the target population and ask them to develop an annual work plan specifying the actions they would contribute to the regulatory program. Although EPA did not adopt this formal method of interest group interaction, the agency did begin an active program of interest group relations. Ron Brand, the first director of OUST, spent a great deal of time in the program's first four years meeting with interest groups and state and local tank regulators, presenting his vision of the UST program and focusing attention on the job of preventing and cleaning up tank leaks. He recognized the importance of involving external organizations in program implementation, but he did not attempt to achieve national-level coordination of their activities.

Over the next decade, EPA developed a strong federal-state partnership to educate UST owners and operators and inspect UST facilities. With this partnership, more than 1 million publications on achieving compliance with the 1988 regulations were distributed. EPA also made electronic versions available so that states could reproduce publications and make state-specific changes. In December 1999, this partnership was used to develop a compliance plan that was mandated by Congress.[21]

The implementation approach that OUST has adopted is similar to the operation of a franchise business. Rather than attempt to control every aspect of the UST program from Washington or even from EPA's regional offices, OUST has opted for the "loose-tight" management style of a franchise business. As Peters and Waterman note, simultaneous loose-tight management involves tight control over the organization's values and standard practices, with loose control over their application in specific situations.[22] OUST effectively initiated a new style of EPA management in both headquarters and the field, and it has in effect established a "sales force" in EPA's regional offices. The goal of this sales force has been to encourage state governments to open up "franchises," or "state-owned and -operated" UST programs. Over the past two decades, every state has developed a program, and in most cases even established state financial assurance funds to provide insurance to tank owners. The role of EPA headquarters in this design has emphasized quality control, research and development, marketing, training, and "product" (or policy) development. With this type of decentralized approach, much of the interest group interaction suggested by the plan has taken place at the state and local, rather than the federal, level. The degree to which this design has been established and has been successful is in many respects the central story of the federal underground tank program.

Required Insurance

With the enactment of SARA in 1986, the UST trust fund was created and tank owners were required to carry insurance. Originally, under HSWA, EPA was to be given a choice on the insurance issue; under SARA, Congress decided to mandate insurance. With its scarce staff and resource base, EPA had to choose between setting up an insurance compliance program or setting up the trust-fund-financed cleanup program. Through 1986 and 1987, EPA chose the latter and focused its efforts on developing cooperative agreements with state governments to fund tank cleanups. Although tank owners were required to carry insurance, in the early days of the program, EPA had not developed a system for administering and enforcing this requirement. However, in 1988 and 1989, the insurance issue came to the forefront, and the heavy emphasis placed on insurance by the strategic regulatory plan was eventually reflected in EPA's program.

In 1988 and 1989, the insurance issue was a major source of frustration to both EPA and the regulated community.[23] Although federal law mandated that EPA enforce an insurance requirement, very few companies were willing to sell insurance. In 1989, a phased-in insurance regulation came into effect, and initially many small businesses were unable to purchase coverage. With estimates that possibly one-third of the nation's tanks were leaking, insurance companies wrote very few policies. In the private words of one insurance executive, "We don't cover [write insurance policies for] burning buildings." In June 1989, a front-page article in the *New York Times* described the problem.[24] In that article, Jerry Ferrara, executive vice president of the New Jersey Gasoline Retailers Association, observed that "the small guy is on the horns of a dilemma. First he's got the problem of his underground tanks, and then he's got to buy insurance, which is not available." In that same article, Brand noted the importance of the insurance requirement and observed that insurance was slowly reemerging in the market. According to him, "The big thing now is the insurance. That has been almost impossible to get for the little guy. But there are signs that problem is beginning to come around."

In the late 1980s through 2000, a market for commercial insurance developed, albeit slowly. Insurers were reluctant to insure tanks, yet there was also a low demand for insurance since state and federal funds were available for cleanup. These state "financial assurance" funds paid for tank abatement and enabled tank owners to claim they had access to cleanup funds and therefore met the legal requirement to demonstrate the financial capacity to clean up tank leaks. This was done without private insurance. The extensive use of these state funds, however, led to solvency problems, which created the need for alternative mechanisms to finance abatement.[25]

In the 1990s, federal LUST fund appropriations declined and state assurance fund revenues increased. By 1993, state funds raised approximately $900 million and increased revenues by 30 percent from 1993 to 1996. Yet data on state claims in the late 1990s reveal outstanding claims amounting to $2.8 billion, with a current balance of $1.3 billion and current income at $1.2 billion per year. Claims were beginning to exceed fund supply. The Association of State Underground Storage Tank Cleanup Funds reported that fourteen states had set dates after which they would no longer cover new releases. Ten of these dates fell before the year 2000, and the association expected more states to make the transition to other finance mechanisms in the future.[26]

With the growing demand for LUST funds, states and industry urged Congress to increase LUST appropriations and broaden the use of the fund. In April 1997, the House passed HR688, the Leaking Underground Storage Tank Amendments Act of 1997, to achieve this goal. The Senate Environment and Public Works Committee reported similar legislation, S555, in October 1998. Since the 105th Congress in 1997–1998, however, there has not been further legislative action on this issue, and it remains unresolved.[27]

With this climate, the demand for commercial liability insurance will grow as more state funds are phased out. This projected demand is also occurring at a time when commercial liability insurance has become affordable and available for tanks that meet all technical requirements. Since most potential insurance customers were covered by state trust funds, there has been a low demand for commercial insurance. This low demand led to severe competition among the five major insurance companies that dominate this market. Such competition led to shorter forms, less cumbersome tests, and lower premiums. Today, there are more commercial insurance providers for storage tank owners, and the average premium is $400 per tank, whereas in the late 1980s, the average premium was about $1,000.[28]

In conclusion, the insurance requirement suggested by the strategic regulatory plan, while not initially a central element of OUST, has become a major focus of the program. EPA's experience with the insurance issue has led to a great deal of policy learning on the part of the agency.

Selective Enforcement

The selective enforcement proposal took a back seat in the early stages of implementation to establish the program's policy and institutional structure. More recently, states have taken measures to ensure that tank owners and operators are complying with the 1998 deadline. As of 2000, twenty states mandated some form of regulatory requirement on fuel delivery companies, including prohibiting fuel delivery to noncompliant tanks, which has proven to be a successful and cost-effective approach to ensuring compliance.[29] In addition, criminal charges have been brought against companies that fail to perform proper testing of UST facilities. For example, on July 24, 2002, the U.S. government filed criminal charges against Tanknology–NDE International, Inc. in ten federal district courts.[30] The company has since pleaded guilty to all ten felony charges that employees falsified statements to federal agencies.[31] EPA is expected to involve state and local governments further in ensuring that tank owners and operators are complying with the law. This will improve EPA's ability to administer the UST program at the federal level.

Explaining Behavior

The difference between the plan's recommendations and EPA action was due to deliberate policy or management choices, the effect of EPA standard practices, and changed conditions. The plan, of course, was a static document. Although it shaped management philosophy at the start of the program, its influence was largely indirect after a few years. When the program began, OUST decided to emphasize program development before actual implementation and devoted most of its resources to designing the program. In large measure, this meant developing the standards and guidelines needed to begin the program. Once those were in place, the emphasis on implementation called for in the plan became truly infused within the organization's culture.

In 1986 and 1987 OUST attempted to assemble a new type of staff to implement a new form of regulatory program. The office was trying to build a headquarters organization that would support, rather than oversee, state, local, and private efforts to improve tank management practices. During the preliminary stages of the UST program, there was less interest in attaining high rates of compliance with specific statutory requirements. Instead, policymakers wanted to reduce the number of underground containers that were leaking and quickly clean up any containers that did leak. The strategy was to focus state and local government efforts on the activities of tank owners and operators. To the extent possible, EPA's resources would be used to support interaction between local government and the regulated community. Thus, OUST's immediate goal was to protect and improve the quality of the environment.

Although this approach was in accord with the general concepts advanced by the planners, Brand initially had a difficult time persuading his staff to follow his direction. His difficulties stemmed from the impact of EPA's standard practices. Despite direct action programs such as Superfund and sewage treatment construction grants, EPA is essentially a regulatory agency. It primarily writes rules and sues private parties to force compliance with those rules. With the exception of pesticides, most of the pollutants that EPA regulates are waste materials. As stated before, the materials stored in the underground tanks are consumer products, and it is in the regulated community's economic self-interest to keep its product from leaking. This was a difference that OUST was determined to exploit.

Brand encountered administrative problems because his staff came from other regulatory programs in EPA and were already used to formulating rules in a certain way. In the development of regulatory programs, they tended to conduct a great deal of technical research, anticipate every loophole in their rules, and carefully specify required behavior. Usually, little effort was invested in trying to understand the likely impact of a rule on actual private behavior.

In OUST's first year, Brand attempted to instill in his staff a greater concern for practical feasibility and environmental improvement. Some of the staff questioned his perspective and insisted on following the traditional approach to regulation. He asked his staff to develop a simple set of tank standards backed up by short turnaround research projects. He found some of his staff unwilling or unable to follow this request. After several months of conflict, the tank regulation effort fell behind schedule, and the head of OUST's regulation branch was transferred out of the program. As the organization evolved, Brand recruited a new regulation chief and staff more willing to try a new approach to rule making. Soon after, a set of simple, practical tank standards was promulgated with great speed and effectiveness.

In addition to difficulty with the drafting of guidelines, OUST experienced problems getting its implementation program underway. The branch responsible for implementation found itself involved in a wide range of critical functions, but it was not able to develop an effective field orientation. Problems beyond the control of the implementation branch delayed program execution. When the effort to draft guidelines faltered, this unit helped draft guidelines. A support contract to augment scarce implementation staff was held up by the contracts office and was awarded over eight months behind schedule. Finally, routine program maintenance tasks such as budget development, space acquisition, and management information also fell to this unit.

The enactment of the trust fund in 1986 dramatically changed OUST's early mission and made it difficult at the outset to adhere closely to the strategic regulatory plan designed at the start of the program. OUST was given a nonregulatory mission and resources that shifted EPA's short-term emphasis from leak prevention to environmental cleanup. As might be expected, the initial effect of this new program was to draw energy and resources away from other parts of the program. With the enactment of the trust fund, OUST had four distinct functions: regulation development, trust fund operations, internal maintenance, and implementation support. OUST was being closely watched and, as a new organization, its competence judged on its ability to complete the first three tasks. If guidelines were late, EPA would probably be sued, and senior management would notice. If the trust fund resources were not spent, Congress would complain, and again senior management would notice. If OUST's budget submission was inadequate, the organization's image inside the agency would suffer. Improved environmental conditions are difficult to measure, and therefore efforts to improve tank management directly were constantly assigned lower priority than the organization's other three functions.

Hence, the first three functions commanded the periodic attention of EPA's senior management while implementation did not. In a more evolved, fully institutionalized program, implementation and quantifiable environmental results would begin to receive senior-level attention. In fact, evidence of this concern exists throughout the 1990s, although other functions dominated early in the program. Staff, of course, respond to the cues of senior management. The best and brightest staff members are usually drawn to the higher-visibility and higher-priority, short-run missions. There is almost a herdlike movement toward high-priority, short-run tasks. To succeed at implementing a longer-term design, a manager must either protect his staff from being drawn away or create an artificial sense of frenzy around discrete pieces of long-term tasks.

In 1988 and 1989, with the basic program structure in place, OUST began to focus nearly all of its attention on implementation. In 1988, it decided to train its staff in the techniques of continuous quality improvement. The logical extension of the emphasis on changing the behavior of polluters was to focus on changing the behavior of regulators. OUST senior management assumed that an emphasis on implementation in the field would not succeed without an effort to develop effective internal work habits.

OUST entered the 1990s with a new and renewed focus on implementation. The large-scale, macro-strategic concerns that guided the 1985 regulatory planning process were replaced by concerns for policy-making on a micro level. The UST program continued to adhere to the overall approach of inducing compliance, but in certain respects this approach has become more of a general philosophy. As an organization matures, its tasks become increasingly specific. With the central tenets of the original plan institutionalized, OUST has placed greater emphasis on implementation. Using the business franchise as a model for working with states and learning the techniques of continuous quality improvement are logical expressions of the concern for implementation expressed in the original plan.

The original plan's strategy of implementation through the states continued into the next decade. In 2000, Fields stressed the importance of state involvement in identifying compliance problems and finding their solutions. He set four priorities for OUST to follow in working with state and federal regulatory agencies: raise the compliance level of UST sites, continue evaluating the efficiency of UST requirements, increase the number of cleanups, and use the UST Fields Initiative to increase cleanups.[32]

This heightened attention toward implementation was also stressed by Congress. On October 13, 1999, Congress directed EPA to prepare and submit a compliance plan for the UST program by May 1, 2000. This plan identified all tanks in temporary closure, determined the ownership of USTs not in compliance, highlighted plans for owners and operators to bring tanks into compliance or out of temporary closure, and described how tanks not in compliance will be brought into compliance. Overall, the report documented much success in terms of closures and abatement. (The findings of this report are discussed below.) The report noted that the key to improvement is regular, particularly annual, inspection. In 2002, most state inspections occurred every three years. States with frequent inspection cycles, every twelve to eighteen months, had higher compliance rates than the national average at that time.[33]

Marianne Horinko, the EPA assistant administrator who succeeded Fields, also stressed the importance of partnerships in implementing her fiscal year 2003 priorities. These priorities, like Fields's, stressed increasing the compliance level of UST sites. Other priorities included enhancing emergency preparedness (counterterrorism), promoting revitalization as a complement to traditional cleanup, developing the One Cleanup Program to unify the management of waste programs at all levels of government, developing OUST's workforce and instituting succession training, educating consumers on making purchasing decisions to benefit the environment, and increasing recycling and energy efforts for hazardous and nonhazardous substances.[34] The remainder of this chapter discusses revisions in the original program and assesses whether the program is working.

Assessing Adherence to the Original Plan

It seems clear that some of the strategic regulatory plan's recommendations were given serious consideration by OUST management and, in fact, influenced the development of the UST program over the past two decades. It is difficult to distinguish the unique approach taken by OUST from the influence of the plan. Clearly, OUST was influenced by the plan; however, it is impossible to measure the exact extent of that influence. A mind-set was beginning to develop in EPA that was shared by OUST and the drafters of the UST plan. In particular, there was a strong desire to move beyond the symbolic gestures that often dominated environmental programs and focus more on concrete environmental improvements. The UST program and the early life of OUST are related elements, and at times it is difficult to identify a direct causal flow. The UST program budget and organization structure described in this chapter are concrete examples of OUST's determination to focus on controlling the behavior of the regulated community.

Relative conformity seems evident, given that a few years after the initiation of the UST program, most of the organization's activities were in pursuit of the broad directions set by the original plan. The emphases on implementation and on insurance were accepted elements of the program, and as the regulations were implemented, activities were underway to target enforcement. While some logistical problems were initially encountered, experience and readjustments led to an operationally and institutionally secure program. This could not have occurred unless significant policy learning had taken place. Rather than revise the strategic regulatory plan, the EPA focused its efforts on narrow tasks, using many of the steps introduced in the planning model to address micro-level issues.

An example of this policy approach took place in spring 1988 as OUST was adopting regulations due in December 1988. These regulations required that all USTs be upgraded with spill, overfill, and corrosion protection; meet new tank standards; or be closed by 1998.[35] Under the UST regulations, tank owners must install leak detection devices or adopt leak detection procedures. This requirement was being phased in, and the first effective date of the requirement was December 23, 1989. At that time, all tanks that were over twenty-five years old were required to have leak detection systems. A team composed of UST staff, state officials, consultants, and others analyzed the obstacles to complying with the new requirement and developed a policy to communicate and implement the rule. Many of the steps outlined in the model presented in this book were pursued. A number of carefully thought-out activities were suggested and begun. This same type of approach took place in a number of other UST program areas throughout the 1990s.

Is the Program Working? Data on UST Implementation

Another important test of the plan's success is whether the behavior of implementers and regulated parties changed as a result of the federal UST program. While Ingram might consider this criterion less important for this type of regulatory approach than policy learning, OUST (as well as NAPA researchers) regarded it as a significant question and published a set of estimates on changes in tank management practices.[36] The estimates included the commitment of state and local resources to administering the UST programs; private investment of funds in UST management; the number and type of tanks installed since 1984; the number of tanks leaking each year; and the number of cleanups initiated each year. Such measures provide an estimate of the overall effectiveness of the policy.

The Commitment of State and Local Resources

The strategies of induced compliance and franchising the federal program to the states require, at a minimum, state authority to regulate USTs. The number of states with their own laws regulating underground tanks has grown dramatically since 1980. The federal government has clearly provided an example to the states. Based on the data, the number of state programs grew from eleven just prior to the enactment of HSWA in 1984 to thirty-two in 2002. By 2002, thirty-one states, as well as the District of Columbia and the Commonwealth of Puerto Rico, had approved state programs. The following states had approved programs: Alabama, Arkansas, Connecticut, Delaware, Georgia, Iowa, Kansas, Louisiana, Maine, Maryland, Massachusetts, Minnesota, Mississippi, Montana, Nevada, New Hampshire, Nebraska, New Mexico, North Carolina, North Dakota, Oklahoma, Rhode Island, South Carolina, South Dakota, Tennessee, Texas, Utah, Vermont, Virginia, Washington, and West Virginia. State program approval (SPA) regulations set criteria for states to garner the authority to operate in lieu of the federal program. "SPA's must meet three criteria: (1) it sets standards for eight performance criteria that are no less stringent than federal standards; (2) it contains provisions for adequate enforcement; and (3) it regulates the same USTs as are regulated under federal statute."[37]

Private Investment of Funds in UST Management

A concrete sign of compliance is when private parties spend money to meet regulatory requirements. The largest private sector investment in tank management was in tank replacement. Most of the major oil companies began major efforts to replace their tanks. With data collected between 1984 and 1988, the EPA reported and projected dramatic increases in private investment in tank management.

Number of Tanks Leaking Each Year

The UST program has two bottom-line indicators of success: the number of tanks leaking and the number of leaks cleaned up. Thus, there is both a prevention and a correction dimension to the program. According to EPA estimates, approximately 46,000 tanks leaked each year prior to regulation in the early 1980s. Since the inception of OUST, confirmed releases average 30,000 annually, with fewer releases over the past few years, a likely result of UST closure or upgrade that met the 1998 compliance deadline.[38]

The Number of Leaking Underground Tanks: Closures and Cleanups

Since 1988, state agencies reported significant results in tank closures and cleanups; approximately 10,000 to 40,000 cleanups are completed each year. As of September 30, 2001, OUST reported that 1.5 million unsafe tanks had been closed. In addition, over 20,000 UST releases were confirmed. Of this number, more than 277,000 cleanups have taken place, and 150,000 cleanups remain. Overall, about eight in ten tanks are in compliance with federal regulations.[39] Table 10.3 highlights the cumulative number of active and closed tanks, reported releases, cleanups initiated and completed, and emergency responses taken in the past decade.

What Do These Data Mean?

There is little question that the management of underground storage containers changed dramatically in the mid–1980s. It is, of course, difficult to attribute this change entirely to the adoption and implementation of HSWA and the strategic regulatory plan. In fact, one could argue that the enactment of HSWA in 1984 alone set in motion all of the improvements documented thus far. Or one could argue that increased levels of environmental awareness contributed to these improvements. Although it is not possible to establish a direct correlation between the strategic regulatory program and changed behavior, the data at a minimum suggest a strong relationship. As long as the trend lines continue in the observed directions, EPA is certainly justified in following the path it has chosen. Similarly, it is reasonable to conclude that compliance is being induced and that the UST program has been a success.

As a preliminary check on these conclusions, a group of graduate students at Columbia University in 1989 analyzed compliance with the new regulations. To make the test as severe as possible, the project focused on owners of underground tanks that did not sell gasoline as a main part of their business. The study team believed that these tank owners would be less informed about the new regulations than the outlets of major oil companies. The students interviewed forty-one tank owners in the New York metropolitan area and found that 61 percent had indeed heard of the regulations, 70 percent intended to comply with the rules, and 37 percent believed they were already in compliance.[40] The study team also found that tank owners had a fairly sophisticated understanding of the UST issue and were surprisingly well informed about the new rules. When the EPA and Columbia University studies are considered together, it seems clear that major behavioral change has taken place and that state activities encouraged by EPA are contributing to that change.

Table 10.3
Cumulative UST data

Date[a]	Number of active tanks	Tanks closed	Confirmed releases	Cleanups initiated	Cleanups completed	Emergency responses
2nd half 2002	697,966	1,525,402	427,307	384,029	284,602	13,615
1st half 2002	698,607	1,519,302	422,573	387,190	277,171	13,207
2nd half 2001	704,717	1,499,167	418,918	379,243	268,833	13,298
1st half 2001	716,018	1,468,626	417,077	375,877	258,638	12,864
2nd half 2000	713,666	1,459,627	412,393	367,603	249,759	12,639
1st half 2000	742,805	1,417,711	405,030	357,268	241,858	12,254
2nd half 1999	760,504	1,377,115	397,821	346,300	228,925	11,874
1st half 1999	824,465	1,325,829	385,927	327,210	211,637	11,455
2nd half 1998	891,686	1,236,007	371,387	314,965	203,247	10,688
1st half 1998	919,540	1,186,431	358,269	301,842	192,065	10,300
2nd half 1997	969,652	1,150,824	341,773	292,446	178,297	9,856
1st half 1997	1,031,960	1,111,266	329,940	276,603	162,431	9,675
2nd half 1996	1,064,478	1,074,022	317,488	252,615	152,683	9,216
1st half 1996	1,093,018	1,043,437	314,720	241,787[b]	141,185	8,863
4th quarter 1995	1,093,105	983,877	303,635	238,671	131,272	8,600
3rd quarter 1995	1,113,872	980,616	295,621	232,703	126,434	8,392
2nd quarter 1995	1,143,755	954,802	288,272	225,341	119,762	8,172
1st quarter 1995	1,161,760	937,778	278,038	216,360	112,071	8,160
4th quarter 1994	1,177,198	907,333	270,567	209,797	107,448	8,045
3rd quarter 1994	1,214,486	892,394	262,829	202,866	101,309	7,815

2nd quarter 1994	1,233,607	868,592	254,253	194,869	96,841	7,699
1st quarter 1994	1,297,929	781,143	245,749	185,135	90,529	7,491
4th quarter 1993	1,307,563	751,921	237,022	171,082	87,065	7,280
3rd quarter 1993	1,312,487	704,990	226,791	79,488	7,173	77,463
2nd quarter 1993	1,355,894	673,985	217,386	165,701	74,655	6,818
1st quarter 1993	1,511,257	584,591	202,418	148,007	69,847	6,487
4th quarter 1992	1,565,613	492,391	184,457	129,074	99,496	55,444
3rd quarter 1992	1,565,613	457,536	166,731	113,774	88,526	44,008
2nd quarter 1992	1,565,613	392,260	156,287	106,157	80,181	38,709
1st quarter 1992	1,365,261	361,053	137,040	86,090	29,723	5,132
4th quarter 1991	1,788,505	314,858	126,816	79,506	58,258	26,666
3rd quarter 1991	Not reported	288,403	116,861	71,166	23,717	47,196
2nd quarter 1991	Not reported	259,654	108,821	65,216	21,278	48,147
1st quarter 1991	Not reported	216,868	95,514	59,177	3,301	40,091

[a]Each fiscal quarter and half year begins in October.
[b]Ohio reported a correction from the previous year of 9,814 cleanups causing a drop in the national number of cleanups
Source: U.S. Environmental Protection Agency, Office of Underground Storage Tanks, "Corrective Action Measures Archive," <www.epa.gov/oust/cat/camarchv.htm>, retrieved June 18, 2003.

Summary

In following step 7 of the strategic regulatory planning model, ex post review and revision, this chapter analyzed EPA's implementation of the UST program since 1984. After applying Ingram's framework, it is evident that the implementation of the UST strategic regulatory plan has been successful. The postimplementation problem of administrative capability predicted by the framework was clearly a large part of the early difficulties experienced by Brand and EPA, affecting implementation of the statute, if only temporarily. Creative leadership on the part of Brand enabled the program to withstand and overcome the logistical problems, with a large amount of policy learning taking place as a result. Oversight and reformulation tactics recommended by Ingram were used in ways that allowed the implementation to proceed as favorably as possible. Furthermore, NAPA researchers and EPA officials were most concerned about achieving compliance with UST rules and improving environmental quality. Given the data reported by OUST, the program has also been successful in attaining these objectives. Further improvements in EPA's administration of the UST program can only help to improve environmental quality.

Conclusion

One purpose of part I of this book was to explain the strategic regulatory plan for the implementation of the UST provisions of HSWA. The Introduction and chapter 1 discussed at length the problems of policy formulation, the tendency of separating policy formulation from implementation, and why policymaking is rarely strategic. Chapter 2 outlined a seven-step model for the development of a strategic regulatory plan: (1) problem recognition, (2) identification of parties, (3) historical analysis, (4) situational analysis, (5) strategic regulation formulation, (6) ex ante review, and (7) ex post review/revision. Chapter 3 expanded on the most significant component of the model, strategic regulation formulation, by introducing a conceptual framework for selecting regulatory devices. Based on the conditions in the regulated community, regulating agency, and outside arena, regulatory devices were thought to occupy varying positions on cost and coercion continua. Different rates of compliance would be achieved depending on which devices were chosen and the overall government effort. Chapter 4 analyzed the strengths and weaknesses of alternative regulatory mechanisms, particularly with respect to the management of USTs. From the start, the long-range objective of the model was the development of a program to achieve a high rate of compliance and improved environmental quality.

Part II applied each step of the strategic regulatory planning model to the MTBE problem. In an effort to explain the emergence of nonstrategic regulatory planning, chapters 5 to 7 examined the reformulated gasoline (RFG) requirements mandated by the 1990 Clean Air Act. Using MTBE contamination as a primary unintended consequence, it was suggested that even science-based policy can be problematic if broader strategic objectives are not clearly understood. Chapter 5 examined the environmental impacts of MTBE in gasoline and its prevalence as a groundwater pollutant. Chapter 6 explored the RFG provisions of the Clean Air Act in an effort to determine why strategic failures occurred. The failures we identified included bureaucratic insulation between regulators working on air quality and regulators working on water quality, a failure to assess the discrete impacts of introducing MTBE into the environment, resistance to emerging evidence of MTBE contamination, and confusing the unique chemical properties of MTBE contamination with the traditional problem of leaking underground storage tanks. Finally, chapter 7 analyzed how the MTBE problem might have been avoided had policymakers followed the strategic regulatory planning model introduced in this study. The strategic model would have permitted regulators to respond more effectively to the MTBE problem as a national concern. The model would have assisted in defining the MTBE problem comprehensively, mitigating MTBE contamination while preserving air quality benefits. In addition, considering the initial 1991 regulatory negotiation that framed the regulatory process, a collaborative process could have been established to work through the strategic response. Finally, the process should work toward the development of a national program that fully accommodates the successes that have occurred across the many affected states.

Part III applied each step of the model to the UST problem. In order to comprehend fully how the different steps of the model were applied, chapter 8 executed steps 1 through 4, in essence, the background work needed to design an effective program for regulating underground tanks. The seriousness and general dynamics of the UST problem were pointed out in this part of the study. Chapter 9 then applied the fifth and sixth phases of the model. Within this context, the framework for the selection of specific regulatory mechanisms (from chapter 3) and the evaluation of various regulatory devices (in chapter 4) were followed. The ex ante review highlighted several potential problems that could hinder the effectiveness of the overall strategic regulatory plan. Step 7, the ex post review/revision stage of the model, was carried out in chapter 10. Based on data collected thus far, the UST program has been a significant influence on the behavior of target groups and must be considered successful.

This chapter ties together several loose ends and offers an analysis of the MTBE and underground tank cases. It begins by discussing a number of general principles of strategic regulatory planning and then assesses the MTBE issue. The study then reviews and evaluates the components of the UST regulatory program, with particular attention paid to the use of liability insurance. This is followed by the limitations of the study and its potential application to other policy areas. Finally, the value of adopting a design perspective in the development of public policy is discussed.

Strategic Regulatory Planning

The strategic approach to policy formulation and implementation, as explained in this study, leads directly to a set of identifiable steps for government officials to follow in structuring effective regulatory programs. The strategic approach places a heavy emphasis on the motivation, resources, and interdependencies among affected parties. In addition, it requires close examination and comprehension of regulatory goals and objectives as set forth by a legislative or other governmental body. In the best-case scenario, substantial interaction occurs between those who are writing laws and those who must execute them. All too frequently, however, this does not happen. The model presented in this study seeks to fit the selected regulatory plan with both the environment from which it is authorized or enforced and the environment from which compliance must result. Only by creating the best possible fit between the plan and these environments can the behavior of the target group be modified most efficiently and effectively and at the least cost.

If this is to be accomplished, policymakers must educate themselves about the dynamics of the regulatory issue in question. It is critical, for example, that policymakers closely research the characteristics of the target group involved, as well as the relevant social, economic, and political circumstances that surround the daily activities of the target group. The conditions in the regulatory agency also deserve careful consideration. Full knowledge of the strengths and weaknesses of available regulatory mechanisms can help avoid costly mistakes and delays in the long run.

In this case, policymakers must determine at the outset how much compliance is required to lead to improved environmental quality. The setting of compliance objectives at different points in time before the plan has been implemented can provide benchmarks for later policy evaluation and modification. Failure to reach predetermined compliance goals can be used by agency officials to justify requests for additional resources or legislation to increase compliance rates.[1]

These requirements for strategic regulatory planning underscore the need to obtain the most accurate data and information available on critical variables. Admittedly, it is difficult to project, for example, what type of technology is likely to be developed in response to regulatory requirements or how many marginal businesses will be forced out of existence by a particular rule. Often it is difficult to measure and understand certain variables. However, policymakers ought to be encouraged to estimate as accurately as possible the impact of key factors on the regulatory process and compliance. Although regulatory impact analyses (RIAs) require the federal government to assess the economic benefits and costs of regulations, they do not provide an assessment of the probability of compliance. Policymakers need to assess the capability of regulated parties to comply and should identify the positive and negative incentives that will be needed to motivate compliant behavior. They should also identify the resources and institutional capability that is needed to generate and deploy these incentives. Some policymakers assume that as long as a rule is formally promulgated and a few violators are punished, compliance will automatically follow. This is not the case most of the time.

This study is not advocating massive data collection efforts. Rather, it is urging that policymakers develop meaningful links to the real world and methods of measuring the impact of their policies on that world. Modest record keeping and the maintenance of realistic program indicators are critical in tracking program progress. Management should travel to the regulated sites and talk to people who have suffered from negative environmental impacts as part of this process. The real world may be summarized in a spreadsheet, but its full dimensions are best perceived firsthand.

Management information systems must be augmented by direct exposure to the regulatory environment. Admittedly, uncertainty increases as the issue becomes more complex.[2] An aim of strategic planning is to reduce uncertainty as much as humanly possible and thereby escape major long-term errors. However, neither people nor institutions learn without making mistakes. The purpose of small-scale pilot projects and crafting strategies is to learn from small mistakes as soon as possible, and thus avoid making serious errors later. To be sure, the federal government spends millions of dollars on testing new military equipment for exactly this reason. It also makes sense to experiment with different approaches in the areas of social and environmental regulation.

One of the most significant characteristics of strategic regulatory planning is that it is a dynamic, tactical, and evolutionary process. The evolutionary nature of the approach, where improvement over previous actions is desired, will require policymakers to return to the model on many occasions. The structure of the model is simple and flexible enough to permit this activity until compliance goals are fulfilled. Despite careful preparation, however, problems are bound to arise during implementation. A well-coordinated but modest evaluation and feedback system, once in place, can help temper the negative impact of unforeseen difficulties and can lead to reasonably quick modifications in program design. Multiple but moderate efforts at data and information gathering therefore remain a crucial and ongoing exercise throughout the life of the regulatory program.

Strategic regulatory planning can be likened to coaching a football team. At the college and professional levels, successful coaches prepare extensively for each game. Offensive and defensive players learn the tendencies of the opposing team based on past records, scouting reports, and films of previous games. A game plan is formulated to take full advantage of the strengths of the coach's team and the weaknesses of the opposing team. Similar to chess, tactics and plays are decided on ahead of time. Once the game begins, substantial and rapid adjustments are made to counter unforeseen behavior. Regardless of whether the team wins or loses, further study and additional modifications are made before the next game and during the course of the season.

In both football and regulatory policymaking, improvement is continuously sought. Several vantages are used to make midcourse corrections during the game itself. Coaches in the press box high above the field of play observe patterns of behavior on the field and communicate their observations to the head coach on the sideline. Reports from players on the field on what is working and not working are factored into play selection. Different approaches are attempted to test the reaction of the opposition. As in football, the strategic regulatory approach requires policymakers to design comprehensive game plans, replete with well-thought-out tactical options, prior to taking the field. However, these plans must be flexible enough to allow for prompt responses to changing conditions.

The perspective taken in strategic regulatory planning runs counter to some of the tenets of incremental policymaking. In contrast to incremental policymaking, strategic regulatory planning necessitates the collection of substantial amounts of data and information regarding the circumstances surrounding a given issue. Rather than being disjointed and remedial, strategic regulatory planning emphasizes rapid institutional learning. Lessons learned are factored into policymaking as rapidly as possible. In a sense, incrementalism is the operation of cybernetic mechanisms until they fail. Strategic planning is the search for new cybernetic mechanisms and new standard operating procedures before they fail. Small-scale experiments are tried in the hope of replacing old standard operating procedures with new, more effective ones. It is not remedial; rather than trying to remedy failures after they occur, an attempt is made to head off expected failures before they occur. The process is characterized by continuous feedback, evaluation, and correction, with progress (i.e., increased compliance) as the objective. In this sense, policymakers are urged to set realistic goals and attempt to build slowly effective ways of reaching those goals. They are encouraged to move toward solutions rather than away from problems, but are not encouraged to believe that a single master plan can ever be used to accomplish a broad aim. The literature and practice of urban planning rejected comprehensive planning because the results were typically large-scale, inhumane housing projects and superhighways that destroyed communities. Yet planning and goal-seeking behavior can take place within the fabric of an organic entity. A series of well-thought-through, small-scale developments can create a city of beauty and human scale. It is therefore possible to take small steps in the direction of predetermined goals, and that is precisely what strategic regulatory planning is designed to do.

In summary, strategic planning requires policymakers to take a tactical approach in developing regulatory programs and to link policy formulation with implementation. They are encouraged to study the entire playing field carefully before deciding on a course of action. The crafting of good public policies necessitates consideration of all facets of the problem without prejudice. Thus, strategic regulatory planning incorporates positive aspects of rational policymaking and incrementalism. The model introduced in this study, while far from being perfect, encourages policymakers to do exactly that.

Employing Outside Organizations

As demonstrated in this study, the involvement of neutral, outside organizations can greatly enhance the strategic planning process.[3] In 1984, the National Academy of Public Administration (NAPA), working closely with EPA, was able to assemble an outstanding panel of professionals and skilled research staff to analyze objectively the various aspects of the UST problem and offer a comprehensive plan. The influence of ideology, individual power brokers, and interest groups, normally substantial in incremental decision making, was kept at a minimum. Deliberations were generally smooth and productive, leading to key insights and prudent policy decisions. When examining EPA's behavior in the MTBE case, one is struck by the narrowness of the perspective taken and the need to listen to outside voices and beyond the beltway analysis.

Some might find fault with employing outside research bodies to craft public policy for the government. One could argue, for example, that the extensive use of research organizations in policymaking is an elitist attempt to circumvent the will of the people.[4] After all, members of these organizations are not elected by the public or appointed to their positions by elected officials. The model outlined in this study, however, encourages policymakers to seek the views of all concerned parties and to consider them in the formulation of a regulatory program. As this study maintains, public support is essential in achieving compliance with UST regulations. It is no less an issue in MTBE regulation. This will frequently be the case in other areas as well.

MTBE Regulation

One of the criticisms commonly heard about EPA is that its medium-specific orientation results in stovepipe thinking that focuses on a single issue to an extreme degree. However, EPA is not simply organized by environmental media. It is also organized geographically, with most of its staff in regional offices. It also includes functional units in enforcement, international affairs, and policy analysis—to name only a few of these nonmedia offices. Still, the agency's success has been built on its ability to focus narrowly on specific sources of pollution and specific targets of pollution such as air, land, and water. The MTBE problem is a classic case of cross-media environmental pollution. A solution to an air pollution problem is the cause of a water pollution problem. In essence, the organizations concerned about protecting groundwater from EPA's Office of Water or from its underground tank office need to deal with an environmental problem that resulted from the actions of another unit of EPA.

Like a drug with untested side effects, one wonders if the cure is worse than the disease. Is MTBE the wrong way to reduce air pollution? Probably so, which raises the questions: What steps could EPA have taken to learn this before allowing MTBE to be added to gasoline? Is the only mechanism the incremental one of waiting until a problem is created for another part of the agency and trust that it will react if the problem becomes serious? Obviously, this study is based on the premise that strategic planning might have prevented the emergence of this problem. Moreover, with the problem identified, strategic thinking could allow policymakers to address this issue and develop a program to protect the nation's air and groundwater simultaneously, while allowing people to continue to drive their SUVs to the market.

It is difficult to know whether MTBE contamination could have been anticipated by a strategic planning process, but it is clear that MTBE policy was developed without the benefit of strategic thinking. It was a policy formulation process dominated by interest group politics and characterized by large-scale adoption of a new technology without the benefit of pilot-testing. At this point, the regulatory process requires the development of a substitute for MTBE. The search for this substitute and an approach to implementing this policy could benefit from a strategic planning process similar to the one developed for leaking underground storage tanks in the mid–1980s.

The Difficulty of Regulating Successfully

Clearly, it is difficult to regulate successfully 100 percent of the time. Several factors affect the ability of regulators to mitigate fully specified problems to the extent statutory goals and objectives might suggest. The regulatory process itself becomes a factor. This, in no small part, is influenced by the separate roles played by Congress and implementing agencies within the executive branch. Congress creates enabling legislation, which provides the statutory framework for problem solving—thereby establishing mandates, standards, and time lines—and assigns implementation authority to a relevant executive agency. Only then do implementing agencies initiate promulgation of regulations. Thus, from the start, implementing officials are hamstrung. Statutory requirements and expectations are often insulated from the realities that implementing officials face on the ground. While most would acknowledge the competitive interest-based bargaining that occurs during the legislative process, a similar process of competing interest-based lobbying takes place during implementation. Chapter 5 discusses the interest-based lobbying and negotiation during the initial implementation of the oxyfuel and reformulated gasoline (RFG) programs.

The public policy literature identifies several factors affecting regulatory success. Information asymmetry is a major problem in technical areas of regulation. The more complex a problem is, the more information is segmented among stakeholders, scientists, and regulators. The different levels of knowledge that may be held by regulatory participants will often result in improper assumptions about the utility of any particular policy tool or in ignorance about a policy tool's negative consequences. The MTBE case study illustrates this well. The support of the National Resources Defense Council and other environmental groups during the RFG regulation negotiation could occur only as a result of their limited knowledge of MTBE's potential for polluting aquifers. In addition, if knowledge is segmented (meaning that no one regulatory participant possesses all of the available knowledge), gaps in alignment between regulatory tools and specified problems will necessarily occur. The broad consensus that MTBE was a win-win solution in early 1991, and the late validation that MTBE was indeed a serious problem, could occur only as a result of the unequal and segmented knowledge that was present in regulatory discussions. EPA's units on air pollution and water pollution had different information, which, if combined, would have brought regulators in the agency to different conclusions.

Successful mitigation assumes target equipment or behavior can be regulated under existing statute. The early UST regulatory framework, for example, had limited legislative authority. Chapter 8 discusses EPA's early attempts to mitigate leaking USTs, an effort hampered by a lack of jurisdiction. Prior to 1984, federal legislation did not allow adequate regulation of USTs. The Resource Conservation and Recovery Act (RCRA) regulates tanks that contain hazardous wastes but not tanks with petroleum or hazardous products. The Clean Water Act requires owners of very large underground tanks (those with a capacity greater than 42,000 gallons) to take certain measures to prevent corrosion and to test tanks periodically. This requirement, however, applies only to tanks that may serve as a direct source of pollution into navigable waters. Since underground containers generally damage groundwater and affect only surface water as a nonpoint source of pollution, the Clean Water Act has not been used to regulate most of them.

The Superfund legislation authorizes EPA to respond whenever hazardous substances are released into the environment. The law has not been used to respond to leaks from oil tanks because petroleum is not defined as a hazardous substance under the act. In addition, Superfund has not been used to prevent most leaks or to set tank standards since its primary function is environmental cleanup. The Safe Drinking Water Act of 1974 ensures that contaminants entering public water systems do not endanger human health. EPA has set maximum levels for contaminants in drinking water, but such standards pertain to tank leaks only when drinking water is directly affected.

After several attempts to rectify the statutory limitations of existing programs, Congress passed the Hazardous and Solid Waste Amendments (HSWA) in November 1984 to regulate USTs. In the decades since, there has been a gradual process of developing and implementing more effective tank regulations. HSWA required EPA to set standards for new tank design and installation, leak detection, spill control, leak cleanup, and tank closure. In addition, the Leaking Underground Storage Tank Trust Fund provided federal resources to clean up leaks when tank owners refused to act and provided funds for the cleanup of abandoned tanks when owners could not be identified.

Alternate Explanations for Regulatory Failure

The regulatory failures illustrated by MTBE include bureaucratic insulation between regulators working on air quality and regulators working on water quality, a failure to assess the discrete impacts of introducing MTBE into the environment, resistance to emerging evidence of MTBE contamination, and confusing the unique chemical properties of MTBE contamination with the traditional problem of leaking underground storage tanks. These regulatory failures are due in large measure to a lack of strategic regulatory planning. Other possible explanations also exist and deserve consideration. Common explanations of the failures of effective policymaking might include, for example, interest-based bargaining and the resulting incrementalist tendencies of American democracy, the cultural baggage that is brought into the regulatory process, the conflation of public policy with economic markets, and, finally, the inherent limitations of policy designs.

Lindblom suggests that the pressure wrought by interest-based politicking constrains policymakers at both the legislative and regulatory levels to make small, incremental (branch) adjustments in policy rather than creative, bold, rational (root) realignments in our approach to problem solving.[5] The UST experience, like so many others, illustrates the point. Industry stakeholders targeted for regulation in the early 1980s argued intensively that not enough was known about the relationship between leaking tanks and groundwater contamination to warrant the immediate development of regulations. These stakeholders (e.g., the American Petroleum Institute and the Steel Tank Institute) formed a vocal ad hoc tank coalition that lobbied heavily and testified at congressional hearings that the problem needed further study before

Congress continued. Their objections, compounded by battles surrounding Superfund reauthorization and RCRA amendments for underground tank regulations, stalled the progress of the legislation.

Other studies suggest that American political culture creates a discomfort with regulating behavior and a preference instead for technical fixes.[6] In the early 1990s MTBE appeared to provide a virtually perfect fit for a technical fix that satisfied all major stakeholders, creating tremendous momentum. The culture of "better living through chemistry"[7] and "technology will rescue us" is consistent with incrementalism in providing an avenue of least resistance, allowing current behaviors to continue as we explore emerging and over-the-horizon technologies. Economists suggest that this dynamic is efficient to the extent it allows market-based solutions to respond to many problems the nation experiences.[8] However, when the problem itself is a result of market failure, policymakers often wait too long to intervene, making mitigation that much more difficult down the road.

Finally, policy design itself may be a factor in regulatory failure. Schneider and Ingram and DeLeon suggest that the structure and design of contemporary public policy discourages active citizen participation.[9] If pluralism is the self-correction that democratic policy environments rely on, then more participation enhances the likelihood of policy success. The regulatory failure surrounding MTBE was not a classic example of minimizing participation. In fact, the 1991 RFG regulation negotiation could be seen as a success in bringing different stakeholders together. However, as chapter 6 points out, the regulatory momentum resulting from the reg-neg consensus made it extraordinarily difficult for critical voices to be heard as the negative impacts of MTBE emerged.

Regulatory policy is always made in an environment of imperfect knowledge. The goal of strategic regulatory planning is to reduce that imperfection as much as possible. The strategic regulatory planning model would have allowed regulators to respond more effectively to the MTBE problem as it emerged as a national concern. The model may have allowed a more complex understanding of the MTBE problem, mitigating MTBE contamination while preserving air quality. The alternate explanations above are not mutually exclusive scenarios; each may have played a role to a greater or lesser extent. Nonetheless, whether the absence of strategic regulatory planning is the primary cause of MTBE regulatory failure, a robust strategic approach would have caught the problem of MTBE contamination much earlier in the process. This would have changed the dynamic of the 1991 RFG regulatory negotiation substantially, slowing—if not halting entirely—the momentum toward MTBE adoption. In short, regulatory strategic planning, while not a silver bullet, is an important tool in the regulatory toolbox.

Finally, strategic regulatory planning is generalizable to other areas that require integrating science and policy. Any policy area that requires a meaningful linkage between complex technical data and regulatory processes would benefit from a strategic regulatory approach. This is especially true in policy domains where accurate risk analysis is essential.[10] The strategic regulatory planning process allows better control of complex data through a formal alignment between data and regulatory goals and objectives early in the regulatory process. Such a process enhances the likelihood of building consensus among diverse stakeholders through a narrowing of the universe of acceptable policy options. In short, it creates an opportunity for collaboration between regulators and target constituencies due to the increased clarity of an evidence-based approach.

The UST Regulatory Program

Throughout the construction of the strategic regulatory plan to control leaking USTs, policymakers kept in mind the size and diversity of the target group. They also remained cognizant of the deeply seated, anti-regulatory attitudes and the tight operating budgets common among small businesses. For the most part, EPA in the mid-1980s was unprepared to regulate such a population, primarily because the agency had few previous experiences dealing with small firms. From EPA's inception in 1970 until the mid-1980s, large corporations had received most of the agency's attention. Political concerns, limited funds, and personnel complicated attempts to develop a successful regulatory program. These factors forced EPA and NAPA planners to be inventive and somewhat experimental in their approach to resolving the UST problem.

As discussed in this study, induced compliance forms the backbone of the regulatory plan recommended to EPA senior management. From the outset, the planners felt the EPA should eschew employment of traditional direct command-and-control mechanisms and adopt instead a carrot-and-stick approach to persuade gently owners of UST systems to obey the law.[11] Admittedly, the UST problem is perceived by some to be less serious and urgent than other contemporary environmental problems, like climate change or even the cleanup of abandoned toxic waste sites. While this makes it difficult for EPA to justify the appropriation of additional monies for enforcing UST regulations, it provided the agency enough time to implement the plan and make modifications. If the least coercive devices had failed to entice owners of USTs to comply with the law, policymakers could have returned to the model, retraced its steps, and selected more coercive devices. This process could be repeated until a satisfactory level of compliance was reached. Fortunately, as chapter 10 indicated, the strategy succeeded: the leaking tank problem has been substantially reduced over the past two decades.

Various circumstances surrounding the UST issue also led to the recommendation that EPA delegate most of the implementation and enforcement duties to state and local governments. This suggestion is in keeping with policies over the past two decades concerning other environmental problems, and it helped minimize obstacles to implementation associated with federal agency funding, staffing, and intervention. The strategy of delegating the program to the states was not without its faults. The fifty states and numerous local governments tend to differ significantly in the amount of resources they possess.[12] Depending on the politics and personalities involved, motivation to control leaking USTs varied across the country too. Furthermore, like many other environmental problems, USTs have been concentrated in large urban communities, thereby placing the greatest financial burden on these jurisdictions. Still, there has been widespread implementation of the program since its enactment. One reason for this is that most of the dollars spent to clean up leaking tanks and improve tank management was spent by the private sector. This occurred because of fear of liability and regulatory enforcement and out of a general sense that it was simply good management to keep valuable products from spilling into the environment.

Another reason for success is that EPA provided tank owners with the time to absorb the costs of upgrade into normal corporate capital planning. In fact, if anything, EPA bent over backwards to accommodate corporate needs. The program waited fourteen years to issue final regulations in 1998 and only then placed heightened stress on compliance with the regulatory deadline. The 1998 deadline was the one that EPA set as the deadline by which all USTs were to be replaced or provided with proper equipment. In the late 1990s, this deadline was frequently noted by administrators at OUST and by Congress, which had directed EPA to provide a detailed compliance plan.

Liability Insurance

As the planners recommended and Congress later mandated, owners of USTs must demonstrate an ability to finance abatement in the event a serious leak occurs. Since most operators of UST systems have limited financial resources and tank replacement and cleanup can be quite costly, external monetary aid is essential. A critical assumption of policy analysts who support the liability insurance requirement is that firms "have an incentive to cooperate with insurance company inspections and adopt recommendations which are made."[13] In addition, insurance allows policymakers to avoid the disadvantages normally associated with direct command-and-control mechanisms (e.g., increased staffing and higher costs).

The experience with insurance over the past two decades has varied significantly. In the 1980s and 1990s, tank insurance was either unavailable or too expensive. To meet the need for this insurance and allow their tank owners to comply with the law, most states developed state financial assurance funds. In essence, states "sold" tank owners a form of insurance that provided a method to pay the unanticipated costs of leaks and liability from leaking tanks. In the early twenty-first century, some of the state funds depleted their resources. However, there also was the reemergence of private insurance. Insurance companies began to see that the cleanup and liability costs of leaking tanks could be predicted, and therefore insurance could be priced and sold at a profit.

Limitations of the Study

As is always the case in social science research, this study has certain limitations. Perhaps most obvious, this study assessed the use of a strategic regulatory planning model involving only two environmental problems, MTBE contamination and leaking USTs. Exactly to what degree the regulatory programs and problem of MTBE and USTs could be transferable to other policy contexts is uncertain.

Two unique characteristics of the UST problem distinguish it from many other areas of environmental regulation. As already discussed, this was one of the first times that EPA has had to deal with an immense and varied target group. Our other case study, MTBE, involved much the same target group. The economic and political issues central to the MTBE and UST cases are likely to differ from those encountered in the regulation of a small number of large industrial firms. This requires researchers and policymakers to adopt a perspective that is sensitive to the dynamics and intricacies generally associated with the regulation of a large population. A regulatory program designed to modify the behavior of individual members of a large target group is likely to be different from one that primarily focuses on a handful of prominent polluters.

Another distinct feature of the MTBE and UST issues is that a commercial product and not a waste is the central object of regulation. As previously explained, most of America's underground storage tanks are in gasoline stations. MTBE is an additive used in gasoline supplies, and it is in the economic self-interest of those selling gasoline to prevent leaks from occurring. Admittedly, the replacement of old, leaking gasoline tanks is very expensive in the short run, and this may cause some owners to ignore small leaks. Overall, however, the fact that it is a valued consumer good that is the subject of regulation may prove to be a strong incentive.

General Application

Policymakers should find the strategic regulatory planning model developed in this study applicable to many other environmental and policy settings. Although the model contains a definite structure and a series of steps that must be followed in chronological order, little in the approach restricts its use to specific issues. The drawbacks of incremental policymaking discussed in chapter 1 are present in nearly every policy context. The model attempts to overcome these problems by encouraging policymakers to take a systematic and tactical but modest approach to the development of regulatory programs and to link policy formulation with implementation. In general, the model will be especially useful in addressing complex regulatory issues.

As discussed in the Introduction and chapter 1, policymaking in the United States tends to be done incrementally, and experimentation is generally avoided. Impatience among leaders and the public, the low priority given social regulation, and an intolerance for failure discourage the kind of policy testing necessary for solving many of society's ills. Instead, policymakers choose to play it safe and follow an incremental approach to problem solving. The strategic regulatory planning model developed in this study allowed EPA to adopt a new and experimental approach to managing leaking USTs. The results after nearly two decades, reported in chapter 10, speak for themselves and suggest that much can be gained from experimentation in policymaking. The MTBE case provides evidence of what happens when government develops new policy without thinking strategically.

Policymakers will probably find the strategic planning process helpful in such areas as education, health care, transportation safety, consumer product regulation, and occupational health and safety. These regulatory policy spheres tend to involve large target populations and intricate issues that require careful scrutiny. Although this investigation centered on two related federal environmental issues, state and local governments should also find strategic planning valuable in their work as well. While the model was applied at the start of a new regulatory program, nothing about the model necessarily prevents it from being adopted at any point in a regulatory effort.[14] As Mercer observes, "Strategy formulation and implementation should be a never-ending process of adapting to changing needs and capabilities."[15] It should be noted, of course, that much of the strategy of any public program is already included in its enabling legislation.

What is likely to vary significantly, however, is the applicability of the specific elements of the final UST program. Clearly, public policy problems have different features and often require different solutions. While insurance might be an appropriate device for controlling leaking USTs, it is hard to see, for example, how it might be used to decrease flight delays by the nation's airlines. Also, some problems, such as sudden spills of toxic chemicals, pose a more immediate and serious threat to the environment and public health than do leaking USTs; undoubtedly, they require swift and direct government intervention. In addition, agencies and individual programs will nearly always vary in available funds and the quantity and quality of personnel. To a large degree, money and personnel dictate what policymakers can and cannot do. The clout of target groups can influence the contents of regulatory programs as well. Attempts to regulate the practice of attorneys and physicians, for example, are likely to receive stiffer and more effective resistance than efforts to regulate the business dealings of less powerful and less organized occupational groups such as gardeners or office messengers. Level of commitment and professional orientation are likely to differ between agencies and across issues. Moreover, outside experts hired to help design a program can have biases against employing certain regulatory approaches (e.g., market mechanisms). Finally, the role and influence of third parties is likely to deviate from one case to the next, thereby producing different solutions to particular problems.

The real contribution of this study is not so much in the specific features of the strategic regulatory approach as it is in the way the approach was applied to the UST program, especially when contrasted to its absence in the MTBE program. Unfortunately, the value of knowing how to design policies has been overlooked until recently. The next section examines the importance of policy design and discusses how such exercises can lead to the formulation of effective public policies.

Policy Design

Cohen and his colleagues argue that policymakers normally take a "garbage can" approach to public policymaking.[16] This approach is characterized by an overreliance on intuition and trial and error, as well as by loose connections between problem recognition, problem analysis, and solution generation. Inputs into the decision are dumped into a "garbage can," and policymakers decide which pieces to retrieve when it suits them. In such an environment, there is little in the way of coordinated problem solving, and decision making tends to be judgmental and unpredictable. In many cases, this results in the development of misdirected and ineffective public policies. In the field of environmental policy, this is often caused by political and scientific uncertainty. As Bressers and Rosenbaum observe, "Many of the most formidable difficulties confronting environmental policymakers arise from the pervasive interplay of uncertain science and political judgment at virtually every stage of the policy process. So much of the scientific research essential for resolving policy conflict and for crafting appropriate policy is unavailable, ambiguous, or preliminary that scientific judgment frequently becomes highly contingent and tentative, almost inevitably contentious."[17]

In an effort to correct this mode of operation, several researchers have called for increased reliance on policy design. Dryzek defines policy design "as the process of inventing, developing, and fine-tuning a course of action with amelioration of some problem or the achievement of some target in mind."[18] Ingraham adds that it is "a process in which causal links between problem and solution are systematically explored."[19] This suggests that "analytical attention will be directed to cause and effect at an early point in formulation activities, and that it be informed and guided by a broad explanatory framework."[20] In essence, policy design attempts to avoid the capricious manner in which choices are made. Instead, it tries to instill order and intelligence in policymaking. These principles were closely adhered to in the development and application of the strategic planning model in this study.

Most existing design methods were developed for employment in formal design tasks in architecture, engineering, urban planning, and product design.[21] The idea of applying such methods to solving social problems was first suggested in the planning literature. Architects and others in the applied sciences associated with urban design were concerned about the organizational problems of modern cities. As Linder and Peters explain, "The basic idea was to externalize the process of creating solutions to insure both its rationality and manipulability."[22]

Several studies, including this one, adopt the design perspective in their analysis of policy formulation at the federal level.[23] Other research primarily addresses the theoretical issues involved in the application of the design approach to the development of public policy.[24] In each instance, the focus has been on systematizing the process of policy formulation to overcome both the prejudices of policymakers and the preferences of most researchers for studying implementation and evaluation.

Important benefits can be gleaned from the policy design process. In Linder and Peters's view:

> Whether the problem is an architectural, mechanical or administrative one, the logic of design is fundamentally similar. The idea is to fashion an instrument that will work in a desired manner. In the context of policy problems, design involves both a systemic process for generating basic strategies and a framework for comparing them. Examining problems from a design perspective offers a more productive way of organizing our thinking and analytical efforts. Systematic attention to design will not only enhance the performance of the alternative eventually chosen, but also expand the opportunities for serious consideration of innovative strategies.[25]

They later add:

> Establishing a logical procedure for designing policy instruments not only reduces the likelihood of errors but also makes explicit the thinking that goes into the development of each design. Complex problems, then, can be reduced to manageable proportions by clarifying basic design requirements and developing plausible strategies for their solution.[26]

A number of obstacles may hinder direct and literal application of design methods to the policy context. Many of these obstacles exist because of the fundamental differences between the applied sciences (e.g., architecture and engineering) and the social sciences. Measurement techniques, for example, are better developed in the applied sciences than in the social sciences. Similarly, it is often difficult to operationalize and quantify certain variables and concepts in policy analysis. In addition, due to economic and political issues, goals are frequently ambiguous or are merely symbolic. Engineers who design and build bridges cannot and do not operate under these conditions. Furthermore, while the human element is not ignored in the applied disciplines, it plays a far more central role in public policymaking. Due to the unpredictable nature of human behavior, the error term in the equation is likely to be larger in the social sciences than in the applied disciplines. In addition, senior bureaucrats may feel confused or even threatened by this new strategy and resist its full-fledged adoption. Finally, policymaking in the United

States is highly departmentalized and often involves different branches of government, different levels of government, and competing bureaucracies.[27] This makes the necessary coordination of policy design efforts difficult, if not impossible.

Most research in the area tends to overlook these problems. Dryzek's work, however, is a notable exception. He explains that "design is no simple matter, and contains numerous pitfalls for the unwary. My contention is that difficulty is no excuse to eschew cogitation. Rather, as the level of hazard in public policy increases, the "fit" of policies to their environment becomes progressively harder to accomplish; hence one must think harder about how to achieve it."[28]

Following Dryzek's line of thought, this study has developed a strategic planning model to address a complicated problem, the regulation of leaking USTs. Despite the complexity of the issue, an effort was made to develop a regulatory program in a rational and methodical fashion. A great deal more research and experimentation is required before the design perspective can be widely adopted in public policymaking. Indeed, the MBTE case demonstrates the difficulties of applying a design perspective to policymaking. Additional information about which aspects of design can be fully exploited and which facets cannot be cleanly grafted needs to be gathered. This study represents a first step in this direction.

Notes

Introduction

1. Kenneth Meier's work on regulation is a notable exception in this regard. See Kenneth J. Meier, *Regulation: Politics, Bureaucracy and Economics* (New York: St. Martin's Press, 1985).

2. Lester M. Salamon, ed., *The Tools of Government: A Guide to the New Governance* (New York: Oxford University Press, 2002).

3. Robert Kagan, *Adversarial Legalism: The American Way of Law* (Cambridge, Mass.: Harvard University Press, 2001).

4. Malcolm Sparrow, *Regulatory Craft: Controlling Risks, Solving Problems, and Managing Compliance* (Washington, D.C.: Brookings Institution, 2000).

5. Cornelius M. Kerwin, *Rulemaking: How Government Agencies Write Law and Make Policy*, 3rd ed. (Washington, D.C.: CQ Press, 2003).

6. David C. Korten, *When Corporations Rule the World* (West Hartford, Conn.: Kumarian Press, 1995); Dan Clawson, Alan Neustadt, and Mark Waller, *Dollars and Votes: How Business Campaign Contributions Subvert Democracy* (Philadelphia: Temple University Press, 1995); Ronald T. Libby, *Eco-Wars: Political Campaigns and Social Movements* (New York: Columbia University Press, 1998).

7. Kerwin, *Rulemaking*.

8. Ibid.

9. Daniel Press and Daniel A. Mazmanian, "Understanding the Transition to a Sustainable Economy," in Norman J. Vig and Michael E. Kraft, eds., *Environmental Policy: New Directions for the Twenty-First Century*, 5th ed. (Washington, D.C.: CQ Press, 2003), pp. 275–298.

10. Theodore J. Lowi, *The End of Liberalism: The Second Republic of the United States*, 2nd ed. (New York: Norton, 1979).

11. Theodore J. Lowi, "Two Roads to Serfdom: Liberalism, Conservatism and Administrative Power," *American University Law Review* 36 (1987): 295.

12. Ibid., p. 296.

13. Ibid., pp. 297–298.

14. Morris P. Fiorina, "Legislative Choice of Regulatory Forms: Legal Process or Administrative Process?" *Public Choice* 39 (1982): 33–66.

15. Ibid.

16. William F. West, "The Politics of Administrative Rulemaking," *Public Administrative Review* 42 (September–October 1982): 420–426; and William F. West, *Administrative Rulemaking: Politics and Processes* (Westport, Conn.: Greenwood Press, 1985).

17. 5 U.S.C. 551 (4).

18. Kerwin, *Rulemaking.*

19. Ibid., p. 2.

20. Ibid.

21. Ibid.

22. West, "The Politics of Administrative Rulemaking"; West, *Administrative Rulemaking*; and Wesley A. Magat, Alan J. Krupnick, and Winston Harrington, *Rules in the Making: A Statistical Analysis of Regulatory Agency Behavior* (Washington, D.C.: Resources for the Future, 1986).

23. Kerwin, *Rulemaking.*

24. Ibid.

25. Harold H. Buff, "The Reagan Era in Retrospect: Presidential Management of Agency Rulemaking," *George Washington Law Review* 57 (January 1989): 533–595; Thomas O. McGarity, *Reinventing Rationality: The Role of Regulatory Analysis in the Federal Bureaucracy* (Cambridge: Cambridge University Press, 1991); Thomas O. McGarity, "The Internal Structure of EPA Rulemaking," *Law and Contemporary Problems* 54 (Autumn 1991): 57–111; Thomas O. McGarity, "Some Thoughts on 'Deossifying' the Rulemaking Process," *Duke Law Journal* 41 (1992): 1385–1462.

26. Kerwin, *Rulemaking.*

27. Ibid.

28. Ibid.

29. Ibid.

30. Philip J. Harter, "Negotiating Regulations: A Cure for Malaise," *Georgetown Law Journal* 71 (1982): 1–118.

31. Ibid.

32. Patricia M. Wald, "ADR and the Courts: An Update," *Duke Law Journal* 46 (1997): 1445–1473.

33. Harter, "Negotiating Regulations."

34. Cary Coglianese, "Assessing Consensus: The Promise and Performance of Negotiated Rulemaking," *Duke Law Journal* 46 (1997): 1255–1349; Philip J.

Harter, "Fear of Commitment: An Affliction of Adolescents," *Duke Law Journal* 46 (1997): 1389–1429.

35. Al Gore, *Creating a Government That Works Better and Costs Less: Report of the National Performance Review* (Washington, D.C.: U.S. Government Printing Office, 1993).

36. Coglianese, "Assessing Consensus."

37. Ibid.

38. His results have been questioned on methodological grounds. See Kerwin, *Rulemaking*.

39. Laura Langbein and Cornelius M. Kerwin, "Regulatory Negotiation: Claims, Counter-Claims and Empirical Evidence," *Journal of Public Administration Research and Theory* 10 (2000): 599–632.

40. Ellen Siegler, "Regulating Negotiations and Other Rulemaking Processes: Strengths and Weaknesses from an Industry Viewpoint," *Duke Law Journal* 46 (1997): 1429–1443.

41. Coglianese, "Assessing Consensus," p. 1335.

42. Cary Coglianese, "The Limits of Consensus," *Environment* (March–April 1999): 28–33; and Cary Coglianese and Laurie K. Allen, "Does Consensus Make Common Sense? An Analysis of EPA's Common Sense Initiative," *Environment* (January–February 2004): 10–25.

43. Cornelius M. Kerwin and Scott R. Furlong, "Time and Rulemaking: An Empirical Test of Theory," *Journal of Public Administration Research and Theory* 2 (April 1992): 113–138.

44. Ibid.

45. Kerwin, *Rulemaking*.

46. Office of Solid Waste and Emergency Response, *The Nation's Hazardous Waste Management Program at a Crossroads* (Washington, D.C.: Environmental Protection Agency, 1990).

47. Ibid.

48. McGarity, "The Internal Structure of EPA Rulemaking." Not everyone agrees with this perspective. For example, see Gary C. Bryner, *Bureaucratic Discretion: Law and Policy in Federal Regulatory Agencies* (Elmsford, N.Y.: Pergamon Press, 1987).

49. McGarity, "The Internal Structure of EPA Rulemaking," p. 111.

50. Kerwin, *Rulemaking*.

51. Coglianese, "Assessing Consensus."

52. Ibid., p. 1293.

53. Harter, "Fear of Commitment."

54. Ibid.

55. Samuel P. Epstein, Lester O. Brown, and Carl Pope, *Hazardous Waste in America* (San Francisco: Sierra Club Books, 1982).

56. Ibid.

57. Walter A. Rosenbaum, *Environmental Politics and Policy*, 6th ed. (Washington, D.C.: CQ Press, 2005), p. 217.

58. Ibid.

59. Ronie Garcia-Johnson, *Exporting Environmentalism: U.S. Multinational Chemical Corporations in Brazil and Mexico* (Cambridge, Mass.: MIT Press, 2000); Press and Mazmanian, "Understanding the Transition to a Sustainable Economy."

60. National Academy of Public Administration Hazardous Waste Management Project, *Implementing Hazardous Waste Regulation: A Summary of the RCRA Framework and Record* (Washington, D.C.: National Academy of Public Administration, 1985), pp. 2–4.

61. Garcia-Johnson, *Exporting Environmentalism*; and Rosenbaum, *Environmental Politics and Policy.*

62. For example, see Sheldon Kamieniecki, George A. Gonzalez, and Robert O. Vos, eds., *Flashpoints in Environmental Policymaking: Controversies in Achieving Sustainability* (Albany: State University of New York Press, 1997); and Martin Janicke and Helge Jorgens, "Strategic Environmental Planning and Uncertainty: A Cross-National Comparison of Green Plans in Industrialized Countries," *Policy Studies Journal* 28 (2000): 612–632.

63. For more information about CERCLA, consult Steven Cohen and Marc Tipermas, "Superfund: Preimplementation Planning and Bureaucratic Politics," in James P. Lester and Ann O'M. Bowman, eds., *The Politics of Hazardous Waste Management* (Durham, N.C.: Duke University Press, 1983), pp. 43–59; Michael Clarke, Sheldon Kamieniecki, and Robert O'Brien, "Decisionmaking in a Complex Socio-Technical Environment: The Case of Toxic Waste Management," in Lloyd Nigro, ed., *Decision Making in the Public Sector* (New York: Marcel Dekker, 1984), pp. 187–207; Steven Cohen, "Defusing the Toxic Time Bomb: Federal Hazardous Waste Programs," in Norman J. Vig and Michael E. Kraft, eds., *Environmental Policy in the 1980s: Reagan's New Agenda* (Washington, D.C.: CQ Press, 1984); Sheldon Kamieniecki, Robert O'Brien, and Michael Clarke, "Environmental Policy and Aspects of Intergovernmental Relations," in David R. Morgan and J. Edwin Benton, eds., *Intergovernmental Relations and Public Policy* (Westport, Conn.: Greenwood Press, 1986), pp. 49–61; Katherine N. Probst, Don Fullerton, Robert E. Litan, and Paul R. Portney, *Footing the Bill for Superfund Cleanups: Who Pays and How?* (Washington, D.C.: Brookings Institution, 1995); and Rosenbaum, *Environmental Politics and Policy.*

64. Juliet Eilperin, "Lack of Funding Slows Cleanup of Hundreds of Superfund Sites," *Washington Post*, November 25, 2004, p. A01.

65. Cohen, "Defusing the Toxic Time Bomb"; Malcolm Getz and Benjamin Walter, "Environmental Policy and Competitive Structure: Implications of the

Hazardous Waste Management Program," *Policy Studies Journal* 9 (Winter 1980): 404–414; Richard Barke, "Policy Learning and the Evolution of Federal Hazardous Waste Policy," *Policy Studies Journal* 14 (September 1985): 123–131; and Benjamin Walter and Malcolm Getz, "Social and Economic Effects of Toxic Waste Disposal," in Sheldon Kamieniecki, Robert O'Brien, and Michael Clarke, eds., *Controversies in Environmental Policy* (Albany: State University of New York Press, 1986), pp. 223–245; and Rosenbaum, *Environmental Politics and Policy*.

66. Christopher Harris, William W. Want, and Morris M. Ward, *Hazardous Waste: Confronting the Challenge* (Westport, Conn.: Greenwood Press, 1987).

67. Rosenbaum, *Environmental Politics and Policy*, p. 183.

68. Gary C. Bryner, *Blue Skies, Green Politics: The Clean Air Act of 1990 and Its Implementation* (Washington, D.C.: CQ Press, 1995). Also see Christopher J. Bailey, *Congress and Air Pollution* (New York: Manchester University Press, 1998).

69. University of California, Davis, *Health and Environmental Assessment of MTBE*, 1998 <www.tsrp.ucdavis.edu/mtbept/homepage.html>.

70. Ibid.

Chapter 1

1. Oil companies are replacing MTBE with ethanol, an ingredient distilled primarily from midwestern corn. The federal government provides a tax subsidy for ethanol use. See Dan Morian, "Ethanol Brings Drop in Gas Tax," *Los Angeles Times*, March 24, 2003, p. B1.

2. Amihai Glazer and Lawrence S. Rothenberg, *Why Government Succeeds and Why It Fails* (Cambridge, Mass.: Harvard University Press, 2001).

3. Gary C. Bryner, *Blue Skies, Green Politics: The Clean Air Act of 1990 and Its Implementation*, 2nd ed. (Washington, D.C.: CQ Press, 1995); and Lawrence S. Rothenberg, *Environmental Choices: Policy Responses to Green Demands* (Washington, D.C.: CQ Press, 2002).

4. David Braybrooke and Charles E. Lindblom, *A Strategy of Decision* (New York: Free Press, 1970), p. 48.

5. John D. Steinbrunner, *The Cybernetic Theory of Decision* (Princeton, N.J.: Princeton University Press, 1974).

6. Ibid., p. 57.

7. Daniel C. McCool, "Conflict and Choice in Policy Theory," in Daniel C. McCool, ed., *Public Policy Theories, Models, and Concepts* (Englewood Cliffs, N.J.: Prentice Hall, 1995), pp. 390–407.

8. Braybrooke and Lindblom, *A Strategy of Decision*, p. 104. Also see Charles A. Lindblom, "The Science of Muddling Through," *Public Administration Review* 19 (Spring 1959): 79–88.

9. Yehezkel Dror, *Public Policymaking Reexamined* (Scranton, Pa.: Chandler Publishing Company, 1968); Charles O. Jones, "Speculative Augmentation in Federal Air Pollution Policymaking," *Journal of Politics* (May 1974): 438–463; and Steinbrunner, *The Cybernetic Theory of Decision.*

10. Rothenberg, *Environmental Choices.*

11. Office of Solid Waste and Emergency Response, *The Nation's Hazardous Waste Management Program at a Crossroads* (Washington, D.C.: Environmental Protection Agency, 1990).

12. Kenneth J. Meier, *Regulation: Politics, Bureacracy and Economics* (New York: St. Martin's Press, 1985), p. 1.

13. C. W. Hoffer and D. Schendel, *Strategy Formulation: Analytic Concepts* (St. Paul, Minn.: West, 1978).

14. Jeffrey L. Pressman and Aaron Wildavsky, *Implementation* (Berkeley: University of California Press, 1973).

15. Meier, *Regulation.*

16. This argument is made in Stephen H. Linder and B. Guy Peters, "A Design Perspective on Policy Implementation: The Fallacies of Misplaced Prescription," *Policy Studies Review* 6 (February 1987): 459–475.

17. However, see ibid.

18. Cornelius M. Kerwin, *Rulemaking: How Government Agencies Write Law and Make Policy*, 3rd ed. (Washington, D.C.: CQ Press, 2003).

19. Theodore J. Lowi, *The End of Liberalism* (New York: Norton, 1969).

20. Kerwin, *Rulemaking.*

21. Meier, *Regulation*, p. 277.

22. Jeffrey Berry and Frank Baumgartner and Beth Leech document the recent rise of citizen groups in their research. Their studies suggest that the sharp increase in the number of such groups has provided an effective counterbalance to the influence of business and industry in the legislative process. Frank R. Baumgartner and Beth L. Leech, *Basic Interests: The Importance of Groups in Politics and in Political Science* (Princeton, N.J.: Princeton University Press, 1998); and Jeffrey M. Berry, *The New Liberalism: The Rising Power of Citizen Groups* (Washington, D.C.: Brookings Institution Press, 1999). Also see David Lowery and Virginia Gray, "A Neopluralist Perspective on Research on Organized Interests," *Political Research Quarterly* 57 (March 2004): 163–175.

23. Kerwin, *Rulemaking.*

24. Daniel Press and Daniel A. Mazmanian, "Understanding the Transition to a Sustainable Economy," in Norman J. Vig and Michael E. Kraft, eds., *Environmental Policy: New Directions for the Twenty-First Century*, 5th ed. (Washington, D.C.: CQ Press, 2003), pp. 275–298.

25. Kerwin, *Rulemaking.*

26. Braybrooke and Lindblom, *A Strategy of Decision.*

27. Thomas J. Peters and Robert H. Waterman, *In Search of Excellence: Lessons from America's Best-Run Companies* (New York: Harper & Row, 1982).

28. Henry Mintzberg, "Crafting Strategy," *Harvard Business Review* 65 (July–August 1987): 66–67.

29. Peter Bachrach and Morton S. Baratz, *Power and Poverty* (New York: Oxford University Press, 1970).

30. Helen Ingram, "Implementation: A Review and Suggested Framework," in Aaron Wildavsky and Naomi B. Lynn, eds., *Public Administration: The State of the Field* (Chatham, N.J.: Chatham House, 1990). In addition, see Robert T. Nakamura and Frank Smallwood, *The Politics of Policy Implementation* (New York: St. Martin's Press, 1980); and Walter A. Rosenbaum, *Environmental Politics and Policy*, 6th ed. (Washington, D.C.: CQ Press, 2005).

31. A. Myrick Freeman III, "Economics, Incentives, and Environmental Policy," in Vig and Kraft, eds., *Environmental Policy*, pp. 201–221.

32. For instance, see John A. Baden and Tim O'Brien, "Bringing Private Management to the Public Lands: Environmental and Economic Advantages," in Sheldon Kamieniecki, George A. Gonzalez, and Robert O. Vos, eds., *Flashpoints in Environmental Policymaking: Controversies in Achieving Sustainability* (Albany: State University of New York Press, 1997), pp. 179–205.

33. This is demonstrated in William T. Gormley, "Intergovernmental Conflict on Environmental Policy: The Attitudinal Connection," *Western Political Quarterly* (June 1987): 285–303.

34. Edward P. Weber, *Bringing Society Back In: Grassroots Ecosystem Management, Accountability, and Sustainable Communities* (Cambridge, Mass.: MIT Press, 2003).

35. Press and Mazmanian, "Understanding the Transition to a Sustainable Economy."

36. Ibid.

37. Dan Beardsley, Terry Davies, and Robert Hersh, "Improving Environmental Management: What Works, What Doesn't," *Environment* (September 1997): 6–9, 28–35. Also consult Alfred Marcus, Donald A. Geffen, and Ken Sexton, *Reinventing Environment Regulation: Lessons from Project XL* (Washington, D.C.: Resources for the Future, 2002).

38. U.S. Environmental Protection Agency, *Partners for the Environment: A Catalogue of the Agency's Partnership Programs* (Washington, D.C.: U.S. Government Printing Office, 1998).

39. Cary Coglianese and Laurie K. Allen, "Does Consensus Make Common Sense? An Analysis of EPA's Common Sense Initiative," *Environment* (January–February 2004): 10–25.

40. Kettl discusses the problems associated with the new partnerships between business and the EPA and the attempt by the agency to reinvent itself. He believes

citizens are being excluded from environmental policymaking and must be brought into the decision-making process. Donald F. Kettl, ed., *Environmental Governance: A Report on the Next Generation of Environmental Policy* (Washington, D.C.: Brookings Institution, 2002). A complete list of partnerships between industry and EPA can be found at www.epa.gov/epahome/industry.

41. Ronie Garcia-Johnson, *Exporting Environmentalism: U.S. Multinational Chemical Corporations in Brazil and Mexico* (Cambridge, Mass.: MIT Press, 2000).

42. Norman Miller, *Environmental Politics: Interest Groups, the Media, and the Making of Policy* (Boca Raton, Fla.: Lewis Publishers, 2002).

43. Garcia-Johnson, *Exporting Environmentalism.*

44. See, for example, Aseem Prakash, *Greening the Firm: The Politics of Corporate Environmentalism* (Cambridge: Cambridge University Press, 2000).

45. Robert T. Nakamura and Thomas W. Church, *Taming Regulation: Superfund and the Challenge of Regulatory Reform* (Washington, D.C.: Brookings Institution, 2003).

46. Paul S. Fischbeck, R. Scott Farrow, and M. Granger Morgan, "Introduction: The Challenge of Improving Regulation," in Paul S. Fischbeck and R. Scott Farrow, eds., *Improving Regulation: Cases in Environment, Health and Safety* (Washington, D.C.: Resources for the Future, 2001), pp. 1–16.

47. In addition, Stikkers analyzes the extent to which regulatory planning was employed in the case of MTBE. He discusses the development of the oxygenate mandate in Congress, how regulators drafted rules that favored MTBE, and the environmental consequences that resulted. He concludes that regulatory planning was highly fragmented in this issue area. David Stikkers, "The Unintended Consequence of Reformulated Gasoline," in Paul S. Fischbeck and R. Scott Farrow, eds., *Improving Regulation: Cases in Environment, Health and Safety* (Washington, D.C.: Resources for the Future, 2001), pp. 70–94.

48. National Academy of Public Administration, *Resolving the Paradox of Environmental Protection* (Washington, D.C.: National Academy of Public Administration. September 1997).

49. Ibid., p. 39.

Chapter 2

1. Stephen H. Linder and B. Guy Peters, "A Design Perspective on Policy Implementation: The Fallacies of Misplaced Prescriptions," *Policy Studies Review* 6 (February 1987): 459–475.

2. Ibid., p. 460. An example is B. W. Hogwood and L. A. Gunn, *Policy Analysis for the Real World* (Oxford: Oxford University Press, 1984).

3. An example of each respective approach is Jeffrey Pressman and Aaron Wildavsky, *Implementation* (Berkeley: University of California Press, 1973); Andrew Dunshire, *Implementation in a Bureaucracy* (New York: St. Martin's Press, 1978); Michael Lipsky, *Street-Level Bureaucracy* (New York: Russell Sage Foundation, 1980); and Daniel Mazmanian and Paul Sabatier, *Implementation and Public Policy* (Glencoe, Ill.: Scott, Foresman, 1983).

4. Linder and Peters, "A Design Perspective on Policy Implementation," p. 468.

5. Ibid., p. 472.

6. Ibid.

7. A discussion of outputs and outcomes appears in Walter Williams, *The Implementation Perspective* (Berkeley: University of California Press, 1980), pp. 83–84.

8. Ian C. MacMillan and Patricia E. Jones, *Strategy Formulation: Power and Politics*, 2nd ed. (St. Paul, Minn.: West, 1986).

9. Charles W. Hoffer and Dan E. Schendel, *Strategy Formulation: Analytic Concepts* (St. Paul, Minn.: West, 1978). Readers should also refer to Sheldon Kamieniecki and Steven A. Cohen, "Strategic Regulatory Planning in the Management of Hazardous Materials," *Policy and Politics* 18 (July 1990): 207–216.

10. Works that represent this general approach include Robert W. Hahn, "The Political Economy of Environmental Regulation: Towards a Unifying Framework," *Public Choice* 65 (April 1990): 21–47; Elinor Ostrom, Roy Gardner, and James Walker, *Rules, Games, and Common-Pool Resources* (Ann Arbor: University of Michigan Press, 1994); Michael C. Munger and Dennis Coates, "Strategizing in Small Group Decision Making: Host State Identification in the Southeast Compact," *Public Choice* 82 (July 1995): 1–15; and Elinor Ostrom and James Walker, "Neither Markets nor States: Linking Transformation Processes in Collective Action Arenas," in Dennis C. Mueller, ed., *Perspectives on Public Choice* (Cambridge: Cambridge University Press, 1997), pp. 35–72.

11. William N. Dunn, *Public Policy Analysis*, 2nd ed. (Englewood Cliffs, N.J.: Prentice Hall, 1994).

12. Ibid., p. 254.

13. Ibid., p. 257.

14. Helen Ingram, "Implementation: A Review and Suggested Framework," in Aaron Wildavsky and Naomi B. Lynn, eds., *Public Administration: The State of the Field* (Chatham, N. J.: Chatham House, 1990).

15. Mazmanian and Sabatier, *Implementation and Public Policy.*

16. Ingram, "Implementation," p. 471.

17. Robert Salisbury and John Heinz, "A Theory of Policy Analysis and Some Preliminary Applications," in Ira Sharkansky, ed., *Policy Analysis in Political Science* (Chicago: Markham, 1970), p. 47.

18. Ingram, "Implementation," p. 476.

Chapter 3

1. Rosemary O'Leary, Robert F. Durant, Daniel J. Fiorino, and Paul S. Weiland, *Managing for the Environment: Understanding the Legal, Organizational, and Policy Challenges* (San Francisco: Jossey-Bass, 1999). Also see Alfred A. Marcus, "Command and Control: An Assessment of Smokestack Emission Regulation," in John Brigham and Don W. Brown, eds., *Policy Implementation: Penalties or Incentives?* (Beverly Hills, Calif.: Sage, 1980), pp. 209–226; Daniel Mazmanian and David Morell, *Beyond Superfailure: America's Toxics Policy for the 1990s* (Boulder, Colo.: Westview Press, 1992); and Shelley H. Metzenbaum, "Measurement That Matters: Cleaning Up the Charles River," in Donald F. Kettl, ed., *Environmental Governance: A Report on the Next Generation of Environmental Policy* (Washington, D.C.: Brookings Institution Press, 2002), pp. 58–117.

2. Steven A. Cohen, "EPA: A Qualified Success," in Sheldon Kamieniecki, Robert O'Brien, and Michael Clarke, eds., *Controversies in Environmental Policy* (Albany: State University of New York Press, 1986), pp. 174–195; and Walter A. Rosenbaum, "Regulation at Risk: The Controversial Politics and Science of Comparative Risk Assessment," in Sheldon Kamieniecki, George A. Gonzalez, and Robert O. Vos, eds., *Flashpoints in Environmental Policymaking: Controversies in Achieving Sustainability* (Albany: State University of New York Press, 1997), pp. 31–61.

3. Frank J. Thompson, "Deregulation by the Bureaucracy: OSHA and the Augean Quest for Error Correction," *Public Administration Review* 42 (May–June 1982): 202–212; Susan J. Tolchin and Martin Tolchin, *Dismantling America: The Rush to Deregulate* (Boston: Houghton Mifflin, 1983); Catherine H. Lovell, "Deregulation of State and Local Government," *Policy Studies Journal* 13 (March 1985): 607–615; William R. Lowry, *The Dimensions of Federalism: State Governments and Pollution Control Policies* (Durham, N.C.: Duke University Press, 1992); Evan J. Ringquist, *Environmental Protection at the State Level: Politics and Progress in Controlling Pollution* (Armonk, N.Y.: M. E. Sharpe, 1993); Denise Scheberle, *Federalism and Environmental Policy: Trust and the Politics of Implementation* (Washington, D.C.: Georgetown University Press, 1997); and Barry G. Rabe, "Power to the States: The Promise and Pitfalls of Decentralization," in Norman J. Vig and Michael E. Kraft, eds., *Environmental Policy: New Directions for the Twenty-First Century*, 5th ed. (Washington, D.C.: CQ Press, 2003), pp. 33–56.

4. Grant McConnell, *Private Power and American Democracy* (New York: Knopf, 1966); and Barry M. Mitnick, *The Political Economy of Regulation* (New York: Columbia University Press, 1980). In contrast, see Jeanne Nienaber Clarke and Daniel C. McCool, *Staking Out the Terrain: Power and Performance among Natural Resource Agencies*, 2nd ed. (Albany: State University of New York Press, 1996).

5. William F. West, "The Politics of Administrative Rulemaking," *Public Administration Review* 42 (September–October 1982): 420–426; Susan J. Tolchin,

"Cost-Benefit Analysis and the Rush to Deregulate: The Use and Misuse of Theory to Effect Policy Change," *Policy Studies Review* 4 (November 1984): 212–218; Rosenbaum, "Regulation at Risk"; and Walter A. Rosenbaum, *Environmental Politics and Policy*, 6th ed. (Washington, D.C.: CQ Press, 2005).

6. Terry Moe, "Regulatory Performance and Presidential Administration," *American Journal of Political Science* 26 (May 1982): 197–224; Dennis L. Soden, ed., *The Environmental Presidency* (Albany: State University of New York Press, 1999); and Norman J. Vig, "Presidential Leadership and the Environment," in Vig and E. Kraft, *Environmental Policy*, pp. 103–125.

7. The few studies that have done this include Malcolm Sparrow, *Regulatory Craft: Controlling Risks, Solving Problems, and Managing Compliance* (Washington, D.C.: Brookings Institution 2000); Lester M. Salamon, ed., *The Tools of Government: A Guide to the New Governance* (New York: Oxford University Press, 2002); and Robert T. Nakamura and Thomas W. Church, *Taming Regulation: Superfund and the Challenge of Regulatory Reform* (Washington, D.C.: Brookings Institution, 2003).

8. Rosenbaum, *Environmental Politics and Policy*. Also see Marcus, "Command and Control."

9. Welford W. Wilms, "Soft Policies for Hard Problems: Implementing Energy Conserving Building Regulations in California," *Public Administration Review* 42 (November–December 1982): 553–561.

10. Ibid., p. 557.

11. Ibid.

12. James Q. Wilson, "The Politics of Regulation," in James W. McKie, ed., *Social Responsibility and the Business Predicament* (Washington, D.C.: Brookings Institution, 1974), pp. 135–169.

13. Stephen Breyer, *Regulation and Its Reform* (Cambridge, Mass.: Harvard University Press, 1982); and Richard J. Tobin, "Safety-Related Defects in Motor Vehicles and the Evaluation of Self-Regulation," *Policy Studies Review* 1 (February 1982): 532–539.

14. Kenneth J. Meier, *Regulation: Politics, Bureaucracy and Economics* (New York: St. Martin's Press, 1985).

15. Aseem Prakash, *Greening the Firm: The Politics of Corporate Environmentalism* (Cambridge: Cambridge University Press, 2000). Also see B. Peter Pashigian, "How Large and Small Plants Fare under Environmental Regulation," *Regulation* 7 (September–October 1983): 19–23.

16. Marver H. Bernstein, *Regulating Business by Independent Commission* (Princeton, N.J.: Princeton University Press, 1955).

17. Marcus, "Command and Control."

18. Robert S. Montjoy and Lawrence J. O'Toole, "Toward a Theory of Policy Implementation: An Organizational Perspective," *Public Administration Review* 39 (September–October 1979): 465–475; George C. Edwards, *Implementing*

Public Policy (Washington, D.C.: Congressional Quarterly Press, 1980); and Daniel Mazmanian and Paul Sabatier, *Implementation and Public Policy* (Glenview, Ill.: Scott, Foresman, 1983).

19. Robert F. Durant, "EPA, TVA, and Pollution Control: Implications for a Theory of Regulatory Policy Implementation," *Public Administration Review* 44 (July–August 1984): 305–315; and Mazmanian and Morell, *Beyond Superfailure.*

20. Tobin, "Safety-Related Defects in Motor Vehicles and the Evaluation of Self-Regulation."

21. Marcus, "Command and Control"; and Prakash, *Greening the Firm.*

22. Steven Cohen, "Employing Strategic Planning in Environmental Regulation," in Kamieniecki, Gonzalez, and Vos, *Flashpoints in Environmental Policymaking*, pp. 109–125. Open communications can sometimes lead to co-optation as well.

23. Paul Sabatier and Daniel Mazmanian, "The Conditions of Effective Implementation: A Guide to Accomplishing Policy Objectives," *Policy Analysis* (Fall 1979): 481–504; Paul Sabatier and Daniel Mazmanian, "The Implementation of Public Policy: A Framework of Analysis," *Policy Studies Journal* 8 (Special Issue 1980): 538–560; Roland N. McKean, "Enforcement Costs in Environmental and Safety Regulations," *Policy Analysis* 6 (Summer 1980): 269–289; and Keith Hawkins, *Environment and Enforcement: Regulation and the Social Definition of Pollution* (Oxford: Clarendon Press, 1984).

24. Francis E. Rourke, *Bureaucracy, Politics and Public Policy*, 3rd ed. (Boston: Little, Brown, 1984).

25. Ibid., pp. 106–107.

26. Cary Coglianese, "Assessing Consensus: The Promise and Performance of Negotiated Rulemaking," *Duke Law Journal* 46 (1997): 1255–1349; and Cornelius M. Kerwin, *Rulemaking: How Government Agencies Write Law and Make Policy*, 3rd ed. (Washington, D.C.: CQ Press, 2003).

27. Richard P. Barke, "Regulatory Delay as Political Strategy," in Howard Ball, ed., *Federal Administrative Agencies: Essays on Power and Politics* (Englewood Cliffs, N.J.: Prentice Hall, 1984), pp. 144–156.

28. West, "The Politics of Administrative Rulemaking."

29. Durant, "EPA, TVA, and Pollution Control."

30. Thompson, "Deregulation by the Bureaucracy."

31. John O'Dell, "Rewrite of Emissions Rule May Roll Out More Hybrids," *Los Angeles Times*, April 7, 2003, p. C2.

32. Sabatier and Mazmanian, "The Condition of Effective Implementation"; Sabatier and Mazmanian, "The Implementation of Public Policy"; McKean, "Enforcement Costs in Environmental and Safety Regulations"; Congressional Quarterly, *Regulation: Process and Politics* (Washington, D.C.: Congressional Quarterly Press, 1982); Meier, *Regulation*; Clarke and McCool, *Staking Out the Terrain.*

33. Florence Heffron and Neil McFeeley, *The Administrative Regulatory Process* (New York: Longman, 1983).

34. Rabe, "Power to the States"; and Rosenbaum, *Environmental Politics and Policy*.

35. Meier, *Regulation*; and J. Clarence Davies and Jan Mazurek, *Pollution Control in the United States: Evaluating the System* (Washington, D.C.: Resources for the Future, 1998).

36. West, "The Politics of Administrative Rulemaking."

37. Kenneth W. Chilton and Murray Weidenbaum, "Government Regulation: The Small Business Burden," *Journal of Small Business Management* 20 (January 1982): 4–10; John D. Aram and Jeffrey S. Coomes, "Public Policy and the Small Business Sector," *Policy Studies Journal* 13 (June 1985): 692–700; and Robert E. Berney and Ed Owens, "A Theoretical Framework for Small Business Policy," *Policy Studies Journal* 13 (June 1985): 681–691.

38. Bruce A. Williams and Albert R. Matheny, "Testing Theories of Social Regulation: Hazardous Waste Regulation in the American States," *Journal of Politics* 46 (May 1984): 428–458.

39. Rosemary O'Leary, "Environmental Policy in the Courts," in Vig and Kraft, *Environmental Policy*, pp. 151–173.

40. Sabatier and Mazmanian, "The Conditions of Effective Implementation"; McKean, "Enforcement Costs in Environmental and Safety Regulations"; Guy Benveniste, *Regulation and Planning: The Case of Environmental Politics* (San Francisco: Boyd and Fraser, 1981); Tolchin and Tolchin, *Dismantling America*; Katherine N. Probst, Don Fullerton, Robert E. Litan, and Paul R. Portney, *Footing the Bill for Superfund Cleanups: Who Pays and How Much?* (Washington, D.C.: Brookings Institution, 1995); and Philip J. Harter, "Fear of Commitment: An Affliction of Adolescents," *Duke Law Journal* 46 (1997): 1389–1429.

41. Edward P. Weber, *Pluralism by the Rules: Conflict and Cooperation in Environmental Regulation* (Washington, D.C.: Georgetown University Press, 1998).

42. Judith A. Hermanson, "Regulatory Reform by Statute: The Implication of the Consumer Product Safety Commission's 'Offeror System,'" *Public Administration Review* 38 (March–April 1978): 151–155.

43. In 1981, Congress abolished the Offeror System and ordered the Consumer Product Safety Commission to rely primarily on voluntary product safety standards. The few mandatory rules that the agency writes are to be established through traditional rule-making channels.

44. Robert M. O'Brien, Michael Clarke, and Sheldon Kamieniecki, "Open and Closed Systems of Decision Making: The Case of Toxic Waste Management," *Public Administration Review* 44 (July–August 1984): 334–340; Riley E. Dunlap, Michael E. Kraft, and Eugene A. Rosa, eds., *Public Reactions to Nuclear Waste: Citizens' Views of Repository Siting* (Durham, N.C.: Duke University Press, 1993); and Edward P. Weber, *Bringing Society Back In: Grassroots Ecosys-*

tem Management, Accountability, and Sustainable Communities (Cambridge, Mass.: MIT Press, 2003).

45. Williams and Matheny, "Testing Theories of Social Regulation."

46. Robert H. Salisbury, "The Analysis of Public Policy: A Search for Theories and Roles," in Austin Ranney, ed., *Political Science and Public Policy* (Chicago: Markham Publishing Company, 1968), pp. 151–175.

47. Wilms, "Soft Policies for Hard Problems."

48. Sabatier and Mazmanian, "The Conditions of Effective Implementation" and "The Implementation of Public Policy."

49. Sabatier and Mazmanian, "The Conditions of Effective Implementation," p. 491. In fact, a lack of integration has hurt hazardous waste cleanup in the Southeast and Wisconsin. See Ann O'M. Bowman, "Hazardous Waste Cleanups and Superfund Implementation in the Southeast," *Policy Studies Journal* 14 (September 1985): 100–110; and William T. Gormley, "Intergovernmental Conflict on Environmental Policy: The Attitudinal Connection," *Western Political Quarterly* 40 (June 1987): 285–303. Also, consult Sheldon Kamieniecki, Robert O'Brien, and Michael Clarke, "Environmental Policy and Aspects of Intergovernmental Relations," in J. Edwin Benton and Daniel R. Morgan, eds., *Intergovernmental Relations and Public Policy* (Westport, Conn.: Greenwood Press, 1986), pp. 49–61.

50. Theodore Lowi, "American Business, Public Policy, Case Studies, and Political Theory," *World Politics* 16 (July 1964): 677–715; and Salisbury, "The Analysis of Public Policy."

51. Salisbury, "The Analysis of Public Policy," p. 158. Actually, Lowi's typology focuses on policy outcomes, while Salisbury's typology centers on decision structures and demand patterns of public policy. This difference in emphasis does not seriously affect the approach taken in this analysis.

52. Robert T. Nakamura and Frank Smallwood, *The Politics of Policy Implementation* (New York: St. Martin's Press, 1980), pp. 178–179; Bjorn Wittrock and Peter DeLeon, "Policy as a Moving Target: A Call for Conceptual Realism," *Policy Studies Review* 6 (August 1986): 44–60; and Cohen, "Employing Strategic Planning in Environmental Regulation."

53. Ibid: Cohen.

54. Sabatier and Mazmanian, "The Conditions of Effective Implementation."

Chapter 4

1. A. Myrick Freeman, "Economics, Incentives, and Environmental Policy," in Norman J. Vig and Michael E. Kraft, eds., *Environmental Policy: New Directions for the Twenty-First Century*, 5th ed. (Washington, D.C.: CQ Press, 2003), pp. 201–221.

2. Ibid., p. 208.

3. Richard J. Tobin, "Safety-Related Defects in Motor Vehicles and the Evaluation of Self- Regulation," *Policy Studies Review* 1 (February 1982): 532–539.

4. Norman Miller, *Environmental Politics: Interest Groups, the Media, and the Making of Policy* (Boca Raton, Fla.: Lewis Publishers, 2002); Walter A. Rosenbaum, *Environmental Politics and Policy*, 6th ed. (Washington, D.C.: CQ Press, 2005); and Alfred A. Marcus, Donald A. Geffen, and Ken Sexton, *Reinventing Environmental Regulation: Lessons from Project XL* (Washington, D.C.: Resources for the Future, 2002).

5. Rosenbaum, *Environmental Politics and Policy*, pp. 155–156.

6. Gary C. Bryner, *Blue Skies, Green Politics: The Clean Air Act of 1990 and Its Implementation,* 2nd ed. (Washington, D.C.: CQ Press, 1995), p. 30.

7. Robert N. Stavens, "What Can We Learn from the Grand Policy Experiment? Lessons from SO_2 Allowance Trading," *Journal of Economic Perspectives* 12 (1998): 69–88; Paul R. Portney and Robert N. Stavins, eds., *Public Policies for Environmental Protection*, 2nd ed. (Washington, D.C.: Resources for the Future, 2000); and U.S. Environmental Protection Agency, Office of Policy, Economics, and Innovation, "The United States Experience with Economic Incentives for Protecting the Environment," EPA 240-R-1-01 (January 2001).

8. Barry M. Mitnick, "Incentive Systems in Environmental Regulation," *Policy Studies Journal* 9 (Winter 1980): 379–394; and Rosenbaum, *Environmental Politics and Policy.*

9. For example, see ibid. Mitnick; Guy Benveniste, *Regulation and Planning: The Case of Environmental Politics* (San Francisco: Boyd and Fraser, 1981); Stephen Breyer, *Regulation and Its Reform* (Cambridge) Mass.: Harvard University Press, 1982); Alfred A. Marcus, Paul Sommers, and Frederic A. Morris, "Alternative Arrangements for Cost Effective Pollution Abatement: The Need for Implementation Analysis," *Policy Studies Review* 1 (February 1982): 477–483; Gregory A. Daneke, "The Future of Environmental Protection: Reflections on the Difference between Planning and Regulating," *Public Administration Review* 42 (May–June 1982): 227–233; and Gregory A. Daneke, "An Adaptive-Learning Approach to Environmental Regulation," *Policy Studies Review* 3 (August 1983): 7–12.

10. Alan Stone, *Regulation and Its Alternatives* (Washington, D.C.: CQ Press, 1982).

11. George C. Eads and Michael Fix, *Relief or Reform? Reagan's Regulatory Dilemma* (Washington, D.C.: Urban Institute, 1984).

12. Kenneth Meier, *Regulation: Politics, Bureaucracy, and Economics* (New York: St. Martins Press, 1985).

13. Welford W. Wilms, "Soft Policies for Hard Problems: Implementing Energy Conserving Building Regulations in California," *Public Administration Review* 42 (November–December 1982): 553–561; and Robert W. Hahn and Gregory J. McRae, "Application of Market Mechanisms to Pollution," *Policy Studies Review* 1 (February 1982): 470–476.

14. Sheldon Kamieniecki, David Shafie, and Julie Silvers, "Forming Partnerships in Environmental Policy: The Business of Emissions Trading in Clean Air Management," *American Behavioral Scientist* 43 (September 1999): 107–123.

15. Gary Polakovic, "Innovative Smog Plan Makes Little Progress," *Los Angeles Times* April 17, 2001, p. B1. Citizens for a Better Environment and other environmental groups have legally challenged the way in which SCAQMD has implemented RECLAIM on environmental justice grounds and have won.

16. Stavins, "What Can We Learn from the Grand Policy Experiment?"

17. Congressional Quarterly, *Regulation: Process and Politics* (Washington, D.C.: CQ Press, 1982).

18. Joseph Ferreira, "Promoting Safety through Insurance," in Eugene Bardach and Robert A. Kagan, eds., *Social Regulation: Strategies for Reform* (San Francisco: Institute for Contemporary Studies, 1982), pp. 267–288.

19. Ibid.

20. Martin T. Katzman, "Pollution Liability Insurance and the Internalization of Environmental Risks," *Policy Studies Review* 5 (February 1986): 614–623.

21. Ibid.

22. Ibid.

23. Katherine N. Probst, Don Fullerton, Robert E. Litan, and Paul R. Portney, *Footing the Bill for Superfund Cleanups: Who Pays and How?* (Washington, D.C.: Brookings Institution, 1995).

24. Katzman, "Pollution Liability Insurance and the Internationalization of Environmental Risks."

25. Ibid., p. 619.

26. Ibid.

27. Ibid., pp. 620–621.

28. Other studies on the use of liability insurance in protective legislation include Michael Baron, *Alternatives to Regulations* (Lexington, Mass.: Lexington Books, 1982); Ferreira, "Promoting Safety through Insurance"; John Scholz, "In Search of Regulatory Alternatives," *Journal of Policy Analysis and Management* 4 (Fall 1984): 113–121; Carol Heimer, *Reactive Risk and Rational Action: Managing Moral Hazard in Insurance Contracts* (Berkeley: University of California Press, 1985); David Hemenway, "Private Insurance as an Alternative to Protective Regulation: The Market for Residential Fire Insurance," *Policy Studies Journal* 15 (March 1987): 415–440; and Probst, Fullerton, Litan, and Portney, *Footing the Bill for Superfund Cleanup*.

29. For example, see W. Kip Viscusi, "The Informational Requirements for Effective Regulatory Review: An Analysis of the EPA Lead Standard," *Policy Studies Review* 1 (May 1982): 686–691.

30. Wilms, "Soft Policies for Hard Problems."

31. Beryl E. Pettus, "OSHA Inspection Costs, Compliance Costs, and Other Outcomes: The First Decade," *Policy Studies Review* 1 (February 1982): 596–614.

32. Paul Sabatier and Daniel Mazmanian, "A Guide to Accomplishing Policy Objectives," *Policy Analysis* 5 (Fall 1979): 481–504; Roland N. McKean, "Enforcement Costs in Environmental and Safety Regulation," *Policy Analysis* 6 (Summer 1980): 271–289; and Keith Hawkins, *Environment and Enforcement: Regulation and the Social Definition of Pollution* (Oxford: Claredon Press, 1984).

33. Hawkins, *Environment and Enforcement.* For a number of years, however, Los Angeles and New York City health officials have found it useful to provide the media with a weekly list of restaurants that are in violation of health codes. The media have cooperated by printing these lists in the newspaper and reporting the names of violators in television news reports.

34. Paul Sabatier and Daniel Mazmanian, "The Implementation of Public Policy: A Framework of Analysis," *Policy Studies Journal* 8 (Special Issue 1980): 538–560.

35. Murry L. Weidenbaum, "The High Cost of Government Regulation," *Challenge* (November–December 1979): 32–39.

36. Stone, *Regulation and Its Alternatives.*

37. Freeman, "Economics, Incentives, and Environmental Policy."

38. Ibid., pp. 212–213.

39. Barry G. Rabe, "Power to the States: The Promise and Pitfalls of Decentralization," in Norman J. Vig and Michael E. Kraft, eds., *Environmental Policy: New Directions for the Twenty-First Century*, 5th ed. (Washington, D.C.: CQ Press, 2003), pp. 33–56.

40. Ibid., p. 40.

41. Weidenbaum, "The High Cost of Government Regulation."

42. For example, see Eads and Fix, *Relief or Reform?*

43. Eugene Bardach, "Self-Regulation and Regulatory Paperwork," in Eugene Bardach and Robert A. Kagan, eds., *Social Regulation: Strategies for Reform* (San Francisco: Institute for Contemporary Studies, 1982), pp. 315–340.

44. Ibid.

45. Rabe, "Power to the States."

46. Barry G. Rabe, "Permitting, Prevention, and Integration: Lessons from the States," in Donald F. Kettl, ed., *Environmental Governance: A Report on the Next Generation of Environmental Policy* (Washington, D.C.: Brookings Institution, 2002), pp. 14–57.

47. Ibid.

48. Congressional Quarterly, *Regulation.*

49. Ibid.

50. Vague and ambiguous rules have hindered compliance in the past. See Sabatier and Mazmanian, "The Conditions of Effective Implementation."

51. McKean, "Enforcement Costs in Environmental and Safety Regulation," p. 286.

52. Mitnick, "Incentive Systems in Environmental Regulation"; Breyer, *Regulation and Its Reform*; and Hawkins, *Environment and Enforcement.*

53. McKean, "Enforcement Costs in Environmental and Safety Regulation," p. 281.

54. Ibid., p. 286.

55. Wilms, "Soft Policies for Hard Problems."

56. McKean, "Enforcement Costs in Environmental Regulation."

57. Mitnick, "Incentive Systems in Environmental Regulation"; and Breyer, *Regulation and Its Reform.*

58. James P. Lester, "Federalism and State Environmental Policy," in James P. Lester, ed., *Environmental Politics and Policy: Theories and Evidence*, 2nd ed. (Durham, N.C.: Duke University Press, 1995), pp. 39–60; and Rosenbaum, *Environmental Politics and Policy.*

59. C. K. Rowland and Roger Marz, "Gresham's Law: The Regulatory Analogy," *Policy Studies Review* 1 (February 1982): 572–580.

60. Frank J. Thompson and Michael J. Scicchitano, "State Enforcement of Federal Regulatory Policy: The Lessons of OSHA," *Policy Studies Journal* 13 (March 1985): 591–598.

61. Benveniste, *Regulation and Planning*; and Beryl Pettus, "OSHA Inspection Costs, Compliance Costs, and Other Outcomes."

62. Eads and Fix, *Relief or Reform?*

63. Ibid.

64. Mitnick, "Incentive Systems in Environmental Regulation"; and David M. Hedge and Donald C. Menzel, "Loosening the Regulatory Ratchet: A Grassroots View of Environmental Regulation," *Policy Studies Review* 13 (March 1985): 599–606. Also see Jeanne Nienaber Clarke and Daniel C. McCool, *Staking Out the Terrain: Power and Performance Among Natural Resource Agencies*, 2nd ed. (Albany, N.Y.: State University of New York Press, 1996).

65. Hawkins, *Environment and Enforcement.*

66. Paul Danaceau, "Developing Successful Enforcement Programs," in Bardach and Kagan, *Social Regulation*, pp. 139–158.

67. Florence Heffron and Neil McFeeley, *The Administrative Regulatory Process* (New York: Longman, 1983).

68. Ibid.

69. Rosemary O'Leary, "Environmental Policy in the Courts," in Vig and Kraft, *Environmental Policy*, pp. 151–173.

70. Ibid.

71. Cornelius M. Kerwin, *Rulemaking: How Government Agencies Write Law and Make Policy*, 3rd ed. (Washington, D.C.: CQ Press, 2003).

Chapter 5

1. Gary C. Bryner, *Blue Skies, Green Politics: The Clean Air Act of 1990 and Its Implementation*, 2nd ed. (Washington, D.C.: CQ Press), pp. 160–161. See also Matthew Cahn, *Environmental Deceptions: The Tension between Liberalism and Environmental Policymaking in the United States* (Albany: State University of New York Press, 1995).

2. U.S. Environmental Protection Agency, "FAQ on MTBE" <http://www.epa.gov/mtbe/gas.htm>, retrieved February 16, 2004.

3. U.S. Environmental Protection Agency, "Methyl Tertiary Butyl Ether (MTBE): Recommendations and Actions," <www.epa.gov/mtbe/action.htm>, retreived February 16, 2004.

4. Arturo Keller, John Froines, Catherine Koshland, John Reuter, Irwin Suffet, and Jerold Last, *Health and Environmental Assessment of MTBE: Report to the Governor and Legislature of the State of California as Sponsored by SB 521* November 1998 <http://tsrtp.ucdavis.edu/mtberpt>.

5. U.S. EPA, fact sheet on MTBE, <http://www.epa.gov/mtbe/faq.htm>; General Motors, fact sheet on tetraethyl lead, <http://www.gm.com/automotive/innovations/altfuel/info/t.htm>, DuPont, Heritage Dupont fact sheet, <http://heritage.dupont.com/floater/fl_tel/floater.shtml>, all retrieved February 16, 2004.

6. Keller et al., *Health and Environmental Assessment of MTBE*, p. 15.

7. Pamela Franklin, "To MTBE, or Not to MTBE," in "Is All Research Created Equal? Institutional Credibility and Technical Expertise in Environmental Policymaking at US EPA" (doctoral dissertation, University of California, Berkeley, 2002), pp. 79–82.

8. Maine Bureau of Health, Maine Bureau of Waste Management and Remediation, and Maine Geological Survey, *The Presence of MTBE and Other Gasoline Compounds in Maine's Drinking Water: A Preliminary Report* (Augusta, ME: Maine Bureau of Health, Maine Bureau of Waste Management and Remediation, Maine Geological Survey, October 13, 1998).

9. U.S. Environmental Protection Agency, internal memorandum, Office of Pollution Prevention and Toxic Substances, April 1987. See Franklin, "All Research Created Equal?" p. 107.

10. Keller et al., *Health and Environmental Assessment of MTBE*, p. 15.

11. Maine Bureau of Health et al., *Presence of MTBE and Other Gasoline Compounds in Maine's Drinking Water.*

12. U.S. Environmental Protection Agency, "Methyl Tertiary Butyl Ether (MTBE): Overview," <www.epa.gov/mtbe/faq.htm>, retrieved February 16, 2004.

13. Ibid.; and Keller et al., *Health and Environmental Assessmental MTBE*, p. 16.

14. U.S. Environmental Protection Agency. "RFG Covered Areas Code List," 2003, <http://www.epa.gov/otaq/regs/fuels/rfg/covareas.pdf>, retrieved February 16, 2004.

15. James E. McCarthy and Mary Tiemann, "MTBE in Gasoline: Clean Air and Drinking Water Issues" (Washington, D.C.: Congressional Research Service, Library of Congress, February 25, 2000); and Keller et al., *Health and Environmental Assessment of MTBE*, p. 15.

16. Northeast States for Coordinated Air Use Management (NESCAUM), RFG/MTBE: *Findings and Recommendations* (Boston, MA: NESCAUM, August 1999), p. 14.

17. U.S. Environmental Protection Agency, "Methyl Tertiary Butyl Ether (MTBE): Advance Notice of Intent to Initiate Rulemaking under the Toxic Substances Control Act to Eliminate or Limit the Use of MTBE as a Fuel Additive in Gasoline; Advance Notice of Proposed Rulemaking." *Federal Register*, part VII, March 24, 2004.

18. NESCAUM, *RFG/MTBE*.

19. U.S. EPA, Environmental Protection Agency, "Methyl Tertiary Butyl Ether (MTBE): Recommendations and Actions."

20. U.S EPA, "MTBE FAQ." See also Franklin, "To MTBE, or Not to MTBE," pp. 75–159. Franklin points out that ethanol receives a federal subsidy of almost $0.54 per gallon.

21. NESCAUM, *RFG/MTBE*, p. 9.

22. McCarthy and Tiemann, "MTBE in Gasoline," p. 2.

23. Franklin, "To MTBE, or Not to MTBE," p. 121.

24. Keller et al., *Health and Environmental Assessment of MTBE*, p. 25.

25. U.S. EPA, "Methyl Tertiary Butyl Ether (MTBE): Recommendations and Actions."

26. McCarthy and Tiemann, "MTBE in Gasoline."

27. Keller et al., *Health and Environmental Assessment of MTBE*, p. 20.

28. U.S. EPA, "MTBE: Advance Notice," p. 16097.

29. Ibid.

30. Energy Information Administration, DOE, "Refiners'/Gas Plant Operators' Monthly Petroleum Product Sales Report" *Petroleum Marketing Annual* 2002.

31. Ibid.; U.S. EPA, "MTBE: Advance Notices," p. 16100.

32. Ibid., p. 16100.

33. Keller et al., *Health and Environmental Assessment of MTBE*, p. 33

34. Ibid., pp. 22, 28.

35. Ibid., p. 38.

36. Ibid., p. 33.

37. Ibid., p. 39.

38. U.S. EPA, MTBE: Advance Notice," p. 16097.

39. Ibid., p. 16100.

40. U.S. EPA, Office of Underground Storage Tanks, OUST Overview <http://www.epa.gov/oust/overview.htm>, retrieved February 16, 2004.

41. U.S. EPA, "MTBE: Advance Notice," p. 16100.

42. Keller et al., *Health and Environmental Assessment of MTBE*, p. 31.

43. Ibid., p. 32.

44. U.S. EPA, "MTBE: Advance Notice," p. 16101.

45. Ibid., p. 16100.

46. Ibid., p. 16099.

47. Ibid.

48. Ibid.

49. Ibid., p. 16101.

50. Ibid.

51. Keller et al., *Health and Environmental Assessment of MTBE*, pp. 33–35.

52. U.S. Environmental Protection Agency, "MTBE Fact Sheet #2: Remediation of MTBE Contaminated Soil and Groundwater" (Washington, D.C.: Office of Solid Waste and Emergency Response, Office of Underground Storage Tanks, January 1998), p. 2.

53. U.S. EPA, "MTBE: Advance Notice," p. 16096.

54. Keller et al., *Health and Environmental Assessment of MTBE*, pp. 35–36.

55. Ibid.

56. U.S. EPA, "MTBE Fact Sheet #2," pp. 1–2.

57. Keller et al., *Health and Environmental Assessment of MTBE*, p. 47.

58. Ibid., p. 48.

59. Ibid.

60. John S. Zogorski, Michael J. Moran, and Pixie A. Hamilton, *USGS Fact Sheet 105–01* (Washington, D.C.: U.S. Geological Survey, October 2001).

61. John E. Reuter, Tahoe Research Group (TRG), University of California, Davis, Research on MTBE <http://trg.ucdavis.edu/research/mtbe.html>, retrieved February 16, 2004.

62. U.S. EPA, "MTBE: Advance Notice," p. 16100.

63. Association of State and Territorial Solid Waste Management Officials, *MTBE and Fuel Oxygenates Workgroup Newsletter* (Summer 2001): 6.

64. New England Interstate Water Pollution Control Commission, "Survey of State Experiences with MTBE Contamination at LUST Sites, August 2000," (Lowell, MA: NEIWPCC, December 15, 2000). This was an EPA-funded survey of all fifty states to determine how MTBE contamination is affecting LUST sites.

65. Ibid.

66. Alabama Department of Environmental Management, "Results Show Alabama Drinking Water Safe from MTBE Contamination," press release, March 9, 2001.

67. Alaska Department of Environmental Conservation, "Technical Review," *Alaska Tank News* 9, no. 1 (Spring 2000): 5.

68. Arizona Department of Environmental Quality, "Report on Methyl Tertiary Butyl Ether (MTBE)," October 1, 1999.

69. Reuter, Research on MTBE.

70. Susie T. Parker, "Mileage Reduction, 'Very Distinctive' Odors Top Denver Area Motorists' MTBE Complaints," *Oil Daily*, October 16, 1991, p. B3.

71. New England Interstate Water Pollution Control Commission, "Survey of State Experiences with MTBE Contamination at LUST Sites."

72. Iowa Department of Natural Resources, "Methyl Tertiary-Butyl Ether (MTBE) Occurrence in Iowa: A Report for the 2000 Session of the Seventy-Eighth General Assembly," February 2000.

73. Ibid.

74. New Jersey Department of Environmental Protection, "MTBE in New Jersey's Environment," December 19, 2000.

75. Ibid.

76. Ibid.

77. New England Interstate Water Pollution Control Commission, "Survey of State Experiences with MTBE Contamination at LUST Sites."

78. Ibid.

79. Ibid.

80. Association of State and Territorial Solid Waste Management Officials, *MTBE and Fuel Oxygenates Workgroup Newsletter* (Fall 2001).

81. Ibid.

82. New England Interstate Water Pollution Control Commission, "Survey of State Experiences with MTBE Contamination at LUST Sites."

83. Ibid.

84. Washington State House of Representatives, "Legislature Bans Gasoline Additive Showing Up in Groundwater," press release, May 9, 2001.

85. U.S. EPA, "Frequently Asked Questions (FAQs) About MTBE and USTs," <http://www.epa.gov/oust/mtbe/mtbefaqs.htm>, retrieved February 16, 2004.

86. Zogorski et al., *USGS Fact Sheet 105–01.*

87. Ibid.

Chapter 6

1. The strategic regulatory model defined in part I is designed precisely to account for these tensions. The creative accommodation of these constraints is the reason for developing the strategy.

2. Pamela Franklin, "To MTBE, or Not to MTBE," from "Is All Research Created Equal? Institutional Credibility and Technical Expertise in Environmental Policymaking at US EPA" (doctoral dissertation, University of California, Berkeley, 2002), pp. 75–159.

3. For a complete discussion of the politics of the 1990 Clean Air Act, see Gary C. Bryner, *Blue Skies, Green Politics: The Clean Air Act of 1990 and Its Implementation*, 2nd ed. (Washington, D.C.: CQ Press, 1995).

4. Walter Rosenbaum, *Environmental Politics and Policy*, 2nd ed. (Washington, D.C.: CQ Press, 1991), pp. 25–26. See also Walter Rosenbaum, *Environmental Politics and Policy*, 6th ed. (Washington, D.C.: CQ Press, 2005). He demonstrates that environmental concern continues to rank high.

5. Ibid.

6. Bryner, *Blue Skies, Green Politics.*

7. Ibid., pp. 160–161.

8. Migdon Segal, *Ethanol and Clean Air: The "Reg-Neg" Controversy and Subsequent Events* (Washington, D.C.: Congressional Research Service, Committee for the National Institute for the Environment, June 22, 1993).

9. The complete list of members is listed in See 56 FR 31176 and includes: EPA, Department of Energy, State and Territorial Air Pollution Program Administrators, Association of Local Air Pollution Control Officials, Northeast States for Coordinated Air Use Management, California Air Resources Board, American Petroleum Institute, National Petroleum Refiners Association, American Independent Refiners Association, Rocky Mountain Small Refiners Association, Clean Fuels Development Coalition (an ethanol trade group), Oxygenated Fuels Association, Renewable Fuels Association (the national trade association for the U.S. ethanol industry), American Methanol Institute, National Council of Farmer Cooperatives, National Corn Growers Association, Petroleum Marketers Association of America, Society of Independent Gasoline Marketers of America, Independent Liquid Terminals Association, Motor Vehicles Manufacturers Association, Association of International Automobile Manufacturers, Citizen Action, Sierra Club, American Lung Association, and Natural Resources Defense Council.

10. Personal e-mail correspondence with Philip Harter, January 27, 2004. See also 57 FR 13416.

11. 57 FR 13416 summarizes the Agreement in Principle: "Generally, the agreed upon reformulated gasoline program would provide refiners with two modeling options and a testing option for determining whether fuels sold in 1995 and 1996 meet the reformulated gasoline requirements. The simpler of the modeling options (the simple model) is detailed in this SNPRM and allows certification based on a fuel's oxygen, benzene, heavy metal and aromatics content and Reid Vapor Pressure (RVP). Under the agreement, EPA would develop a more complex model (the complex model) through a rulemaking to be completed by March 1, 1993. The complex model is expected to provide a method of certification based on the above parameters plus sulfur, olefins and the temperature at which 90 percent of the fuel vaporizes (T90), as well as any other parameters for which sufficient data is available regarding their effects on ozone-forming volatile organic compounds (VOC), toxic air pollutants (toxics) or oxides of nitrogen (NOx) emissions. In the first two years of the program, testing would only be permitted to determine the NOx emission effects of oxygenates other than Methyl Tertiary Butyl Ether (MTBE). Testing would eventually be permitted to qualify for inclusion in the models the emission effects of such other parameters or the effects of fuel parameters beyond the range covered in the models."

"The agreed upon program would allow refiners to produce reformulated gasoline, either by meeting the applicable standards on a per gallon basis or by meeting the standards on average. The agreed upon averaging program ensures that averaging will not result in smaller overall reductions in pollutants than if averaging were not permitted. It does so through the use of adjusted emission and fuel composition standards for averaged fuels, caps on per gallon levels of the relevant parameters, and compliance surveys to be performed at retail stations."

"The outline contains two options for compliance with the requirement that conventional gasoline not cause greater emissions of certain pollutants than occurred in 1990. During 1995 and 1996 each refiner and importer may either use the complex model to show that its conventional fuel does not have greater toxics emissions than its fuel had in 1990 or meet certain exhaust benzene and fuel compositional caps. After 1997 each producer and importer must show using the complex model that its conventional fuel has no more emissions of exhaust toxics and NOx than its 1990 annual average."

12. Franklin, "To MTBE, or Not to MTBE," p. 92.

13. M. K. Landy, M. J. Roberts, and S. R. Thomas, *The Environmental Protection Agency: Asking the Wrong Questions from Nixon to Clinton* (New York: Oxford University Press, 1994); Franklin, "To MTBE, or Not to MTBE," pp. 75–159.

14. Franklin, "To MTBE, or Not to MTBE," p. 101.

15. Matthew Cahn, *Environmental Deceptions: The Tension between Liberalism and Environmental Policymaking in the United States* (Albany: State University of New York Press, 1995).

16. Franklin, "To MTBE, or Not to MTBE," p. 92.

17. For example, ibid.

18. Arturo Keller et al., "Volume I: Summary and Recommendations," *Health and Environmental Assessment of MTBE: Report to the Governor and Legislature of the State of California as Sponsored by SB 521* (November 1998).

19. Quoted in Franklin, "To MTBE, or Not to MTBE," pp. 112–113; from a personal interview between Franklin and a senior official from the U.S. EPA Office of Air and Radiation.

20. U.S. Environmental Protection Agency, *Assessment of Potential Health Risks of Gasoline Oxygenated with Methyl Tertiary Butyl Ether (MTBE)* (Washington, D.C.: Office of Research and Development, November 1993).

21. Centers for Disease Control and Prevention, *An Investigation of Exposure to Methyl Tertiary Butyl Ether among Motorists and Exposed Workers in Stamford, Connecticut* (Atlanta, Ga.: U.S. Department of Health and Human Services, National Center for Environmental Health, September 14, 1993); Centers for Disease Control and Prevention, *An Investigation of Exposure to Methyl Tertiary Butyl Ether in Oxygenated Fuel in Fairbanks, Alaska* (Atlanta, Ga.: U.S. Department of Health and Human Services, National Center for Environmental Health, October 22, 1993); Centers for Disease Control and Prevention, *An Investigation of Exposure to MTBE and Gasoline among Motorists and Exposed Workers in Albany, New York* (Atlanta, Ga.: U.S. Department of Health and Human Services, National Center for Environmental Health, August 4, 1993).

22. U.S. Environmental Protection Agency, *Health Risk Perspectives on Fuel Oxygenates* (Washington, D.C.: Office of Research and Development, 1994).

23. Franklin, "To MTBE, or Not to MTBE," pp. 114–117.

24. Health Effects Institute, *The Potential Health Effects of Oxygenates Added to Gasoline: A Review of the Current Literature* (Cambridge, Mass.: Health Effects Institute, April 1996).

25. Ibid.

26. U.S. Water News Online, "Santa Monica Water Supply Threatened by MTBE," July 1996, <http://www.uswaternews.com/archives/arcquality/6smonica.html>, retrieved February 17, 2004. Also see U.S. EPA, "LA Regional Water, Endorse Santa Monica Water Agreement: Charnock Sub-Basin to Be Cleaned of Petroleum Contaminants," *Water Quality and Environment News*, <http://www.waterchat.com/News/Environment/03/Q4/env_031205–02.htm>, retrieved February 17, 2004.

27. Members of the EPA Blue Ribbon Panel on Oxygenates in Gasoline, 1999, included: Dan Greenbaum, Health Effects Institute, chair; Mark Buehler, Metropolitan Water District, Southern California; Robert Campbell, CEO, Sun Oil; Patricia Ellis, hydrogeologist, Delaware Department of Natural Resources and Environmental Conservation; Linda Greer, Natural Resources Defense Council; Jason Grumet, NESCAUM; Anne Happel, Lawrence Livermore National

Laboratory; Carol Henry, American Petroleum Institute; Michael Kenny, California Air Resources Board; Robert Sawyer, University of California, Berkeley; Todd Sneller, Nebraska Ethanol Board; Debbie Starnes, Lyondell Chemical; Ron White, American Lung Association; Robert Perciasepe, Air and Radiation, U.S. EPA (Nonvoting); Roger Conway, U.S. Department of Agriculture (nonvoting); Cynthia Dougherty, Drinking Water, U.S. EPA (nonvoting); William Farland, Risk Assessment, U.S. EPA (nonvoting); Barry McNutt, U.S. Department of Energy (nonvoting); Margo Oge, Mobile Sources, U.S. EPA (nonvoting); Samuel Ng, Underground Tanks, U.S. EPA (nonvoting); Mary White, ATSDR (nonvoting); and John Zogorski, USGS (nonvoting).

28. U.S. Environmental Protection Agency, "Achieving Clean Air and Clean Water: The Report of the Blue Ribbon Panel on Oxygenates in Gasoline," September 15, 1999.

29. Ibid.

30. Franklin, "To MTBE, or Not to MTBE," pp. 125–126. See also Segal, *Ethanol and Clean Air.*

31. Charles. Pope, "Interest Groups Weigh In as Congress Seeks Solution to Gasoline Additive Pollution," *CQ Weekly*, February 5, 2000, p. 253.

32. Northeast States for Coordinated Air Use Management, *RFG/MTBE: Findings and Recommendations*, August 1999, p. 5.

33. Pope, "Interest Groups Weigh In," p. 253.

34. Keller et al., "Volume I: Summary and Recommendations."

35. Sierra Club, press release, August 14, 2000, "Interim Guidance on the Use of MTBE in Gasoline" <http://www.sierraclub.org/cleanair/factsheets/mtbe.asp>; NRDC, press release, March 20, 2000, "NRDC Supports EPA's Action on Gasoline Additive MTBE" <http://www.nrdc.org/media/pressReleases/MTBErelease.asp>.

36. Neil Franz, "California Energy Commission Says MTBE Ban Premature," *Chemical Week*, March 6, 2002.

37. Franklin, "To MTBE, or Not to MTBE," pp. 127–128.

38. Ibid., pp. 131–132.

39. Health Effects Institute, "The Potential Health Effects of Oxygenates Added to Gasoline: A Review of the Current Literature: A Special Report of the Institute's Oxygenates Evaluation Committee," April 1996, <http://www.healtheffects.org/Pubs/oxysum.htm>.

40. Maine Department of Environmental Protection, "The Presence of MTBE and Other Gasoline Compounds in Maine's Drinking Water: A Preliminary Report" (Augusta, ME: Maine Department of Environmental Protection. October 13, 1998).

41. Joan Lowy, "Congress Moves to Protect Oil Firms on Gas Additive," Scripps Howard News Service, October 10, 2002, <http://www.shns.com/shns/g_index2.cfm?action=detail&pk=MTBELIABILITY-10-10-02>.

42. Ibid.

43. Charles Lindblom, "The 'Science' of Muddling Through," *Public Administration Review* 19 (1959): 79–88.

44. Eugene Bardach, *A Practical Guide for Policy Analysis: The Eightfold Path to More Effective Problem Solving* (New York: Chatham House, 2000).

45. For example, see Health Effects Institute, "The Potential Health Effects of Oxygenates Added to Gasoline"; and Keller et al., "Volume I: Summary and Recommendations."

46 Helen Ingram, "Implementation: A Review and Suggested Framework," in Naomi B. Lynn and Aaron Wildavsky, eds., *Public Administration: The State of the Discipline* (Chatham, N.J.: Chatham House, 1990), pp. 462–480.

Chapter 7

1. Peter Kiernan, "MTBE Phaseout May Boost Refining Margins on Supply Shortfalls," *Oil Daily*, June 5, 2002, p. 107.

2. Andrew Wood, "MTBE Green Image Challenged," *Chemical Week*, October 27, 1993, p. 42.

3. Alaska Department of Environmental Conservation, "Technical Review," *Alaska Tank News* no. 9.1 (Spring 2000): 5.

4. California Air Resources Board, "Proposed Modifications to the Proposed Regulation Order, Showing the Complete Proposed Regulation Order as Modified. Amendments to the California Phase 3 Gasoline (CaRFG3) Regulations to Refine the Prohibitions of MTBE and Specified Other Oxygenates in California Gasoline Starting December 31, 2003," 15-Day Notice version, released December 23, 2002.

5. Association of State and Territorial Solid Waste Management Officials, *MTBE and Fuel Oxygenates Workgroup Newsletter* (Summer 2001).

6. Association of State and Territorial Solid Waste Management Officials, *MTBE and Fuel Oxygenates Workgroup Newsletter* (Fall 2001).

7. Indiana Department of Environmental Management, MTBE Remediation Information, "About Underground Storage Tanks and Their Related Contaminants" <http://www.in.gov/idem/land/lust/pdf/mtberemediation.pdf>.

8. Iowa Department of Natural Resources, "Methyl Tertiary-Butyl Ether (MTBE) Occurrence in Iowa: A Report for the 2000 Session of the Seventy-Eighth General Assembly," Underground Storage Tank Section (February 2000).

9. Illinois Corn, "MTBE Case Studies," <http://www.ilcorn.org/Ethanol/MTBE_Cases/mtbe_cases.html>, retrieved December 30, 2002.

10. Iowa General Assembly, "HF 2294," 2000, <http://www.legis.state.ia.us/cgi-bin/Legislation/File_only.pl?FILE=/usr/ns-home/docs/GA/78GA/Legislation/HF/02200/HF02294/000216.html>, retrieved July 5, 2002.

11. Maine Office of the Governor, "King Praises EPA Decision to Drop MTBE in Gasoline," press release, July 27, 1999.

12. Association of State and Territorial Solid Waste Management Officials, *MTBE and Fuel Oxygenates Workgroup Newsletter* (Fall 2001): 15.

13. Association of State and Territorial Solid Waste Management Officials, *MTBE and Fuel Oxygenates Workgroup Newsletter* (Summer 2001).

14. New Hampshire Department of Environmental Services, "New Hampshire's Application for Relief from Federally Preempted Gasoline Standards," December 7, 2001.

15. U.S. Department of Energy, Energy Information Administration, "Motor Gasoline Outlook and State MTBE Bans," April 6, 2003, <http://www.eia.doe.gov/emeu/steo/pub/special/mtbeban.html>.

16. Illinois Corn, "MTBE Case Studies."

17. Kiernan,"MTBE Phaseout May Boost Refining Margins on Supply Shortfalls," *Oil Daily*, June 5, 2002, p. 107.

18. Association of State and Territorial Solid Waste Management Officials, *MTBE and Fuel Oxygenates Workgroup Newsletter* (Fall 2001): 24.

19. Northeast States for Coordinated Air Use Management, *RFG/MTBE: Findings and Recommendations* (1999).

20. Northeast States for Coordinated Air Use Management, "Northeast States Announce Unified MTBE Strategy," press release, January 19, 1999.

21. Connecticut Department of Environmental Protection, "Use of Methyl Tertiary Butyl Ether (MTBE) as a Gasoline Additive: Report to the Joint Standing Committees on Public Health and the Environment, Connecticut General Assembly," February 2000.

22. U.S. Environmental Protection Agency, *Federal Register* 62 FR 52193 (Oct. 6, 1997); 63 FR 10274 (March 2, 1998).

23. U.S. Environmental Protection Agency, drinking water contaminant candidate list, <http://www.epa.gov/safewater/ccl/cclfs.html>, retrieved April 10, 2004.

24. U.S. Environmental Protection Agency, "Methyl Tertiary Butyl Ether (MTBE): Recommendations and Actions," <http://www.epa.gov/mtbe/action.htm>, retrieved April 7, 2004.

25. U.S. Environmental Protection Agency, 2000 *Federal Register* 40 CFR Part 755.

26. U.S. Environmental Protection Agency, "Methyl Tertiary Butyl Ether (MTBE): Advance Notice of Intent to Initiate Rulemaking under the Toxic Substances Control Act to Eliminate or Limit the Use of MTBE as a Fuel Additive in Gasoline; Advance Notice of Proposed Rulemaking," *Federal Register*, Part VII, March 24, 2000; 40 CFR Part 755, p. 16103.

27. Ibid.

28. Ibid., p. 16104.

29. Ibid.

30. Association of State and Territorial Solid Waste Management Officials, *MTBE and Fuel Oxygenates Workgroup Newsletter* (Fall 2001): 20–23.

31. Office of Water, proposed rule received by OMB 1/11/2000, completed 2/16/2000—withdrawn by agency; Association of State and Territorial Solid Waste Management Officials, *MTBE and Fuel Oxygenates Workgroup Newsletter* (Spring 2001): 23.

32. Office of Air and Radiation, proposed rule received by OMB 1/19/2001, Completed 2/14/2000—withdrawn by agency; ASTSWMO.

33. Office of Air and Radiation, final rule received by OMB 1/19/2001, Completed 2/1/2001—Withdrawn by agency; ASTSWMO.

34. Association of State and Territorial Solid Waste Management Officials, *MTBE and Fuel Oxygenates Workgroup Newsletter* (Fall 2001): 3.

35. Ibid.

36. Ibid., pp. 2–3.

37. U.S. Conference of Mayors,"MTBE Liability Provisions Could Be Largest Unfunded Mandate in Recent Years," press release, November 17, 2003, <http://www.usmayors.org/uscm/news/press_releases/documents/mtbestatement_111703.pdf>, retrieved April 10, 2004; Reuters, "US Senators' Say Can Block MTBE's Liability Shield," October 10, 2003.

38. Associated Press, "Bush Reversed Regulatory Effort on Gas Additive," <http://www.cnn.com/2004/US/02/16/fuel.fight.ap/>, retrieved February 29, 2004.

39. See section 563, Negotiated Rulemaking Act 1990, 5 U.S.C. sections 561–570.

40. James E. MCarthy and Mary Tiemann, "MTBE in Gasoline: Clean Air and Drinking Water Issues," *CRS Report for Congress* (Washington, D.C.: Congressional Research Service, Library of Congress, February 25, 2000); Northeast States for Coordinated Air Use Management, *RFG/MTBE: Findings and Recommendations,* p. 14.

41. The complete list of the 1991 EPA RFG Regulation Negotiation membership is listed in See 56 FR 31176 and included: U.S. Environmental Protection Agency, Department of Energy, State and Territorial Air Pollution Program Administrators, Association of Local Air Pollution Control Officials, Northeast States for Coordinated Air Use Management, California Air Resources Board, American Petroleum Institute, National Petroleum Refiners Association, American Independent Refiners Association, Rocky Mountain Small Refiners Association, Clean Fuels Development Coalition (an ethanol trade group), Oxygenated Fuels Association, Renewable Fuels Association (the national trade association for the U.S. ethanol industry), American Methanol Institute, National Council of Farmer Cooperatives, National Corn Growers Association, Petroleum

Marketers Association of America, Society of Independent Gasoline Marketers of America, Independent Liquid Terminals Association, Motor Vehicles Manufacturers Association, Association of International Automobile Manufacturers, Citizen Action, Sierra Club, American Lung Association, and Natural Resources Defense Council.

42. 5 U.S.C. App. C.

43. U.S. Environmental Protection Agency, "About the EPA Science Advisory Board" <http://www.epa.gov/sab/about.htm>.

44. Health Effects Institute, "The Potential Health Effects of Oxygenates Added to Gasoline: A Review of the Current Literature: A Special Report of the Institute's Oxygenates Evaluation Committee," April 1996, <http://www.healtheffects.org/Pubs/oxysum.htm>.

45. "Program Summary: Research on Oxygenates Added to Gasoline," April 1996, <http://www.healtheffects.org/Pubs/oxyprog.htm>, retrieved April 8, 2004.

46. Ibid.

47. Arturo Keller et al., "Volume I: Summary and Recommendations," in *Health and Environmental Assessment of MTBE: Report to the Governor and Legislature of the State of California as Sponsored by SB 521* (November 1998) executive summary, <http://tsrtp.ucdavis.edu/mtberpt/vol1.pdf>, retrieved April 8, 2004.

48. Ibid.

49. U.S. Environmental Protection Agency, "Executive Summary and Recommendations," from *The Blue Ribbon Panel on Oxygenates in Gasoline*, July 27, 1999, pp. 2–3.

50. Ibid., emphasis in the original.

51. Ibid.

52. Ibid., pp. 3–6.

53. Ibid., p. 6.

54. Aaron B. Wildavsky, *Speaking Truth to Power: The Art and Craft of Policy Analysis* (New Brunswick, N.J.: Transaction Books, 1987).

Chapter 8

1. V. Feticiano, "Leaking Underground Storage Tanks: A Potential Environmental Problem," Congressional Research Service, January 11, 1984, p. 1; and U.S. Environmental Protection Agency, Office of Water, "Leaking Underground Storage Tanks," April 1985, p. 1.

2. Wayne B. Solley, Robert R. Pierce, and Howard Perlman, *Estimated Use of Water in the United States in 1995* (Washington, D.C.: U.S. Government Printing Office, 1998).

3. John E. Blodgett and Claudia Copeland, “Environmental Protection Issues of the 99th Congress” (Washington D.C.: Congressional Research Service, (January 1985), p. 56.

4. U.S. Environmental Protection Agency, “Factoids: Drinking Water and Ground Water Statistics for 2002,” <http://www.epa.gov/safewater/data/pdfs/02factoids.pdf>, retrieved June 17, 2003.

5. U.S. Environmental Protection Agency, “Ground Water Primer—Introduction,” <http://www.epa.gov/seahome/groundwater/src/intro.htm>, retrieved June 17, 2003.

6. American Society of Civil Engineers, “Issue Brief: Underground Storage Tanks,” <http://www.asce.org/reportcard/pdf/kentucky5.pdf>, retrieved April 18, 2003.

7. V. Feticiano, “Leaking Underground Storage Tanks: A Potential Environmental Problem,” Congressional Research Service, January 11, 1984.

8. U.S. Environmental Protection Agency, Office of Underground Storage Tanks, “Summary of State Reports on Releases from Underground Storage Tanks,” August 1986.

9. National Academy of Public Administration, *A Strategy for Implementing Federal Regulation of Underground Storage Tanks* (Washington, D.C.: National Academy of Public Administration, 1986), p. 69.

10. William C. Blackman, Jr., *Basic Hazardous Waste Management* (Boca Raton, Fla.: Lewis Publishers, 2001), p. 378.

11. U.S. Environmental Protection Agency, Office of Underground Storage Tanks, “Summary of State Reports on Releases from Underground Storage Tanks,” August 1986. The rate may have been higher since the tests conducted could not reveal all cases of leakage.

12. National Academy of Public Administration, *A Strategy for Implementing Federal Regulation of Underground Storage Tanks*, p. 70.

13. U.S. Environmental Protection Agency, *Report to Congress on a Compliance Plan for the Underground Storage Tank Program*, <http://www.epa.gov/OUST/pubs/rtc_0600.pdf>, retrieved June 17, 2003. By September 1999, about 400,000 releases from federally regulated USTs had been reported. Of these, work had begun on nearly 346,000 and had been completed at about 229,000 USTs.

14. Glenn Smith, Vermont Department of Fire Prevention, Hazardous Materials Team, telephone interview, March 15, 1986.

15. Blodgett and Copeland, “Environmental Protection Issues of the 99th Congress,” p. 56.

16. U.S. Environmental Protection Agency, *Report to Congress on a Compliance Plan for the Underground Storage Tank Program*, pp. 7–8.

17. U.S. Environmental Protection Agency, Office of Toxic Substances, “National Survey of Underground Motor Fuel Storage Tanks” (2000).

18. U.S. Environmental Protection Agency, Office of Underground Storage Tanks, "Summary of State Reports on Releases from Underground Storage Tanks," August 1986.

19. Ibid.

20. For a good summary of these legislative enactments, see Harvey Lieber, "Federalism and Hazardous Waste Policy," in James P. Lester and Ann O'M. Bowman, eds., *The Politics of Hazardous Waste Management* (Durham, N.C.: Duke University Press, 1983), pp. 60–72; Steven Cohen, "Defusing the Toxic Time Bomb: Federal Hazardous Waste Programs," in Norman J. Vig and Michael E. Kraft, eds., *Environmental Policy in the 1980's: Reagan's New Agenda* (Washington, D.C.: Congressional Quarterly Press, 1984), pp. 273–291; Walter A. Rosenbaum, *Environmental Politics and Policy* (Washington, D.C.: Congressional Quarterly Press, 1985); Thomas G. Ingersoll and Bradley R. Brockbank, "The Role of Economic Incentives in Environmental Policy," in Sheldon Kamieniecki, Robert O'Brien, and Michael Clarke, eds., *Controversies in Environmental Policy* (Albany: State University of New York Press, 1986), pp. 201–222; Benjamin Walter and Malcolm Getz, "Social and Economic Effects of Toxic Waste Disposal," in Kamieniecki, O'Brien, and Clarke, *Controversies in Environmental Policy*, pp. 223–245; Daniel Mazmanian and David Morell, "The Elusive Pursuit of Toxics Management," *Public Interest*, no. 90 (Winter 1988): 81–98; Arlene Elgart Mirsky, Richard J. Conway, Jr., and Geralyn G. Humphrey, "The Interface Between Bankruptcy and Environmental Laws," *Business Lawyer*, 46 (February 1991): 623–690; Rosemary O'Leary, Robert F. Durant, Daniel J. Fiorino, and Paul S. Weiland, *Managing for the Environment* (San Francisco: Jossey-Bass, 1999); Carolyn Merchant, *The Columbia Guide to American Environmental History* (New York: Columbia University Press, 2002); and Glen Sussman, Byron W. Daynes, and Jonathan P. West, *American Politics and the Environment* (New York: Longman, 2002).

21. For an excellent analysis of President Reagan's environmental policies and the political issues surrounding those policies, consult: Vig and Kraft, *Environmental Policy in the 1980's: Reagan's New Agenda*; Henry C. Kenski and Helen M. Ingram, "The Reagan Administration and Environmental Regulation: The Constraint of the Political Market," in Kamieniecki, O'Brien, and Clarke, *Controversies in Environmental Policy*, pp. 275–298; William E. Kovacic, "The Reagan Judiciary and Environmental Policy: The Impact of Appointments to the Federal Courts of Appeals," *Boston College Environmental Affairs Law Review* 18 (June 1991): 669–713; and Paul Boyer, ed., *Reagan as President: Contemporary Views of the Man, His Politics, and His Policies* (Chicago: Ivan R. Dee, 1990), pp. 177–187.

22. Ingersoll and Brockbank, "The Role of Economic Incentives in Environmental Policy," pp. 204–205; and Mirsky, Conway, and Humphrey, "The Interface between Bankruptcy and Environmental Laws."

23. Mary Tiemann, "Leaking Underground Storage Tank Cleanup Issues," Congressional Research Service Report 97-471, February 17, 1999.

24. Ibid.

25. For an in-depth description of the insurance industry's position, refer to National Academy of Public Administration, "Providing Financial Assurance for Storage Tanks," August 1985, pp. 1–39; and "Deep Down Facts about Underground Storage Tanks," *Journal of American Insurance* (Third Quarter 1990): 17–21.

26. For more information about the use of insurance in regulation, see Joseph Ferreira, "Promoting Safety through Insurance," in Eugene Bardach and Robert A. Kagan, eds., *Social Regulation: Strategies for Reform* (San Francisco: Institute for Contemporary Studies, 1982), pp. 267–288; Carol Heimer, *Reactive Risk and Rational Action: Managing Moral Hazard in Insurance Contracts* (Berkeley: University of California Press, 1985); David Hemenway, "Private Insurance as an Alternative to Protective Regulation: The Market for Residential Fire Insurance," *Policy Studies Journal* 15 (March 1987): 415–440; and U.S. EPA Underground Storage Tanks. "Dollars and Sense: Financial Responsibility Requirements for Underground Storage Tanks," July 1995, <http://www.epa.gov/swerust1/pubs/dol&sens.pdf>, retrieved April 18, 2003.

27. National Academy of Public Administration, *A Strategy for Implementing Federal Regulation of Underground Storage Tanks*, pp. 82–86.

28. Ibid., pp. 82–83.

29. Ibid., pp. 24–25. According to U.S. General Accounting Office, "Recommendations for Improving the Underground Storage Tank Program," March 25, 2003, most states now run their own programs; the EPA is responsible for regulating tanks only in Idaho, lands controlled by Native Americans, and some areas in New York State. Compliance among state and federally regulated tanks is increasing, although certain barriers still exist, including funding shortfalls, lack of inspection visits within the mandated time, lack of ability to prevent deliveries to noncompliant tanks (according to Tiemann, *Leaking Underground Storage Tank Cleanup Issues*, however, several large petroleum companies have begun to stop deliveries to noncompliant tank owners), and location of abandoned and unidentified tanks. Also, according to U.S. General Accounting Office, "MTBE Contamination from Underground Storage Tanks," May 21, 2002, further implementation problems come from the tendency of states to use federal monies rather than their own to pay for staff, and the common practice of states not to report leaking tanks until shortly before removal.

Chapter 9

1. National Academy of Public Administration, "A Strategy for Implementing Federal Regulation of Underground Storage Tanks," January 1986, p. 2.

2. Robert Cameron Mitchell, "Public Opinion and Environmental Politics in the 1970's and 1980's," in Norman Vig and Michael Kraft, eds., *Environmental Policy in the 1980's: Reagan's New Agenda* (Washington, D.C.: Congressional Quarterly Press, 1984), pp. 51–74.

3. Given the antiregulatory climate among small businesses, it was assumed that direct command-and-control regulations would probably be resisted. This probably would have a negative impact on compliance rates.

4. National Academy of Public Administration, "A Strategy for Implementing Federal Regulation of Underground Storage Tanks," p. 52.

5. Ibid., pp. 22–29. Evidence of this can also be found in James Boyd and Howard Kunreuther, "Retroactive Liability and Future Risk: The Optimal Regulation of Underground Storage Tanks," http://www.rff.org/CFDOCS/disc_papers/PDF_files/9602.pdf, retrieved June 17, 2003. They wrote, "In order for firms to reduce their insurance premiums, they are induced to make efficient safety investments on their own rather than being forced to do so by the government. Correspondingly, it is in the best interest of insurers to verify and monitor the technical compliance of those operators they underwrite" (p. 7). While they found that state assurance funds are beneficial for cleanup of past spills, they believe that it is inefficient for future ones.

6. Ibid., pp. 31, 59.

7. Ibid., pp. 30–34.

8. Ibid., pp. 34.

9. Ibid., pp. 34–35.

10. Ibid.

11. Ibid., p. 13.

12. Ibid., p. 35.

13. Ibid.

14. Ibid. For an extensive analysis of the UST insurance issue, consult National Academy of Public Administration, "Providing Financial Assurance for Storage Tanks," August 1985. Also see Helen Ingram, "Implementation: A Review and Suggested Framework," in Naomi B. Lynn and Aaron Wildavsky, eds., *Public Administration: The State of the Discipline* (Chatham, N.J.: Chatham House, 1990), pp. 462–480; Robert W. Adler, Jessica C. Landman, and Diane M. Cameron, *The Clean Water Act: 20 Years Later* (Washington, D.C.: Island Press, 1993); John A. Hird, *Superfund: The Political Economy of Environmental Risk* (Baltimore Md.: Johns Hopkins University Press, 1994); Thomas W. Church, *Cleaning Up the Mess: Implementation Strategies in Superfund* (Washington, D.C.: Brookings Institution, 1993); Victor B. Flatt, "A Dirty River Runs through It (The Failure of Enforcement in the Clean Water Act)," *Boston College Environmental Affairs Law Review* 25 (October 1997): 1–45; and Robert T. Nakamura and Thomas W. Church, *Taming Regulation: Superfund and the Challenge of Regulatory Reform* (Washington, D.C.: Brookings Institution, 2003).

Chapter 10

1. Richard J. Tobin, "Revising the Clean Air Act: Legislative Failure and Administrative Success," in Norman J. Vig and Michael E. Kraft, eds., *Environmental Policy in the 1980's: Reagan's New Agenda* (Washington, D.C.: Congressional Quarterly Press, 1984), pp. 227–249. Also see Charles O. Jones, "Speculative Augmentation in Federal Air Pollution Policymaking," *Journal of Politics* 36 (May 1974): 438–464; Charles O. Jones, *Clean Air: The Policies and Politics of Pollution Control* (Pittsburgh: University of Pittsburgh Press, 1975); Gary C. Bryner, *Blue Skies, Green Politics: The Clean Air Act of 1990 and Its Implementation*, 2nd ed. (Washington, D.C.: CQ Press, 1995); and U.S. EPA, "Clean Air Act, 1990," <http://www.epa.gov/oar/caa/caa.txt>, retrieved April 25, 2003.

2. This point also is made in Steven A. Cohen, "EPA: A Qualified Success," in Sheldon Kamieniecki, Robert O'Brien, and Michael Clarke, eds., *Controversies in Environmental Policy* (Albany: State University of New York Press, 1986), pp. 174–195. Generally, litigation and judicial decisions have ameliorated environmental decision making. Rosemary O'Leary observes that "the impact of court decisions on the EPA is problematic. Compliance with court orders has become one of the agency's top priorities, at times overtaking congressional mandates and threatening representative democracy. Clearly litigation is not the best way to formulate environmental policy or to determine our nation's environmental priorities." See Rosemary O'Leary, *Environmental Change: Federal Courts and the EPA* (Philadelphia: Temple University Press 1993), p. 170.

3. Helen Ingram, "Implementation: A Review and Suggested Framework," in Naomi B. Lynn and Aaron Wildavsky, eds., *Public Administration: The State of the Discipline* (Chatham, NJ: Chatham House, 1990), pp. 462–480. We deeply appreciate the assistance provided by Kathy Huber in applying Ingram's framework to the implementation of the UST program. See Kathy Huber, Sheldon Kamieniecki, and Steven A. Cohen, "The Implementation of Federal Underground Storage Tank Regulations: Some Preliminary Findings" (paper prepared for presentation to the 1990 Annual Meeting of the American Political Science Association, San Francisco, Aug. 29–Sept. 2).

4. Ibid., p. 471.

5. Ibid., p. 474.

6. National Academy of Public Administration, *A Strategy for Implementing Federal Regulation of Underground Storage Tanks* (Washington, D.C.: National Academy of Public Administration, 1986).

7. U.S. Environmental Protection Agency, "Leaking Underground Storage Tank Fund," <www.epa.gov/oust/ltffacts.html>, retrieved June 4, 2002.

8. U.S. Environmental Protection Agency, "Leaking Underground Storage Tank Fund." <www.epa.gov/oust/ltffacts.html>, retrieved April 18, 2003.

9. U.S. Environmental Protection Agency, *Fiscal Year 1988 Program Guidance* (Washington, D.C.: U.S. Environmental Protection Agency, 1987).

10. Ibid., p. 30, emphasis in original.

11. Ibid.

12. Ibid., p. 33.

13. This approach is likely to work because HSWA itself has certain "self-implementing" provisions. Unlike RCRA, many of HSWA's provisions can be put into effect without EPA action. The law provides for regulation by statute in the case of underground storage tanks. HSWA includes an interim prohibition against installing certain types of underground tanks. The stringent standards included in the act remain in effect until EPA's requirements are formally promulgated.

14. U.S. Environmental Protection Agency, Office of Solid Waste and Emergency Response, "Underground Storage Tank Program Initiatives," memo from Timothy Fields to Regional UST Division Directors, October 23, 2000.

15. U.S. Environmental Protection Agency, OUST, "UST Fields Initiative," <www.epa.gov/oust/ustfield/index.html>, retrieved August 2, 2002; U.S. Environmental Protection Agency, OUST, "EPA's New UST Fields Pilots: Questions and Answers," <www.epa.gov/oust>, retrieved July 2002; U.S. Environmental Protection Agency, OUST, "EPA Announces $3.8 million to Clean Up Petroleum from Underground Storage Tank Sites at Gas Stations in 26 States," news release, July 1, 2002, <www.epa.gov/oust/ustfield/40pr.pdf>, retrieved August 2002.

16. Ibid.

17. Ibid.

18. U.S. Environmental Protection Agency, OUST, "Status of State Fund Programs," <www.epa.gov/oust/states/fndstatus.html>, retrieved June 4, 2002; U.S. Environmental Protection Agency, "State Funds in Transition: Models for Underground Storage Tank Assurance Funds," January 1997, p. 30, <ww.epa.gov/oust/states/statefnd.html>, retrieved June 13, 2002.

19. U.S. Environmental Protection Agency, "Status of State Fund Programs."

20. Steven Cohen worked closely with OUST to develop this program budget. He was no longer associated with NAPA at this time.

21. U.S. Environmental Protection Agency, "Report to Congress on a Compliance Plan for the Underground Storage Tank Program," June 2000.

22. Thomas J. Peters and Robert H. Waterman, *In Search of Excellence: Lessons from America's Best Run Companies* (New York: Harper and Row, 1982). See also Rosalyn Kulick, "Mission Impossible: Being a Manager Today," *Employee Assistance Program Networker* 11, no. 4 (November 2002), <http://www.hr.wayne.edu/eap/ValueOptions/networker/v11_no4.html>, retrieved April 18, 2003; and CFO—The Business End of Business, Elizabeth Fry, "Virtual CFO," March 1, 1997, <http://www.cfoweb.com.au/stories/19970301/7228.asp>, retrieved April 18, 2003.

23. Patrick Lee, "New EPA Rules Scare Owners of Gas Stations: High Cost of Insurance for Storage Tanks May Drive Many Out of Business," *Los Angeles Times*, July 24, 1989, IV:1; Adolfo Pesquera, "Law Dries Up Gas Tanks: Service

Station Owners Stumble over Deadline for Safety Certification," *San Antonio Express-News*, May 10, 2001, p. 1E; and Patti Bond, "Need to Replace Tanks May Shut Gas Stations: Before Dec. 22, All Underground Storage Must Be Upgraded or Removed, a Job Too Costly for Many Small Firms," *Atlanta Journal and Constitution*, August 1, 1998, p. 6A.

24. "Fuel-Leak Rules May Hasten End of Mom and Pop Service Stations," *New York Times*, June 19, 1989, I:1.

25. U.S. Environmental Protection Agency, OUST, "State Funds in Transition: Models for Underground Storage Tank Assurance Funds," January 1997, pp. 1–31, <www.epa.gov/oust/states/statefnd.html>, retrieved June 13, 2002.

26. Ibid.

27. CRS Report for Congress, "Leaking Underground Storage Tank Cleanup Issues," Mary Tiemann, Specialist in Environmental Policy Resources, Science, and Industry Division. Updated February 17, 1999.

28. Ibid.; U.S. Environmental Protection Agency, "Financial Responsibility for Underground Storage Tanks: A Reference Manual," January 2000, p. 87.

29. U.S. Environmental Protection Agency, "Report to Congress on a Compliance Plan for the Underground Storage Tank Program."

30. U.S. Environmental Protection Agency, "Tanknology-NDE, International, Inc Criminal Plea," <www.epa.gov/compliance/resources/cases/civil/rcra/tanknology.html>, retrieved August 2, 2002.

31. Ibid.

32. U.S. Environmental Protection Agency, OUST, "How Much Work Remains to Be Done?" <www.epa.gov/oust/faqs/remain.html>, retrieved July 2002.

33. U.S. Environmental Protection Agency, "Report to Congress on a Compliance Plan for the Underground Storage Tank Program."

34. Remarks by Marianne Lamont Horinko, 14th Annual UST/LUST Conference Opening Plenary Session, March 11, 2002, <www.epa.gov/oust/aaspeech.html>, retrieved June 5, 2002.

35. U.S. Environmental Protection Agency, OUST, "Report to Congress on a Compliance Plan for the Underground Storage Tank Program."

36. U.S. Environmental Protection Agency, Office of Solid Waste and Emergency Response, *Measuring Progress in UST Management* (Washington, D.C.: United States Environmental Protection Agency, 1988). Steven Cohen served as a consultant to OUST on this project.

37. U.S. Environmental Protection Agency, OUST, "State Underground Storage Tank Programs," <http://www.epa.gov/swerust1/fsstates.htm>, retrieved April 18, 2003.

38. U.S. Environmental Protection Agency, OUST, "How Have the UST Requirements Helped Protect the Environment?" <www.epa.gov/oust/faqs/topfour.html>, retrieved August 21, 2002; and U.S. Environmental Protection

Agency, "Section IV: Managing Underground Storage Tanks RCRA Subtitle I" (2000).

39. U.S. Environmental Protection Agency, OUST, "Cleaning Up UST System Releases," <www.epa.gov/oust/cat/index.html>, retrieved June 7, 2002; and "Remarks by Marianne Lamont Horinko."

40. Columbia University, Graduate Program in Public Policy and Administration, *Final Report: Workshop Project on Leaking Underground Storage Tanks* (New York: N.Y.: School of International and Public Affairs, 1989). Steven Cohen was the faculty adviser to this student group project.

Conclusion

1. Of course, this is a double-edged sword. Opponents of the program can point to such failures as evidence that the law is flawed and should be changed or even repealed.

2. For a good discussion of the relationship between complexity and uncertainty in policy formulation, see John S. Dryzek, "Don't Toss Coins in Garbage Cans: A Prologue to Policy Design," *Journal of Public Policy* 3 (October 1983): 345–367; and Emery Roe, *Narrative Policy Analysis: Theory and Practice* (Durham, N.C.: Duke University Press, 1994).

3. Neutral outside research organizations also have been effectively used in water quality planning. See Sheldon Kamieniecki, *Public Representation in Environmental Policymaking: The Case of Water Quality Management* (Boulder, Colo.: Westview Press, 1980).

4. This argument is forcefully made in Daniel Guttman and Barry Willner, *Shadow Government* (New York: Pantheon Books, 1976). See also James G. McGann and R. Kent Weaver, *Think Tanks and Civil Society: Catalysts for Ideas and Action* (New Brunswick, N.J.: Transaction Publishers, 2000), p. 17; and Diane Stone, *Capturing the Political Imagination: Think Tanks and the Policy Process* (Midsomer Norton, Avon, UK: Bookcraft Ltd., 1996), pp. 28–29.

5. Charles Lindblom, "The Science of Muddling Through," *Public Administration Review* (Spring 1959): 79–88.

6. See, for example, Lester W. Milbrath, *Envisioning a Sustainable Society: Learning Our Way Out* (Albany: State University of New York Press, 1989); and Matthew A. Cahn, *Environmental Deceptions* (Albany: State University of New York Press, 1995).

7. The phrase "better living through chemistry" is a variation of DuPont chemical company's advertising slogan, "Better Things for Better Living . . . through Chemistry." The slogan was used between 1939 and the early 1980s when "through chemistry" was dropped.

8. For a broad discussion on the balance between market efficiency and market failure, see David Weimer and Aidan Vining, *Policy Analysis: Concepts and Practice*, 4th ed. (Upper Saddle River, N.J.: Prentice Hall, 2005).

9. Anne Larason Schneider and Helen Ingram, *Policy Design for Democracy* (Lawrence: University of Kansas Press, 1997); and Peter DeLeon, *Democracy and the Policy Sciences* (Albany: State University of New York, 1997).

10. Mark R. Powell, *Science at EPA: Information in the Regulatory Process* (Washington, D.C.: Resources for the Future, 1999).

11. The dangers of overregulation are discussed in John M. Mendeloff, *The Dilemma of Toxic Substance Regulation: How Overregulation Causes Underregulation* (Cambridge, Mass.: MIT Press, 1988); and Marie-Louise Bemelmans-Videc, Ray C. Rist, and Evert Vedung, *Carrots, Sticks, and Sermons: Policy Instruments and Their Evaluation* (New Brunswick, N.J.: Transaction Publishers, 1998), pp. 59–60.

12. Charles Davis and James Lester found that most of the states did not replace federal aid cuts in the environmental policy area with their own source funds during the 1981–1984 period. Charles E. Davis and James P. Lester, "Decentralizing Federal Environmental Policy: A Research Note," *Western Political Quarterly* 40 (September 1987): 555–565.

13. Council of Economic Advisors, *Economic Report of the President* (Washington, D.C.: U.S. Government Printing Office, 1982), p. 44. Corey Stein, "Pollution Insurance Comes of Age," *Public Management* (July–August 1999): 14–17, notes that liability insurance is an effective incentive for corporate behavior, while Michael C. Pruett, "Environmental Cleanup Costs and Insurance: Seeking a Solution," *Georgia Law Review* 24 (March 1990): 705–732, is not convinced. The insurance requirement is an effective tool when used in combination with other tools.

14. Sheldon Kamieniecki and Steven A. Cohen, "Strategic Regulatory Planning in the Management of Hazardous Materials," *Policy and Politics* 18 (July 1990): 207–216.

15. James L. Mercer, *Strategic Planning for Public Managers* (New York: Quorum Books, 1991), p. 140.

16. Michael D. Cohen, James G. March, and Johan P. Olsen, "A Garbage Can Model of Organizational Choice," *Administrative Science Quarterly* 17 (March 1972): 1–25.

17. Hans Th. A. Bressers and Walter A. Rosenbaum, "Innovation, Learning, and Environmental Policy: Overcoming 'A Plague of Uncertainties,'" *Policy Studies Journal* 28, no. 3 (2000). They discuss the difficulty of coordinating scientific data and environmental policy.

18. Dryzek, "Don't Toss Coins in Garbage Cans," p. 346.

19. Patricia W. Ingraham, "Toward More Systemic Consideration of Policy Design," *Policy Studies Journal* 15 (June 1987): 625.

20. Ibid.

21. Ernest R. Alexander, "Design in the Decisionmaking Process," *Policy Sciences* 14 (June 1982): 279–292.

22. Stephan H. Linder and B. Guy Peters, "From Social Theory to Policy Design," *Journal of Public Policy* 4 (August 1984): 239. In addition, consult Stephen H. Linder and B. Guy Peters, "The Analysis of Design or the Design of Analysis?" *Policy Studies Review* 7 (Summer 1988): 738–750.

23. For instance, see Frederick C. Mosher, "The Changing Responsibilities and Tactics of the Federal Government," *Public Administration Review* 40 (November–December 1980), pp. 541–548; Lester M. Salamon, "Rethinking Public Management: Third Party Government and the Changing Forms of Government Action," *Public Policy* 29 (Summer 1981): 255–275; Harold Wolman, "The Determinants of Program Success and Failure," *Journal of Public Policy* 1 (October 1981): 433–464; Anne Larason Schneider and Helen Ingram, *Policy Design for Democracy* (Lawrence: University Press of Kansas, 1997); and Frederic Varone and Bernard Aebischer, "Energy Efficiency: The Challenges of Policy Design," *Energy Policy* 29 (June 2001): 615–629.

24. For example, see Alexander, "Design in the Decisionmaking Process"; Linder and Peters, "From Social Theory to Policy Design"; Stephen H. Linder and B. Guy Peters, "A Design Perspective on Policy Implementation: The Fallacies of Misplaced Prescription," *Policy Studies Review* 6 (February 1987): 459–475; Ingraham, "Toward More Systematic Consideration of Policy Design"; Mark E. Rushefsky, *Public Policy in the United States* (Armonk, N.Y.: M. E. Sharpe, 2002); and Schneider and Ingram, *Policy Design for Democracy*. Schneider and Ingram note that "policy design is inherently a purposeful and normative enterprise through which the elements of policy are arranged to serve particular values, purposes, and interests" (p. 3).

25. Linder and Peters, "From Social Theory to Policy Design," p. 253.

26. Ibid., p. 254.

27. Evidence of this can be found in Allan W. Lerner and John Wonat, "Fuzziness and Bureaucracy," *Public Administration Review* 43 (November–December 1983): 500–509; Carol H. Weiss, *Organizations for Policy Analysis* (Newbury Park, Calif.: Sage, 1992), pp. 6–7; and Charles F. Bonser, Eugene B. McGregor, and Clinton V. Oster, *Policy Choices and Public Action* (Upper Saddle River, N.J.: Prentice Hall, 1996), pp. 22–23.

28. Dryzek, "Don't Toss Coins in Garbage Cans," pp. 362–363. Also refer to David B. Bobrow and John S. Dryzek, *Policy Analysis by Design* (Pittsburgh: University of Pittsburgh Press, 1987); and John S. Dryzek and Brian Ripley, "The Ambitions of Policy Design," *Policy Studies Review* 7 (Summer 1988): 705–719. Also see John S. Dryzek, "Policy Analysis and Planning: From Science to Argument," in Frank Fischer and John Forester, eds., *The Argumentative Turn in Policy Analysis and Planning* (Durham, N.C.: Duke University Press, 1993).

Bibliography

Adler, Robert W., Jessica C. Landman, and Diane M. Cameron. *The Clean Water Act: 20 Years Later.* Washington, D.C.: Island Press, 1993.

Alabama Department of Environmental Management. "Results Show Alabama Drinking Water Safe from MTBE Contamination," press release, March 9, 2001.

Alaska Department of Environmental Conservation. "Technical Review." *Alaska Tank News* 9, no. 1 (Spring 2000): 5.

Alexander, Ernest R. "Design in the Decisionmaking Process." *Policy Sciences* 14 (June 1982): 279–292.

American Society of Civil Engineers. "Issue Brief: Underground Storage Tanks." Available on-line at <http://www.asce.org/reportcard/pdf/kentucky5.pdf>, retrieved April 18, 2003.

Aram, John D., and Jeffrey S. Coomes. "Public Policy and the Small Business Sector." *Policy Studies Journal* 13 (June 1985): 692–700.

Arizona Department of Environmental Quality. "Report on Methyl Tertiary Butyl Ether (MTBE)." October 1, 1999.

"Assessment of Potential Health Risks of Gasoline Oxygenated with Methyl Tertiary Butyl Ether (MTBE)." Washington, D.C.: Office of Research and Development, U.S. Environmental Protection Agency, November, 1993.

Associated Press. "Bush Reversed Regulatory Effort on Gas Additive." Available on-line at <http://www.cnn.com/2004/US/02/16/fuel.fight.ap/>, retrieved February 19, 2004.

Association of State and Territorial Solid Waste Management Officials. *MTBE and Fuel Oxygenates Workgroup Newsletter* (Summer 2001).

Association of State and Territorial Solid Waste Management Officials. *MTBE and Fuel Oxygenates Workgroup Newsletter* (Fall 2001).

Bachrach, Peter, and Morton S. Baratz. *Power and Poverty.* New York: Oxford University Press, 1970.

Baden, John A., and Tim O'Brien. "Bringing Private Management to the Public Lands: Environmental and Economic Advantages." In *Flashpoints in*

Environmental Policymaking: Controversies in Achieving Sustainability. Eds. Sheldon Kamieniecki, George A. Gonzalez, and Robert O. Vos. Albany: State University of New York Press, 1997.

Bardach, Eugene. "Self-Regulation and Regulatory Paperwork." In *Social Regulation: Strategies for Reform*. Eds. Eugene Bardach and Robert A. Kagan. San Francisco: Institute for Contemporary Studies, 1982.

Bardach, Eugene. *A Practical Guide for Policy Analysis: The Eightfold Path to More Effective Problem Solving*. New York, Chatham House, 2000.

Barke, Richard P. "Regulatory Delay as Political Strategy." In *Federal Administrative Agencies: Essays on Power and Politics*. Ed. Howard Ball. Englewood Cliffs, N.J.: Prentice Hall, 1984.

Baron, Michael. *Alternatives to Regulations*. Lexington, Mass.: Lexington Books, 1982.

Baumgartner, Frank R., and Beth L. Leech. *Basic Interests: The Importance of Groups in Politics and in Political Science*. Princeton, N.J.: Princeton University Press, 1998.

Beardsley, Dan, Terry Davies, and Robert Hersh. "Improving Environmental Management: What Works, What Doesn't." *Environment* (September 1997): 6–9, 28–35.

Bemelmans-Videc, Marie-Louise, Ray C. Rist, and Evert Vedung. *Carrots, Sticks, and Sermons: Policy Instruments and Their Evaluation*. New Brunswick, N.J.: Transaction Publishers, 1998.

Benveniste, Guy. *Regulation and Planning: The Case of Environmental Politics*. San Francisco: Boyd and Fraser, 1981.

Berney, Robert E., and Ed Owens. "A Theoretical Framework for Small Business Policy." *Policy Studies Journal* 13 (June 1985): 681–691.

Bernstein, Marver H. *Regulating Business by Independent Commission*. Princeton, N.J.: Princeton University Press, 1955.

Berry, Jeffrey M. *The New Liberalism: The Rising Power of Citizen Groups*. Washington, D.C.: Brookings Institution Press, 1999.

Blackman, William C. *Basic Hazardous Waste Management*. Boca Raton, Fla.: Lewis Publishers, 2001.

Blodgett, John E., and Claudia Copeland. *Environmental Protection Issues of the 99th Congress*. Report Number 85-517. Washingon, D.C.: Congressional Research Service, Environment and Natural Resources Policy Division, January 1985.

Bobrow, David B., and John S. Dryzek. *Policy Analysis by Design*. Pittsburgh: University of Pittsburgh Press, 1987.

Bond, Patti "Need to Replace Tanks May Shut Gas Stations: Before Dec. 22, All Underground Storage Must Be Upgraded or Removed, A Job Too Costly for Many Small Firms." *Atlanta Journal and Constitution*, August 1, 1998, p. 6A.

Bonser, Charles F., Eugene B. McGregor, and Clinton V. Oster. *Policy Choices and Public Action*. Upper Saddle River, N.J.: Prentice Hall, 1996.

Bowman, Ann O'M. "Hazardous Waste Cleanups and Superfund Implementation in the Southeast." *Policy Studies Journal* 14 (September 1985): 100–110.

Boyd, James, and Howard Kunreuther. *Retroactive Liability and Future Risk: The Optimal Regulation of Underground Storage Tanks.* Available on-line at <http://www.rff.org/CFDOCS/disc_papers/PDF_files/9602.pdf>, retrieved June 17, 2003.

Boyer, Paul, ed. *Reagan as President: Contemporary Views of the Man, His Politics, and His Policies.* Chicago: Ivan R. Dee, 1990.

Braybrooke, David, and Charles E. Lindblom. *A Strategy of Decision.* New York: Free Press, 1970.

Bressers, Hans Th. A., and Walter A. Rosenbaum. "Innovation, Learning, and Environmental Policy: Overcoming 'A Plague of Uncertainties.'" *Policy Studies Journal* 28, no. 3 (2000): 668–671.

Breyer, Stephen. *Regulation and Its Reform.* Cambridge, Mass.: Harvard University Press, 1982.

Bryner, Gary C. *Blue Skies, Green Politics: The Clean Air Act of 1990 and Its Implementation.* 2nd ed. Washington, D.C.: CQ Press, 1995.

Cahn, Matthew. *Environmental Deceptions: The Tension between Liberalism and Environmental Policymaking in the United States.* Albany: State University of New York Press, 1995.

California Air Resources Board. "Proposed Modifications to the Proposed Regulation Order, Showing the Complete Proposed Regulation Order as Modified. Amendments to the California Phase 3 Gasoline (CaRFG3) Regulations to Refine the Prohibitions of MTBE and Specified Other Oxygenates in California Gasoline Starting December 31, 2003." 15-day notice version, released December 23, 2002.

Centers for Disease Control and Prevention. "An Investigation of Exposure to MTBE and Gasoline among Motorists and Exposed Workers in Albany, New York." Atlanta Ga.: U.S. Department of Health and Human Services, National Center for Environmental Health, August 4, 1993.

Centers for Disease Control and Prevention. "An Investigation of Exposure to Methyl Tertiary Butyl Ether among Motorists and Exposed Workers in Stamford, Connecticut." Atlanta, Ga.: U.S. Department of Health and Human Services, National Center for Environmental Health, September 13, 1993.

Centers for Disease Control and Prevention. "An Investigation of Exposure to Methyl Teriary Butyl in Oxygenated Fuel in Fairbanks, Alaska." Atlanta, Ga.: U.S. Department of Health and Human Services, National Center for Environmental Health, October 22, 1993.

Chilton, Kenneth W., and Murray Weidenbaum. "Government Regulation: The Small Business Burden." *Journal of Small Business Management* 20 (January 1982): 4–10.

Church, Thomas W. *Cleaning Up the Mess: Implementation Strategies in Superfund.* Washington, D.C.: Brookings Institution, 1993.

Clarke, Jeanne Nienaber, and Daniel C. McCool. *Staking Out the Terrain: Power and Performance among Natural Resource Agencies.* 2nd ed. Albany, N.Y.: SUNY Press, 1996.

Coglianese, Cary. "Assessing Consensus: The Promise and Performance of Negotiated Rulemaking." *Duke Law Journal* 46 (1997): 1255–1349.

Coglianese, Cary, and Laurie K. Allen. "Does Consensus Make Common Sense? An Analysis of EPA's Common Sense Initiative." *Environment* (January–February 2004): 10–25.

Cohen, Michael D., James G. March, and Johan P. Olsen. "A Garbage Can Model of Organizational Choice." *Administrative Science Quarterly* 17 (March 1972): 1–25.

Cohen, Steven A. "Defusing the Toxic Time Bomb: Federal Hazardous Waste Programs." In *Environmental Policy in the 1980's: Reagan's New Agenda.* Eds. Norman J. Vig, and Michael E. Kraft. Washington, D.C.: Congressional Quarterly Press, 1984.

Cohen, Steven A. "Environmental Protection Agency: A Qualified Success." In *Controversies in Environmental Policy.* Eds. Sheldon Kamieniecki, Robert O'Brien, Michael Clarke. Albany: State University of New York Press, 1986.

Cohen, Steven A. "Employing Strategic Planning in Environmental Regulation." In *Flashpoints in Environmental Policymaking: Controversies in Achieving Sustainability.* Eds. Sheldon Kamieniecki, George A. Gonzalez, and Robert O. Vos. Albany: State University of New York Press, 1997.

Columbia University. Graduate Program in Public Policy and Administration. *Final Report: Workshop Project on Leaking Underground Storage Tanks.* New York: School of International and Public Affairs, 1989.

Congressional Quarterly. *Regulation: Process and Politics.* Washington, D.C.: CQ Press, 1982.

Connecticut Department of Environmental Protection. "Use of Methyl Tertiary Butyl Ether (MTBE) as a Gasoline Additive: Report to the Joint Standing Committees on Public Health and the Environment, Connecticut General Assembly." February 2000.

Council of Economic Advisors. *Economic Report of the President.* Washington, D.C.: U.S. Government Printing Office, 1982.

Danaceau, Paul. "Developing Successful Enforcement Programs." In *Social Regulation: Strategies for Reform.* Eds. Eugene Bardach and Robert A. Kagan. San Francisco: Institute for Contemporary Studies, 1982.

Daneke, Gregory A. "The Future of Environmental Protection: Reflections on the Difference between Planning and Regulating." *Public Administration Review* 42 (May–June 1982): 27–33.

Daneke, Gregory A. "An Adaptive-Learning Approach to Environmental Regulation." *Policy Studies Review* 3 (August 1983): 7–12.

Davies, J. Clarence, and Jan Mazurek. *Pollution Control in the United States: Evaluating the System.* Washington, D.C.: Resources for the Future, 1998.

Davis, Charles E., and James P. Lester, "Decentralizing Federal Environmental Policy: A Research Note." *Western Political Quarterly* 40 (September 1987): 555–565.

"Deep Down Facts about Underground Storage Tanks." *Journal of American Insurance* (Third Quarter, 1990): 17–21.

DeLeon, Peter. *Democracy and the Policy Sciences*. Albany: State University of New York, 1997.

Department of Environmental Protection. *Use of Methyl Tertiary Butyl Ether (MTBE) as a Gasoline Additive: Report to the Joint Standing Committees on Public Health and the Environment, Connecticut General Assembly*. February 2000.

Dror, Yehezkel. *Public Policymaking Reexamined*. Scranton, Pa.: Chandler Publishing Co., 1968.

Dryzek, John S. "Don't Toss Coins in Garbage Cans: A Prologue to Policy Design." *Journal of Public Policy* 3 (October 1983): 345–367.

Dryzek, John S. "Policy Analysis and Planning: From Science to Argument." In *The Argumentative Turn in Policy Analysis and Planning*. Eds. Frank Fischer and John Forester. Durham, N.C.: Duke University Press, 1993.

Dryzek, John S., and Brian Ripley. "The Ambitions of Policy Design." *Policy Studies Review* 7 (Summer 1988): 705–719.

Dunlap, Riley E., Michael E. Kraft, and Eugene A. Rosa, eds. *Public Reactions to Nuclear Waste: Citizens' Views of Repository Siting*. Durham, N.C.: Duke University Press, 1993.

Dunn, William N. *Public Policy Analysis*. 2nd ed. Englewood Cliffs, N.J.: Prentice Hall, 1994.

Dunshire, Andrew. *Implementation in a Bureaucracy*. New York: St. Martin's Press, 1978. "Dupont factsheet." DuPont, Heritage [cited 16 February 2004]. Available on-line at <http://heritage.dupont.com/floater/fl_tel/floater.shtml>.

Durant, Robert F. "EPA, TVA, and Pollution Control: Implications for a Theory of Regulatory Policy Implementation." *Public Administration Review* 44 (July–August 1984): 305–315.

Eads, George C., and Michael Fix. *Relief or Reform? Reagan's Regulatory Dilemma*. Washington, D.C.: Urban Institute, 1984.

Edwards, George C. *Implementing Public Policy*. Washington, D.C.: Congressional Quarterly Press, 1980.

Employee Assistance Program Networker 11 no. 4 (November 2002).

Energy Information Administration. *Motor Gasoline Outlook and State MTBE Bans*. Washington, D.C.: U.S. Department of Energy, April 6, 2003. Available on-line at: <http://www.eia.doe.gov/emeu/steo/pub/special/mtbeban.html>, retrieved April 7, 2004.

Ferreira, Joseph. "Promoting Safety through Insurance." In *Social Regulation: Strategies for Reform*. Eds. Eugene Bardach and Robert A. Kagan. San Francisco: Institute for Contemporary Studies, 1982.

Feticiano, V. "Leaking Underground Storage Tanks: A Potential Environmental Problem." Congressional Research Service, January 11, 1984.

Fischbeck, Paul S., R. Scott Farrow, and M. Granger Morgan. "Introduction: The Challenge of Improving Regulation." In *Improving Regulation: Cases in Environment, Health and Safety*. Eds. Paul S. Fischbeck and R. Scott Farrow. Washington, D.C.: Resources for the Future, 2001.

Flatt, Victor B. "A Dirty River Runs through It (The Failure of Enforcement in the Clean Water Act)." *Boston College Environmental Affairs Law Review* 25 (October 1997): 1–46.

Franklin, Pamela. 2002. "To MTBE, or Not to MTBE. Is All Research Created Equal? Institutional Credibility and Technical Expertise in Environmental Policymaking at US EPA." Doctoral dissertation, University of California, Berkeley.

Franz, Neil. 2002. "California Energy Commission Says MTBE Ban Premature." *Chemical Week*, March 6, 2002.

Freeman, A. Myrick. "Economics, Incentives, and Environmental Policy." In *Environmental Policy: New Directions for the Twenty-First Century*. 5th ed. Eds. Norman J. Vig and Michael E. Kraft. Washington, D.C.: CQ Press, 2003.

Fry, Elizabeth. "Virtual CFO." *CFO—The Business End of Business*, March 1, 1997. Available on-line at <http://www.cfoweb.com.au/stories/19970301/7228.asp>, retrieved April 18, 2003.

"Fuel-Leak Rules May Hasten End of Mom and Pop Service Stations." *New York Times*, June 19, 1989, I: 1.

Garcia-Johnson, Ronie. *Exporting Environmentalism: U.S. Multinational Chemical Corporations in Brazil and Mexico*. Cambridge, Mass.: MIT Press, 2000.

General Motors. "Fact Sheet on Tetraethyl Lead." Available on-line at <http://www.gm.com/automotive/innovations/altfuel/info/t.htm>, retrieved April 19, 2003.

Glazer, Amihai, and Lawrence S. Rothenberg. *Why Government Succeeds and Why It Fails*. Cambridges, Mass.: Harvard University Press, 2001.

Gormley, William T. "Intergovernmental Conflict on Environmental Policy: The Attitudinal Connection." *Western Political Quarterly* 40 (June 1987): 285–303.

Guttman, Daniel, and Barry Willner. 1976. *Shadow Government*. New York: Pantheon Books, 1976.

Hahn, Robert W., "The Political Economy of Environmental Regulation: Towards a Unifying Framework." *Public Choice* 65 (April 1990): 21–47.

Hahn, Robert W., and Gregory J. McRae. "Application of Market Mechanisms to Pollution." *Policy Studies Review* 1 (February 1982): 470–476.

Hamilton, Pixie A., Michael J. Moran, and John S. Zogorski. "USGS Fact Sheet 105–01." U.S. Geological Survey, October 2001.

Harter, Philip J. "Fear of Commitment: An Affliction of Adolescents." *Duke Law Journal* 46 (1997): 1389–1429.

Hawkins, Keith. *Environment and Enforcement: Regulation and the Social Definition of Pollution.* Oxford: Claredon Press, 1984.

Health Effects Institute. *The Potential Health Effects of Oxygenates Added to Gasoline: A Review of the Current Literature: A Special Report of the Institute's Oxygenates Evaluation Committee.* April 1996. Available on-line at <http://www.healtheffects.org/Pubs/oxysum.htm>, retrieved April 9, 2004.

Health Effects Institute. *Program Summary: Research on Oxygenates Added to Gasoline.* April 1996. Available on-line at <http://www.healtheffects.org/Pubs/oxyprog.htm>, retrieved April 8, 2004.

Hedge, David M., and Donald C. Menzel. "Loosening the Regulatory Ratchet: A Grassroots View of Environmental Regulation." *Policy Studies Review* 13 (March 1985): 599–606.

Heffron, Florence, and Neil McFeeley. *The Administrative Regulatory Process.* New York: Longman, 1983.

Hemenway, David. "Private Insurance as an Alternative to Protective Regulation: The Market for Residential Fire Insurance." *Policy Studies Journal* 15 (March 1987): 415–440.

Hermanson, Judith A. "Regulatory Reform by Statute: The Implication of the Consumer Product Safety Commission's 'Offeror System.'" *Public Administration Review* 38 (March–April 1978): 151–155.

Hird, John A. *Superfund: Political Economy of Environmental Risk.* Baltimore, Md.: Johns Hopkins University Press, 1994.

Hoffer, Charles W., and Dan E. Schendel. *Strategy Formulation: Analytic Concepts.* St. Paul, Minn.: West, 1978.

Hogwood, B. W., and L. A. Gunn. *Policy Analysis for the Real World.* Oxford: Oxford University Press, 1984.

Huber, Kathy, Sheldon Kamieniecki, and Steven A. Cohen. "The Implementation of Federal Underground Storage Tank Regulations: Some Preliminary Findings." Paper prepared for presentation to the 1990 Annual Meeting of the American Political Science Association, San Francisco, August 29–September 2, 1990.

Illinois Corn. *MTBE Case Studies.* Available on-line at: <http://www.ilcorn.org/Ethanol/MTBE_Cases/mtbe_cases.html>, retrieved December 30, 2002.

Indiana Department of Environmental Management. "MTBE Remediation Information." Available on-line at <http://www.in.gov/idem/land/lust/pdf/mtberemediation.pdf>, retrieved December 15, 2004.

Ingersoll, Thomas G., and Bradley R. Brockbank. "The Role of Economic Incentives in Environmental Policy." In *Controversies in Environmental Policy.* Eds.

Kamieniecki, Sheldon, Robert O'Brien and Michael Clarke. Albany: State University of New York Press, 1986.

Ingraham, Patricia W. "Toward More Systemic Consideration of Policy Design." *Policy Studies Journal* 15 (June 1987): 611–628.

Ingram, Helen. "Implementation: A Review and Suggested Framework." In *Public Administration: The State of the Field*. Eds. Aaron Wildavsky and Naomi B. Lynn. Chatham, N.J.: Chatham House, 1990.

Ingram, Helen, and Anne Larason Schneider. *Policy Design for Democracy*. Lawrence: University of Kansas Press, 1997.

Iowa Department of Natural Resources. *Methyl tertiary-Butyl Ether (MTBE) Occurrence in Iowa: A Report for the 2000 Session of the Seventy-Eighth General Assembly*. February 2000.

Iowa General Assembly. *HF 2294*. 2000. "A Bill for an Art Prohibiting Methyl-Tertiary Butyl Ether Eliminating a Conflicting Provision, Providing Penalties, and Providing an Effective Date." Available on-line at <http://www.legis.state.ia.us/cgi-bin/Legislation/File_only.pl?FILE=/usr/ns-home/docs/GA/78GA/Legislation/HF/02200/HF02294/000216.html>, retrieved July 5, 2002.

Jones, Charles O. "Speculative Augmentation in Federal Air Pollution Policy-making." *Journal of Politics* 36 (May 1974): 438–463.

Jones, Charles O. *Clean Air: The Policies and Politics of Pollution Control*. Pittsburgh: University of Pittsburgh Press, 1975.

Kagan, Robert. *Adversarial Legalism: The American Way of Law*. Cambridge, Mass.: Harvard University Press, 2001.

Kamieniecki, Sheldon. *Public Representation in Environmental Policymaking: The Case of Water Quality Management*. Boulder, Colo.: Westview Press, 1980.

Kamieniecki, Sheldon, and Steven A. Cohen. "Strategic Regulatory Planning in the Management of Hazardous Materials." *Policy and Politics* 18 (July 1990): 207–216.

Kamieniecki, Sheldon, Robert O'Brien, and Michael Clarke. "Environmental Policy and Aspects of Intergovernmental Relations." In *Intergovernmental Relations and Public Policy*. Eds. J. Edwin Benton and Daniel R. Morgan. Westport, Conn.: Greenwood Press, 1986.

Kamieniecki, Sheldon, David Shafie, and Julie Silvers. "Forming Partnerships in Environmental Policy: The Business of Emissions Trading in Clean Air Management." *American Behavioral Scientist* 43 (September 1999): 107–123.

Katzman, Martin T. "Pollution Liability Insurance and the Internalization of Environmental Risks." *Policy Studies Review* 5 (February 1986): 614–623.

Keller, Arturo, John Froines, Catherine Koshland, John Reuter, Irwin Suffet, and Jerold Last. *Health and Environmental Assessment of MTBE: Report to the Governor and Legislature of the State of California as Sponsored by SB 521*. Davis: University of California Systemwide Toxic Substances Research and Teaching

Program, November 1998. Available on-line at <http://tsrtp.ucdavis.edu/mtberpt>, retrieved April 8, 2004.

Kenski, Henry C., and Helen M. Ingram. "The Reagan Administration and Environmental Regulation: The Constraint of the Political Market." In *Controversies in Environmental Policy.* Eds. Sheldon Kamieniecki, Robert O'Brien, and Michael Clarke. Albany: State University of New York, Press, 1986.

Kerwin, Cornelius M. *Rulemaking: How Government Agencies Write Law and Make Policy*. 3rd ed. Washington, D.C.: CQ Press, 2003.

Kerwin, Cornelius M., and Scott R. Furlong, "Time and Rulemaking: An Empirical Test of Theory." *Journal of Public Administration Research and Theory* 2 (April 1992): 113–138.

Kettl, Donald F., ed. *Environmental Governance: A Report on the Next Generation of Environmental Policy.* Washington, D.C.: Brookings Institution, 2002.

Kiernan, Peter. "MTBE Phaseout May Boost Refining Margins on Supply Shortfalls." *Oil Daily*, June 5, 2002, p. 107.

Kovacic, William E. "The Reagan Judiciary and Environmental Policy: The Impact of Appointments to the Federal Courts of Appeals." *Boston College Environmental Affairs Law Review* 18 (June 1991): 669–713.

Kulick, Rosalyn. "Mission Impossible: Being a Manager Today." *Employee Assistance Program Networker* 11, no. 4 (November 2002). Available on-line at <http://www.hr.wayne.edu/eap/ValueOptions/networker/v11_no4.html>, retrieved April 18, 2003.

Landy, M. K., M. J. Roberts, and S. R. Thomas. *The Environmental Protection Agency: Asking the Wrong Questions from Nixon to Clinton.* New York: Oxford University Press.

"LA Regional Water, Endorse Santa Monica Water Agreement: Charnock Sub-Basin to Be Cleaned of Petroleum Contaminants." Water Quality and Environment News, U.S. Environmental Protection Agency, Region 9, November 25, 2003. Available on-line at <http://www.waterchat.com/News/Environment/03/Q4/env_031205-02.htm>.

Lee, Patrick. "New EPA Rules Scare Owners of Gas Stations: High Cost of Insurance for Storage Tanks May Drive Many Out of Business." *Los Angeles Times*, July 24, 1989, IV: 1.

"Legislature Bans Gasoline Additive Showing Up in Groundwater." Washington State House of Representatives, press release, May 9, 2001.

Lerner, Allan W., and John Wonat. "Fuzziness and Bureaucracy." *Public Administration Review* 43 (November–December 1983): 500–509.

Lester, James P. "Federalism and State Environmental Policy." In *Environmental Politics and Policy: Theories and Evidence.* 2nd ed. James P. Lester. Durham, N.C.: Duke University Press, 1995.

Lieber, Harvey. "Federalism and Hazardous Waste Policy." In *The Politics of Hazardous Waste Management.* Eds. James P. Lester, and Ann O'M. Bowman. Durham, N.C.: Duke University Press, 1983.

Lindblom, Charles A. "The Science of Muddling Through." *Public Administration Review* 19 (Spring 1959): 79–88.

Linder, Stephan H., and B. Guy Peters. "From Social Theory to Policy Design." *Journal of Public Policy* 4 (August 1984): 237–259.

Linder, Stephen H., and B. Guy Peters. "A Design Perspective on Policy Implementation: The Fallacies of Misplaced Prescription." *Policy Studies Review* 6 (February 1987): 459–475

Linder, Stephen H., and B. Guy Peters. "The Analysis of Design or the Design of Analysis?" *Policy Studies Review* 7 (Summer 1988): 738–750.

Lipsky, Michael. *Street-Level Bureaucracy.* New York: Russell Sage Foundation, 1980.

Lovell, Catherine H. "Deregulation of State and Local Government." *Policy Studies Journal* 13 (March 1985): 607–615.

Lowery, David, and Virginia Gray. "A Neopluralist Perspective on Research on Organized Interests." *Political Research Quarterly* 57 (March 2004): 163–175.

Lowi, Theodore. "American Business, Public Policy, Case Studies, and Political Theory." *World Politics* 16 (July 1964): 677–715.

Lowi, Theodore J. *The End of Liberalism.* New York: Norton, 1969.

Lowry, William R. *The Dimensions of Federalism: State Governments and Pollution Control Policies.* Durham, N.C.: Duke University Press, 1992.

Lowy, Joan. "Congress Moves to Protect Oil Firms on Gas Additive." Scripps Howard News Service, October 10, 2002. Available on-line at <http://www.shns.com/shns/g_index2.cfm?action=detail&pk=MTBELIABILITY-10-10-02>, retrieved April 8, 2004.

MacMillan, Ian C., and Patricia E. Jones. *Strategy Formulation: Power and Politics.* 2nd ed. St. Paul, Minn.: West, 1986.

Maine Bureau of Health. "Presence of MTBE and Other Gasoline Compounds in Maine's Drinking Water Supplies—A Preliminary Report." Augusta, ME: Maine Bureau of Health, Department of Human Services; Bureau of Waste Management and Remediation, Department of Environmental Protection; Maine Geological Survey, Department of Conservation, October 13, 1998.

Maine Office of the Governor. "King Praises EPA Decision to Drop MTBE in Gasoline," press release, July 27, 1999.

Marcus, Alfred A. "Command and Control: An Assessment of Smokestack Emission Regulation." In *Policy Implementation: Penalties or Incentives?* Eds. John Brigham and Don W. Brown. Beverly Hills, Calif.: Sage, 1980.

Marcus, Alfred, Donald A. Geffen, and Ken Sexton. *Reinventing Environment Regulation: Lessons from Project XL.* Washington, D.C.: Resources for the Future, 2002.

Marcus, Alfred A., Paul Sommers, and Frederic A. Morris. "Alternative Arrangements for Cost Effective Pollution Abatement: The Need for Implementation Analysis." *Policy Studies Review* 1 (1982): 477–483.

Mazmanian, Daniel, and David Morell. "The Elusive Pursuit of Toxics Management." *Public Interest*, no. 90 (Winter 1988): 81–98.

Mazmanian, Daniel, and David Morell. *Beyond Superfailure: America's Toxics Policy for the 1990s*. Boulder, Colo.: Westview Press, 1992.

Mazmanian, Daniel, and Paul Sabatier. "The Conditions of Effective Implementation: A Guide to Accomplishing Policy Objectives." *Policy Analysis* 5 (Fall 1979): 481–504.

Mazmanian, Daniel, and Paul Sabatier. "The Implementation of Public Policy: A Framework of Analysis." *Policy Studies Journal* 8 (Special Issue 1980): 538–560.

Mazmanian, Daniel, and Paul Sabatier. *Implementation and Public Policy*. Glenview, Ill.: Scott, Foresman, 1983.

McCarthy, James E., and Mary Tiemann. *MTBE in Gasoline: Clean Air and Drinking Water Issues*. Washington, D.C.: Congressional Research Service, Library of Congress, February 25, 2000.

McConnell, Grant. *Private Power and American Democracy*. New York: Knopf, 1966.

McCool, Daniel C. "Conflict and Choice in Policy Theory." In *Public Policy Theories, Models, and Concepts*. Ed. Daniel C. McCool. Englewood Cliffs, N.J.: Prentice Hall, 1995.

McGann, James G., and R. Kent Weaver. *Think Tanks and Civil Society: Catalysts for Ideas and Action*. New Brunswick, N.J.: Transaction Publishers, 2000.

McKean, Roland N. "Enforcement Costs in Environmental and Safety Regulation." *Policy Analysis* 6 (Summer 1980): 271–289.

Meier, Kenneth J. *Regulation: Politics, Bureaucracy and Economics*. New York: St. Martin's Press, 1985.

Mendeloff, John M. *The Dilemma of Toxic Substance Regulation: How Overregulation Causes Underregulation*. Cambridge, Mass.: MIT Press, 1998.

Mercer, James L. *Strategic Planning for Public Managers*. New York: Quorum Books, 1991.

Merchant, Carolyn. *The Columbia Guide to American Environmental History*. New York: Columbia University Press, 2002.

"Methyl Tertiary Butyl Ether (MTBE): Recommendations and Actions." U.S. Environmental Protection Agency. Available on-line at <www.epa.gov/mtbe/action.htm>, retrieved February 16, 2004.

"Methyl Tertiary Butyl Ether (MTBE): Advance Notice of Intent to Initiate Rulemaking Under the Toxic Substances Control Act to Eliminate or Limit the Use of MTBE as a Fuel Additive in Gasoline; Advance Notice of Proposed Rulemaking." *Federal Register*, Part VII, March 24, 2000. 40 CFR Part 755.

"Methyl Tertiary-Butyl Ether (MTBE) Occurrence in Iowa: A Report for the 2000 Session of the Seventy-Eighth General Assembly." Des Moines, IA: Iowa Department of Natural Resources, Underground Storage Tank Section, February 2000.

Metzenbaum, Shelley H. "Measurement That Matters: Cleaning Up the Charles River." In *Environmental Governance: A Report on the Next Generation of Environmental Policy*. Ed. Donald F. Kettl. Washington, D.C.: Brookings Institution Press, 2002.

Milbrath, Lester W. *Envisioning a Sustainable Society: Learning Our Way Out*. Albany: State University of New York Press, 1989.

Miller, Norman. *Environmental Politics: Interest Groups, the Media, and the Making of Policy*. Boca Raton, Fla.: Lewis Publishers, 2002.

Mintzberg, Henry. "Crafting Strategy." *Harvard Business Review* 65 (July–August 1987): 66–67.

Mirsky, Arlene Elgart, Richard J. Conway, Jr., and Geralyn G. Humphrey. "The Interface between Bankruptcy and Environmental Laws." *Business Lawyer* 46 (February 1991): 623–691.

Mitchell, Robert Cameron. "Public Opinion and Environmental Politics in the 1970's and 1980's." In *Environmental Policy in the 1980's: Reagan's New Agenda*. Eds. Norman Vig, and Michael Kraft. Washington, D.C.: Congressional Quarterly Press, 1984.

Mitnick, Barry M. *The Political Economy of Regulation*. New York: Columbia University Press, 1980.

Mitnick, Barry M. "Incentive Systems in Environmental Regulation." *Policy Studies Journal* 9 (Winter 1980): 379–394.

Moe, Terry. "Regulatory Performance and Presidential Administration." *American Journal of Political Science* 26 (May 1982): 197–224.

Montjoy, Robert S., and Lawrence J. O'Toole. "Toward a Theory of Policy Implementation: An Organizational Perspective." *Public Administration Review* 39 (September–October 1979): 465–475.

Morian, Dan. "Ethanol Brings Drop in Gas Tax." *Los Angeles Times*, March 24, 2003, p. B1.

Mosher, Frederick C. "The Changing Responsibilities and Tactics of the Federal Government." *Public Administration Review* 40 (November–December 1980): 541–548.

Munger, Michael C., and Dennis Coates. "Strategizing in Small Group Decision Making: Host State Identification in the Southeast Compact." *Public Choice* 82 (July 1995): 1–15.

Murry, L. Weidenbaum. "The High Cost of Government Regulation." *Challenge* (November–December 1979): 32–39.

Nakamura, Robert T., and Thomas W. Church. *Taming Regulation: Superfund and the Challenge of Regulatory Reform*. Washington, D.C.: Brookings Institution, 2003.

Nakamura, Robert T., and Frank Smallwood. *The Politics of Policy Implementation.* New York: St. Martin's Press, 1980.

National Academy of Public Administration. *Resolving the Paradox of Environmental Protection.* Washington, D.C.: National Academy of Public Administration, September 1997.

National Academy of Public Administration. *Providing Financial Assurance for Storage Tanks.* Washington, D.C.: National Academy of Public Administration, August 1985.

National Academy of Public Administration. *A Strategy for Implementing Federal Regulation of Underground Storage Tanks.* Washington, D.C.: National Academy of Public Administration, January 1986.

New England Interstate Water Pollution Control Commission. "Survey of State Experiences with MTBE Contamination at Leaking UST Sites." New England Interstate Water Pollution Control Commission, August 2000.

New Hampshire Department of Environmental Services. *New Hampshire's Application for Relief from Federally Preempted Gasoline Standards.* December 7, 2001.

New Jersey Department of Environmental Protection, MTBE Workgroup and Division of Science, Research and Technology. "MTBE in New Jersey's Environment." December 19, 2000.

Northeast States for Coordinated Air Use Management. Press release, January 19, 1999.

Northeast States for Coordinated Air Use Management. *RFG/MTBE: Findings and Recommendations.* 1999.

NRDC. Press release [online]. "NRDC Supports EPA Action on Gasoline Additive MTBE." NRDC, March 20, 2000. Available on-line at <http://www.nrdc.org/media/pressReleases/MTBErelease.asp>.

O'Brien, Robert M., Michael Clarke, and Sheldon Kamieniecki. "Open and Closed Systems of Decision Making: The Case of Toxic Waste Management." *Public Administration Review* 44 (July–August 1984): 334–340.

O'Dell, John. "Rewrite of Emissions Rule May Roll Out More Hybrids." *Los Angeles Times*, April 7, 2003, p. C2.

Office of Solid Waste and Emergency Response. *The Nation's Hazardous Waste Management Program at a Crossroads.* Washington, D.C.: Environmental Protection Agency, 1990.

Office of Air and Radiation. "Proposed rule received by OMB 1/19/2001, Completed May 2000—Withdrawn by Agency: Association of State and Territorial Solid Waste Management Officials (ASTSWMO)."

Office of Water. "Proposed Rule Received by OMB 1/11/2000, Completed 2/16/2000—Withdrawn by Agency: Association of State and Territorial Solid Waste Management Officials (ASTSWMO)." *ASTSWMO MTBE and Fuel Oxygenates Workgroup Newsletter* 4, no. 1 (Spring 2001): 23. Available on-line at <http://www.astswmo.org/Publications/MSWord/mtbe11.pdf>.

O'Leary, Rosemary. *Environmental Change: Federal Courts and the EPA.* Philadelphia: Temple University Press, 1993.

O'Leary, Rosemary. "Environmental Policy in the Courts." In *Environmental Policy: New Directions for the Twenty-First Century.* 5th ed. Eds. Norman J. Vig and Michael E. Kraft. Washington, D.C.: CQ Press, 2003.

O'Leary, Rosemary, Robert F. Durant, Daniel J. Fiorino, and Paul S. Weiland. *Managing for the Environment: Understanding the Legal, Organizational, and Policy Challenges.* San Francisco: Jossey-Bass, 1999.

Ostrom, Elinor, Roy Gardner, and James Walker. *Rules, Games, and Common-Pool Resources.* Ann Arbor: University of Michigan Press, 1994.

Ostrom, Elinor, and James Walker. "Neither Markets nor States: Linking Transformation Processes in Collective Action Arenas." In *Perspectives on Public Choice.* Ed. Dennis C. Mueller. Cambridge: Cambridge University Press, 1997.

Parker, Susie T. "Mileage Reduction, 'Very Distinctive' Odors Top Denver Area Motorists' MTBE Complaints." *Oil Daily*, October 16, 1991, p. B3.

Pashigian, B. Peter. "How Large and Small Plants Fare under Environmental Regulation." *Regulation* 7 (September–October 1983): 19–23.

Pesquera, Adolfo. "Law Dries Up Gas Tanks: Service Station Owners Stumble over Deadline for Safety Certification." *San Antonio Express-News*, May 10, 2001, p. 1E.

Peters, Thomas J., and Robert H. Waterman. In *Search of Excellence: Lessons from America's Best-Run Companies.* New York: Harper & Row, 1982.

Pettus, Beryl E. "OSHA Inspection Costs, Compliance Costs, and Other Outcomes: The First Decade." *Policy Studies Review* 1 (February 1982): 596–614.

Polakovic, Gary. "Innovative Smog Plan Makes Little Progress." *Los Angeles Times*, April 17, 2001, p. B1.

Pope, Charles. "Interest Groups Weigh In as Congress Seeks Solution to Gasoline Additive Pollution." *CQ Weekly*, February 5, 2000.

Portney, Paul R., and Robert N. Stavins, eds. *Public Policies for Environmental Protection.* 2nd ed. Washington, D.C.: Resources for the Future, 2000.

"The Potential Health Effects of Oxygenates Added to Gasoline: A Review of the Current Literature: A Special Report of the Institute's Oxygenates Evaluation Committee." Mass.: Health Effects Institute, April 1996. Available on-line at <http://www.healtheffects.org/Pubs/oxysum.htm>, retrieved April 18, 2004.

Powell, Mark R. *Science at EPA: Information in the Regulatory Process.* Washington, D.C.: Resources for the Future, 1999.

Prakash, Aseem. *Greening the Firm: The Politics of Corporate Environmentalism.* Cambridge: Cambridge University Press, 2000.

Probst, Katherine N., Don Fullerton, Robert E. Litan, and Paul R. Portney. *Footing the Bill for Superfund Cleanups: Who Pays and How?* Washington, D.C.: Brookings Institution, 1995.

Press, Daniel, and Daniel A. Mazmanian. "Understanding the Transition to a Sustainable Economy." In *Environmental Policy: New Directions for the Twenty-First Century*. 5th ed. Eds. Norman J. Vig and Michael E. Kraft. Washington, D.C.: CQ Press, 2003.

Pressman, Jeffrey L., and Aaron Wildavsky. *Implementation*. Berkeley: University of California Press, 1973.

Pruett, Michael C. "Environmental Cleanup Costs and Insurance: Seeking a Solution." *Georgia Law Review* 24 (March 1990): 705–732.

Rabe, Barry G. "Permitting, Prevention, and Integration: Lessons from the States." In *Environmental Governance: A Report on the Next Generation of Environmental Policy*. Ed. Donald F. Kettl. Washington, D.C.: Brookings Institution, 2002.

Rabe, Barry G. "Power to the States: The Promise and Pitfalls of Decentralization." In *Environmental Policy: New Directions for the Twenty-First Century*. 5th ed. Eds. Norman J. Vig and Michael E. Kraft. Washington, D.C.: CQ Press, 2003.

"Refiners'/Gas Plant Operators' Monthly Petroleum Product Sales Report." In Energy Information Administration, DOE, Petroleum Marketing Annual 2002. Washington, D.C.: U.S. Government Printing Office, 2002.

Reuter, John E. Tahoe Research Group. *Research on MTBE*. University of California, Davis. [cited 16 February 2004]. Available on-line at: <http://trg.ucdavis.edu/research/mtbe.html>.

Ringquist, Evan J. *Environmental Protection at the State Level: Politics and Progress in Controlling Pollution*. Armonk, N.Y.: M. E. Sharpe, 1993.

Roe, Emery. *Narrative Policy Analysis: Theory and Practice*. Durham, N.C.: Duke University Press, 1994.

Rosenbaum, Walter A. *Environmental Politics and Policy.* Washington, D.C.: Congressional Quarterly Press, 1985.

Rosenbaum, Walter. *Environmental Politics and Policy.* 2nd ed. Washington, D.C.: CQ Press, 1991.

Rosenbaum, Walter A. "Regulation at Risk: The Controversial Politics and Science of Comparative Risk Assessment." In *Flashpoints in Environmental Policymaking: Controversies in Achieving Sustainability*. Eds. Sheldon Kamieniecki, George A. Gonzalez, and Robert O. Vos. Albany: State University of New York Press, 1997.

Rosenbaum, Walter. *Environmental Politics and Policy.* 6th ed. Washington, D.C.: CQ Press, 2005.

Rothenberg, Lawrence S. *Environmental Choices: Policy Responses to Green Demands*. Washington, D.C.: CQ Press, 2002.

Rourke, Francis E. *Bureaucracy, Politics and Public Policy.* 3rd ed. Boston: Little, Brown, 1984.

Rowland, C. K., and Roger Marz. "Gresham's Law: The Regulatory Analogy." *Policy Studies Review* 1 (February 1982): 572–580.

Rushefsky, Mark E. *Public Policy in the United States.* Armonk, N.Y.: M. E. Sharpe, 2002.

Sabatier, Paul, and Daniel Mazmanian. "A Guide to Accomplishing Policy Objectives." *Policy Analysis* 5 (Fall 1979): 481–504.

Salamon, Lester M. "Rethinking Public Management: Third Party Government and the Changing Forms of Government Action." *Public Policy* 29 (Summer 1981): 255–275.

Salamon, Lester M. *The Tools of Government: A Guide to the New Governance.* New York: Oxford University Press, 2002.

Salisbury, Robert H. "The Analysis of Public Policy: A Search for Theories and Roles." In *Political Science and Public Policy.* Ed. Austin Ranney. Chicago: Markham Publishing Co., 1968.

Salisbury, Robert, and John Heinz. "A Theory of Policy Analysis and Some Preliminary Applications." In *Policy Analysis in Political Science.* Ed. Ira Sharkansky. Chicago: Markham, 1970.

"Santa Monica Water Supply Threatened by MTBE." *U.S. Water News Online,* July 1996. Available on-line at <http://www.uswaternews.com/archives/arcquality/6smonica.html>, retrieved February 17, 2004.

Scheberle, Denise. *Federalism and Environmental Policy: Trust and the Politics of Implementation.* Washington, D.C.: Georgetown University Press, 1997.

Schneider, Anne Larason, and Helen Ingram. *Policy Design for Democracy.* Lawrence: University Press of Kansas, 1997.

Scholz, John. "In Search of Regulatory Alternatives." *Journal of Policy Analysis and Management* 4 (Fall 1984): 113–121.

Segal, Migdon. *Ethanol and Clean Air: The "Reg-Neg" Controversy and Subsequent Events.* Washington, D.C.: Congressional Research Service, Committee for the National Institute for the Environment, Washington, June 22, 1993.

Sierra Club, press release, August 14, 2000. Available on-line "Interim Guidance on the Use of MTBE in Gasoline." at <http://www.sierraclub.org/cleanair/factsheets/mtbe.asp>.

Smith, Glenn. Vermont Department of Fire Prevention, Hazardous Materials Team, telephone interview, March 15, 1986.

Soden, Dennis L., ed. *The Environmental Presidency.* Albany: State University of New York Press, 1999.

Solley, Wayne B. Pierce, Robert R., and Perlman, Howard. *Estimated Use of Water in the United States in 1995.* Washington, D.C.: U.S. Government Printing Office, 1998.

Sparrow, Malcolm. *Regulatory Craft: Controlling Risks, Solving Problems, and Managing Compliance.* Washington, D.C.: Brookings Institution, 2000.

Stavens, Robert N. "What Can We Learn from the Grand Policy Experiment? Lessons from SO_2 Allowance Trading." *Journal of Economic Perspectives* 12 (1998): 69–88.

Stein, Corey. "Pollution Insurance Comes of Age." *Public Management*, (July–August 1999): 14–17.

Steinbrunner, John D. *The Cybernetic Theory of Decision.* Princeton, N.J.: Princeton University Press, 1974.

Stikkers, David. "The Unintended Consequence of Reformulated Gasoline." In *Improving Regulation: Cases in Environment, Health and Safety.* Eds. Paul S. Fischbeck and R. Scott Farrow. Washington, D.C.: Resources for the Future, 2001.

Stone, Alan. *Regulation and Its Alternatives.* Washington, D.C.: CQ Press, 1982.

Stone, Diane. *Capturing the Political Imagination: Think Tanks and the Policy Process.* Avon, U.K.: Bookcraft, 1996.

Sussman, Glen, Byron W. Daynes, and Jonathan P. West. *American Politics and the Environment.* New York: Longman, 2002.

Thompson, Frank J. "Deregulation by the Bureaucracy: OSHA and the Augean Quest for Error Correction." *Public Administration Review* 42 (May–June 1982): 202–212.

Thompson, Frank J., and Michael J. Scicchitano. "State Enforcement of Federal Regulatory Policy: The Lessons of OSHA." *Policy Studies Journal* 13 (March 1985): 591–598.

Tiemann, Mary. *Leaking Underground Storage Tank Cleanup Issues.* Washington, D.C.: Congressional Research Service, Report, February 17, 1999.

Tobin, Richard J. "Safety-Related Defects in Motor Vehicles and the Evaluation of Self-Regulation." *Policy Studies Review* 1 (February 1982): 532–539.

Tolchin, Susan J. "Cost-Benefit Analysis and the Rush to Deregulate: The Use and Misuse of Theory to Effect Policy Change." *Policy Studies Review* 4 (November 1984): 212–218.

Tolchin, Susan J., and Martin Tolchin. *Dismantling America: The Rush to Deregulate.* Boston: Houghton Mifflin, 1983.

U.S. Conference of Mayors. "MTBE Liability Provisions Could Be Largest Unfunded Mandate in Recent Years." Press release, November 17, 2003. Available on-line at <http://www.usmayors.org/uscm/news/press_releases/documents/mtbestatement_111703.pdf>, retrieved April 10, 2004.

U.S. Environmental Protection Agency, Office of Administration Law Judges. *Fiscal Year 1988 Program Guidance.* Washington, D.C.: U.S. Environmental Protection Agency, 1987.

U.S. Environmental Protection Agency, "Executive Summary and Recommendations." The Report of the Blue Ribbon Panel on Oxygenates in Gasoline. July 27, 1999.

U.S. Environmental Protection Agency, Office of Air and Radiation."Methyl Tertiary Butyl Ether (MTBE): Advance Notice of Intent to Initiate Rulemaking Under the Toxic Substances Control Act to Eliminate or Limit the Use of MTBE as a Fuel Additive in Gasoline; Advance Notice of Proposed Rulemaking." *Federal Register*, March 24, 2000, p. 16103.

U.S. Environmental Protection Agency. "Clean Air Act." Available on-line at <http://www.epa.gov/oar/caa/caa.txt>, retrieved April 25, 2003.

U.S. Environmental Protection Agency, Office of Air and Radiation. "Methyl Tertiary Butyl Ether (MTBE): Overview. Available on-line at <www.epa.gov/mtbe/faq.htm>, retrieved September 17, 2003.

U.S. Environmental Protection Agency. "Factoids: Drinking Water and Ground Water Statistics for 2002." Available on-line at <http://www.epa.gov/safewater/data/pdfs/02factoids.pdf>, retrieved June 17, 2003.

U.S. Environmental Protection Agency. "Ground Water Primer—Office of Groundwater and Drinking Water Introduction." Available on-line at <http://www.epa.gov/seahome/groundwater/src/intro.htm>, retrieved June 17, 2003.

U.S. Environmental Protection Agency, Office of Policy, Economics, and Innovation. *The United States Experience with Economic Incentives for Protecting the Environment.* Washington, D.C.: Environmental Protection Agency, January 2001.

U.S. Environmental Protection Agency. *Assessment of Potential Health Risks of Gasoline Oxygenated with Methyl Tertiary Butyl Ether (MTBE).* November 1993.

U.S. Environmental Protection Agency. *Health Risk Perspectives on Fuel Oxygenates.* Washington, D.C.: Office of Research and Development, 1994.

U.S. Environmental Protection Agency, Office of Research and Development. *Partners for the Environment: A Catalogue of the Agency's Partnership Programs.* Washington, D.C.: Environmental Protection Agency, Spring 1998.

U.S. Environmental Protection Agency, Office of Research and Development. *Achieving Clean Air and Clean Water: The Report of the Blue Ribbon Panel on Oxygenates in Gasoline.* September 15, 1999.

U.S. Environmental Protection Agency, Office of Solid Waste and Emergency Response. *Measuring Progress in UST Management.* Washington, D.C.: U.S. Environmental Protection Agency, 1988.

U.S. Environmental Protection Agency, Office of Solid Waste and Emergency Response, Office of Underground Storage Tanks. "MTBE Fact Sheet #2: Remediation of MTBE Contaminated Soil and Groundwater." January 1998.

U.S. Environmental Protection Agency, Office of Solid Waste and Emergency Response. "Underground Storage Tank Program Initiatives." Memo from Timothy Fields to Regional UST division directors, October 23, 2000.

U.S. Environmental Protection Agency, Office of Transportation and Air Quality. "2003 RFG Covered Areas Code List." Available on-line at <http://www.epa.gov/otaq/regs/fuels/rfg/covareas.pdf>.

U.S. Environmental Protection Agency, Office of Underground Storage Tanks. *National Survey of Underground Storage Tanks*, 1991.

U.S. Environmental Protection Agency, Office of Underground Storage Tanks. *Summary of State Reports on Releases from Underground Storage Tanks.* August 1986.

U.S. Environmental Protection Agency, Office of Underground Storage Tanks. "Dollars and Sense: Financial Responsibility Requirements for Underground Storage Tanks." July 1995. Available on-line at <http://www.epa.gov/swerust1/pubs/dol&sens.pdf>, retrieved April 18, 2003.

U.S. Environmental Protection Agency, Office of Underground Storage Tanks. "State Funds in Transition: Models for Underground Storage Tank Assurance Funds." January 1997. Available on-line at <www.epa.gov/oust/states/statefnd.html>, retrieved June 13, 2002.

U.S. Environmental Protection Agency. "Section IV: Managing Underground Storage Tanks RCRA Subtitle I." 2000.

U.S. Environmental Protection Agency, Office of Underground Storage Tanks. *Financial Responsibility for Underground Storage Tanks: A Reference Manual.* January 2000.

U.S. Environmental Protection Agency, Office of Underground Storage Tanks. *Report to Congress on a Compliance Plan for the Underground Storage Tank Program.* June 2000. Available on-line at <http://www.epa.gov/swerust1/pubs/rtc_0600.pdf>, retrieved August 21, 2002.

U.S. Environmental Protection Agency. "Fact Sheet on MTBE." Available on-line at <http://www.epa.gov/mtbe/faq.htm>, retrieved February 25, 2004.

U.S. Environmental Protection Agency, Office of Underground Storage Tanks. *Report to Congress on a Compliance Plan for the Underground Storage Tank Program.* June 2000.

U.S. Environmental Protection Agency, Office of Underground Storage Tanks. "Remarks by Marianne Lamont Horinko, 14th Annual UST/LUST Conference, Opening Plenary Session," March 11, 2002. Available on-line at <www.epa.gov/oust/aaspeeck.html>, retrieved June 5, 2002.

U.S. Environmental Protection Agency. "Leaking Underground Storage Tank Fund." Available on-line at <www.epa.gov/oust/ltffacts.html>, retrieved June 4, 2002.

U.S. Environmental Protection Agency, Office of Underground Storage Tanks. "Status of State Fund Programs." Available on-line at <www.epa.gov/oust/states/fndstatus.html>, retrieved June 4, 2002.

U.S. Environmental Protection Agency, Office of Underground Storage Tanks. "Cleaning Up UST System Releases." Available on-line at <www.epa.gov/oust/cat/index.html>, retrieved June 7, 2002.

U.S. Environmental Protection Agency, Office of Underground Storage Tanks. "EPA's New UST Fields Pilots: Questions and Answers." Available on-line at <www.epa.gov/oust>, retrieved July 2002.

U.S. Environmental Protection Agency, Office of Underground Storage Tanks. "How Much Work Remains to Be Done?" Available on-line at <www.epa.gov/oust/faqs/remain.html>, retrieved July 2002.

U.S. Environmental Protection Agency, Office of Underground Storage Tanks. "EPA Announces $3.8 Million to Clean Up Petroleum from Underground Storage Tank Sites at Gas Stations in 26 States." Press release, July 1, 2002. Available on-line at <www.epa.gov/oust/ustfield/40pr.pdf>, retrieved August 2002.

U.S. Environmental Protection Agency, Office of Underground Storage Tanks. "Tanknology-NDE, International, Inc Criminal Plea." Available on-line at <www.epa.gov/compliance/resources/cases/civil/rcra/tanknology.html>, retrieved August 2, 2002.

U.S. Environmental Protection Agency, OUST. "UST Fields Initiative." Available on-line at <www.epa.gov/oust/ustfield/index.html>, retrieved August 2, 2002.

U.S. Environmental Protection Agency, Office of Underground Storage Tanks. "How Have the UST Requirements Helped Protect the Environment?" Available on-line at <www.epa.gov/oust/faqs/topfour.html>, retrieved August 21, 2002.

U.S. Environmental Protection Agency, Office of Underground Storage Tanks. "State Underground Storage Tank Programs." Available on-line at <http://www.epa.gov/swerust1/fsstates.htm>, retrieved April 18, 2003.

U.S. Environmental Protection Agency. *Report to Congress on a Compliance Plan for the Underground Storage Tank Program.* Available on-line at <http://www.epa.gov/OUST/pubs/rtc_0600.pdf>, retrieved June 17, 2003.

U.S. Environmental Protection Agency, Office of Underground Storage Tanks. "Corrective Action Measures Archive." Available on-line at <www.epa.gov/oust/cat/camarchv.htm>, retrieved June 18, 2003.

U.S. Environmental Protection Agency, Office of Underground Storage Tanks. "USEPA, Frequently Asked Questions (FAQs) about MTBE and USTs." Available on-line at <http://www.epa.gov/oust/mtbe/mtbefaqs.htm>, retrieved February 16, 2004.

U.S. Environmental Protection Agency. "US EPA Office of Underground Storage Tanks." Available on-line at <http://www.epa.gov/oust/overview.htm>, retrieved February 16, 2004.

U.S. Environmental Protection Agency, Office of Water. "Leaking Underground Storage Tanks." April 1985.

U.S. Environmental Protection Agency. "Status of State Funds." Available on-lined at <http://www.epa.gov/oust/states/fndstatus.htm>, retrieved June 18, 2003.

U.S. Environmental Protection Agency, Office of Water. "LA Regional Water, Endorse Santa Monica Water Agreement: Charnock Sub-Basin to Be Cleaned of Petroleum Contaminants." *Water Quality and Environment News*, November 25, 2003 Available on-line at <http://www.waterchat.com/News/Environment/03/Q4/env_031205–02.htm>, retrieved February 17, 2004.

U.S. Environmental Protection Agency, "About the Science Advisory Board." Available on-line at <http://www.epa.gov/sab/about.htm>, retrieved April 17, 2004.

"US Senators' Say Can Block MTBE's Liability Shield." Reuters, 2003. October 10, 2003. Available on-line at <http://www.forbes.com/markets/newswire/2003/10/10/rtr1106383.html>, retrieved March 18, 2005.

U.S. Water News Online. "Santa Monica Water Supply Threatened by MTBE." July 1996. Available on-line at <http://www.uswaternews.com/archives/arcquality/6smonica.html>, retrieved February 17, 2004.

Varone, Frederic, and Bernard Aebischer, "Energy Efficiency: The Challenges of Policy Design." *Energy Policy* 29 (June 2001): 615–629.

Vig, Norman J. "Presidential Leadership and the Environment." In *Environmental Policy: New Directions for the Twenty-First Century*. 5th ed. Eds. Norman J. Vig and Michael E. Kraft. Washington, D.C.: CQ Press, 2003.

Vig, Norman J., and Michael Kraft, eds. *Environmental Policy in the 1980's: Reagan's New Agenda*. Washington, D.C.: Congressional Quarterly Press, 1984.

Viscusi, W. Kip. "The Informational Requirements for Effective Regulatory Review: An Analysis of the EPA Lead Standard." *Policy Studies Review* 1 (May 1982): 686–691.

Walter, Benjamin, and Malcolm Getz. "Social and Economic Effects of Toxic Waste Disposal." In *Controversies in Environmental Policy*. Eds. Sheldon, Kamieniecki, Robert O'Brien, and Michael Clarke. Albany: State University of New York Press, 1986.

Weber, Edward P. *Pluralism by the Rules: Conflict and Cooperation in Environmental Regulation*. Washington, D.C.: Georgetown University Press, 1998.

Weber, Edward P. *Bringing Society Back In: Grassroots Ecosystem Management, Accountability, and Sustainable Communities*. Cambridge, Mass.: MIT Press, 2003.

Weimer, David, and Aidan Vining. *Policy Analysis: Concepts and Practice*. 4th ed. Upper Saddle River, N.J.: Prentice Hall, 2005.

West, William F. "The Politics of Administrative Rulemaking." *Public Administration Review* 42 (September–October 1982): 420–426.

Weiss, Carol H. *Organizations for Policy Analysis*. Newbury Park, Calif.: Sage, 1992.

Wildavsky, Aaron B. *Speaking Truth to Power: The Art and Craft of Policy Analysis.* New Brunswick, N.J.: Transaction Books, 1987.

Williams, Bruce A., and Albert R. Matheny. "Testing Theories of Social Regulation: Hazardous Waste Regulation in the American States." *Journal of Politics* 46 (May 1984): 428–458.

Williams, Walter. *The Implementation Perspective.* Berkeley: University of California Press, 1980.

Wilms, Welford W. "Soft Policies for Hard Problems: Implementing Energy Conserving Building Regulations in California." *Public Administration Review* 42 (November–December 1982): 553–561.

Wilson, James Q. "The Politics of Regulation." In *Social Responsibility and the Business Predicament.* Ed. James W. McKie. Washington, D.C.: Brookings Institution, 1974.

Wittrock, Bjorn, and Peter deLeon. "Policy as a Moving Target: A Call for Conceptual Realism." *Policy Studies Review* 6 (August 1986): 44–60.

Wolman, Harold. "The Determinants of Program Success and Failure." *Journal of Public Policy* 1 (October 1981): 433–464.

Wood, Andrew. "MTBE Green Image Challenged." *Chemical Week*, October 27, 1993, p. 42.

Index